Re-Careering in Turbulent Times: SKILLS AND STRATEGIES FOR SUCCESS IN TODAY'S JOB MARKET

Ronald L. Krannich, Ph.D.

IMPACT PUBLICATIONS

Dedicated to my parents, Louis and Florence Krannich

RE-CAREERING IN TURBULENT TIMES: SKILLS AND STRATEGIES FOR SUCCESS IN TODAY'S JOB MARKET

Library of Congress Number: 82-82720

ISBN 0-942710-02-9

For information on distribution or quantity discount rates, call 703/361-7300 or write to Sales Department, IMPACT PUBLICATIONS, 10655 Big Oak Circle, Manassas, Virginia 22111.

CONTENTS

vi

PREFACE

The 1980's have proven to be one of the most challenging decades for government, business, and individuals. Political institutions appear paralyzed; public policy is in disarray; and government is expected to do more with less. Politicians and bureaucrats, lacking coherent policies and effective programs, hope for better days. In the meantime, they are doing what was considered unthinkable a decade ago — cutting government programs and personnel.

Business, the great hope of the 1980's, fared no better than government. A stagnant and declining economy led to a record number of bankruptcies and layoffs. Productivity, the buzzword of the 80's, took on new meaning as the survivors began practicing more of what they preached — efficiency. However, cleaning out deadwood was not enough; many businesses continued running in the red.

For individuals, both government and business lacked answers to the economic afflictions besetting the country. With 12 million people unemployed and business failures mounting, no one expected easy answers or quick results.

Since the 1970's, the American economy had been undergoing major restructuring. Turbulent changes would affect most individuals by the end of the 1980's. A technological revolution was taking place at the same time the world economy was undergoing major changes in response to energy and monetary crises.

Many displaced workers in 1983 had become victims of the larger structural changes taking place in both the international and domestic economies. Their skills were becoming increasingly obsolete for the jobs of tomorrow. While many of the unemployed expected to return to work once the economy improved, many would not because they lacked appropriate skills to function in the job markets of the 80's and 90's. Unfortunately, they were not likely to acquire the necessary skills, because they failed to take initiative, and neither the public nor private sectors were preparing them for new jobs. In the meantime, high unemployment existed in the midst of major labor shortages.

So why write another career planning and job search book? Because there is a need for a different approach to employment for the future. Previous approaches have not prepared individuals for the coming changes in American society. Educational institutions primarily exist to provide employment for educators rather than to train individuals for jobs and careers. Government mainly provides training programs for the hardcore unemployed — the ones least likely to be trainable or benefit from training. Business continues to maximize short-run profits and views training as a luxury or perk to be given primarily to supervisors and managers. And career counselors still preach the doctrine of *"anyone can find a job if they only know how to find a job."* Consequently, they continue to train people in developing and utilizing *job search skills* regardless of whether they have marketable *job performance skills*.

This book was written to fill the need for a new perspective on employment in the 1980's and beyond. For the problem of jobs, careers, and employment is not being addressed from a comprehensive, integrated, realistic, and future-oriented perspective. Most experts tend to "stand where they sit." Educators, for example, believe people need to come to them and their institutions for training when, in fact, educators are facing one of the most critical employment problems of any group in society. Politicians and bureaucrats tend to think in the narrow terms of creating another government program which they hope *"this time"* will produce results. Today they propose a *"jobs training program"* for the hardcore unemployed and a few displaced workers. Tomorrow they will probably suggest another *"tax credit incentive program"* for the middle and upper classes. Career counselors and futurists are unprepared to provide practical guidance to unemployed workers in the depressed economies of Detroit, Cleveland, and Peoria. At a loss for solutions, many advise migration to Houston, Dallas, Tulsa, Albuquerque, or Salt Lake City.

The perspective I develop in this book synthesizes the skills training and job search approaches within the framework of a society undergoing major social, economic, and political restructuring. Beginning with a realistic understanding of politics, public policy, and bureaucracy, I place full responsibility for employment and training squarely on the shoulders of the *individual*. No one owes anyone a job or a career, and few people have valid excuses for not acquiring the education and training necessary to function effectively in the job market. Therefore, you must be responsible for your own employment fate. You shape your own future by the decisions you made yesterday and today as well as by those you will make tomorrow. This book is designed to prepare you for turbulent times by giving you the necessary knowledge to *make informed choices* about your future.

I believe we are in the midst of a profoundly revolutionary period which will require individuals to re-career several times during their work lives. Knowing job search skills alone will be insufficient to function effectively in the turbulent times ahead. Such skills must accompany concrete work-content skills. Individuals, therefore, must continuously acquire new skills in order to adjust to job market realities. The *"one job, one career, one work life"* phenomenon has all but ended for many occupations. The *"15 jobs, 5 careers, and many work lives"* phenomenon is now upon us in a new re-careering era.

The process I call re-careering recognizes the need to prepare for an uncertain future by *linking work skills to job search skills*. Re-careering prepares individuals for dealing with the turbulent job markets of today and tomorrow. The chapters that follow outline how you can re-career in the decades ahead. More important, they show you how to turn turbulence into new and, hopefully, exciting opportunities in the world of work.

Ronald L. Krannich
Manassas, Virginia
March 1, 1983

ACKNOWLEDGEMENTS

I am especially indebted to five individuals for this book. Caryl Rae Krannich encouraged me to finally put the subject into writing and then endured neglect. Yet, she spent an incredible number of hours critiquing and editing the manuscript while also building a house; both the book and the house exhibit her sense of style, quality, craftsmanship, and purpose. Throughout the text I refer to "we," which indicates our joint effort.

William J. Banis got me started in career planning when I was teaching political science and public administration in the university classroom. Without his friendship and assistance in introducing me to his field, I might still be in the classroom doing political science rather than experiencing the joys of re-careering.

Edwin and Richard Phelps provided opportunities and a re-careering bridge which helped support this project from beginning to end.

Marlene Hassell typeset the manuscript with a rare and wonderful combination of speed, accuracy, judgment, and humor. In the end, we all got through it, including our machines, without experiencing burnout or having to re-career in the process.

PART I

Re-Careering
Times

Chapter One
APPROACHING NEW REALITIES

What skills should I have for today's job market? How relevant will my skills be for tomorrow's job market? If I lose my job, what should I do? How can I best prepare for the jobs and careers of tomorrow? What strategies are most effective for finding employment and changing careers?

These questions are important for individuals seeking success in today's job market. They require a thorough understanding of how jobs and careers are changing as well as how the job market functions in the 1980's. More important, these questions reveal a need for new approaches to the emerging realities of jobs in the 1980's and 1990's.

CHANGING TIMES

Unemployment reached nearly 11 percent in 1982 — the first time since the Great Depression. As the unemployed anxiously awaited better times, few understood the permanent nature of this phenomenon; many sat idle, hopeful that an improved economy would carry them back to full employment. Others, depressed, dropped out of the unemployment lines altogether.

Economic problems in the 1980's seemed to baffle even the best minds. While politicians and economists debated the causes of

1

unemployment and devised strategies for creating more jobs, the relatively depressed economy was undergoing major restructuring. Although some thinking about employment began to change, most continued to be based upon outmoded theories and approaches to creating jobs and finding employment.

The causes of unemployment in the 1980's are varied and complex. While it has economic causes, unemployment in the end is political and thus controversial. Excessive public spending, the Vietnam War, Wall Street, irresponsible labor unions and corporations, the rich and the poor, liberals, conservatives, Democrats, Republicans, FDR, and the Japanese are all touted as possible culprits.

Solutions to the unemployment problem are equally varied, complex, and controversial. Except for the training emphasis of the 1982 Jobs Training Partnership Act, which replaces the controversial CETA jobs program, America lacks a national employment and training policy. The relatively nondirected, fragmented, and decentralized economic and political systems are somehow supposed to resolve the paradoxical unemployment/labor shortage problem: high unemployment persists at the same time major labor shortages exist.

LIVING IN A DUAL SOCIETY

Signs of an economy and job market undergoing major restructuring are apparent everywhere. As millions of Americans join the ranks of the unemployed, millions of jobs also go unfilled because individuals lack the necessary skills to function in a newly emerging post-industrial, high-tech society. Like the dual societies of Third World countries — one rural/agricultural and another urban/industrial — America is quickly becoming a dual society of a different type.

The emerging dual society in America consists of two sectors. The first and most traditional sector is located mainly in the older urban centers of the Northeast and North Central regions. Based largely on manufacturing and related service industries, this sector is characterized by stagnation, decline, and high levels of unemployment and underemployment. A disproportionate number of poor and unskilled people live in these aging communities which also have serious problems with deteriorating infrastructure, excessive welfare burdens, and high costs of living. The state of Michigan led this sector in 1983 with a depressing 18 percent unemployment rate. Ohio, Illinois, West Virginia, Indiana, and Pennsylvania were not far behind.

The second sector points us toward a more promising yet unpredictable future. It is located mainly in younger suburban areas and in the rapidly growing cities of the Southern and Western regions. It is based on high-tech, communication, and related service industries. In contrast to the first sector, this one is characterized by dynamic growth and relatively high employment. This sector is populated by a disproportionate number of affluent and skilled people who live in the boom towns of the 1980's. Yet, growth of this sector is constrained by shortages of highly skilled workers and the overall depressed nature of the national economy.

UNDERSTANDING STRUCTURAL DYNAMICS

Much of the unemployment problem is structural in nature. For the American economy has entered into a major period of *structural unemployment*. While the normal pattern of unemployment is *cyclical* — people lose their jobs because of temporary business downturns and then are rehired when business rebounds — structural unemployment has permanent features. Moreover, this type of unemployment has far reaching consequences for the economy, workers, and employment strategies.

Structural unemployment is caused when industries and skills become obsolete due to technological advances. In the past, street sweepers, buggy-whip makers, tailors, and shoemakers became victims of such unemployment. More recently, aerospace scientists and engineers, auto workers, tire makers, steel workers, and farm laborers have experienced structural unemployment. Like their buggy-whip maker and shoemaker counterparts of yesterday, the recent victims must acquire new skills and change careers in order to join the ranks of the gainfully employed.

Unfortunately, few people are prepared or willing to deal with the changing structure of employment in America. Many unemployed auto workers, for example, still believe their condition is due to cyclical unemployment, with Japanese competition and a recession being the major culprits. They expect to be rehired when the business cycle improves again. While union leaders are just beginning to recognize the significance of structural unemployment by negotiating for more job security, give backs, and retraining programs for their members, management introduces the latest industrial robot technology in a major effort to improve the productivity and competitiveness of the American auto industry. General Motors, a case in point, laid off 130,000 workers and then announced in 1982 that it would spend $1 billion to install 14,000 robots on its assembly lines by 1990. Chrysler and Ford announced similar intentions. The end result will be permanently displaced workers who must acquire new skills if they hope to survive and prosper in the job markets of today and tomorrow.

TAKING INITIATIVE

Some experts estimate that somewhere between 50 and 75 percent of American factory workers will be displaced by robots by the end of this century! Peter Drucker confirms such estimates by projecting that 10 to 15 million manufacturing jobs will disappear during the 1980's and 1990's.

But few people, especially displaced workers, are taking the initiative to provide or acquire the necessary skills training and retraining. As structural unemployment becomes more pervasive, the problem of what to do with millions of unemployed workers with obsolete skills may become a national crisis. Some believe a major national training and retraining program, which goes far beyond the limited scope of the Jobs Training Partnership Act, is desperately needed. Others see this as naive and nearly impossible to implement.

What will displaced factory workers do — many of whom are highly skilled in older technologies? What actions can be taken now, and by whom, to make a positive transition to the job market of the high-tech society?

We believe the answers to these questions primarily lie with the *individual* rather than with government or corporations. Indeed, our major purpose in writing this book is to see that you become *self-reliant and effective* in dealing with the job markets of today and tomorrow. While government and the private sector may provide incentives and opportunities, the individual ultimately must be responsible for his or her own employment fate. We assume that both government and the private sector will be slow in responding to the obvious training and retraining needs. In the meantime, a serious national employment and economic development crisis is brewing, and many people are being hurt by public and private sector inaction. Individuals, therefore, must take their own initiative to acquire the necessary skills for success in the job markets of today and tomorrow.

PREDICTING CHANGE

The American dream of a stable family, home ownership, a

good job, and early retirement is being severely challenged by new economic and social realities: high divorce rates, low levels of home ownership, high unemployment, and a severely strained social security system. Futurists and soothsayers predict different scenarios ranging from Armageddon to the promised land. The Armageddons predict the collapse of the economy, massive unemployment, widespread hunger, riots in the streets, major energy shortages, and nuclear disaster.

The new utopians envision a more advanced society riding the waves of a high-tech revolution; a booming economy experiencing major labor shortages lies just around the corner — especially for the 1990's.

However, predictors have a notorious record for being inaccurate. How can they accurately predict when there are so many variables and unexpected developments, such as the development and corresponding impact of the revolutionary microprocessing chip? Predictors, at best, identify trends which may or may not become salient. But one thing is always certain about the future — it is unpredictable. Like a blind date, you don't know what you will get until you meet.

FACING TURBULENT TIMES

We no doubt live in turbulent times. Daniel Bell calls this the "post-industrial" era. Alvin Toffler terms it the era of "The Third Wave," a profoundly revolutionary period; we are moving from a mainly industrial to a highly technological and anti-industrial civilization.

The predicted transformations are indeed dramatic. While the agricultural revolution took thousands of years, the industrial revolution only took 300 years. The newest revolution — The Third Wave — began in the late 1940's and early 1950's and will be completed within a few years. As revolutionary changes become compressed into the space of 20 to 30 years — a quantum jump in history — the results can be disruptive for many individuals. At the same time, new opportunities arise during such periods for individuals who understand and adapt to rapid changes.

Peter Drucker in *Managing in Turbulent Times* similarly views this as a period of extremely revolutionary changes — "sea changes" as he terms it. Changing population dynamics coupled with the post-World War II technological revolution will result in a dramatically altered economy and corresponding changes in the job market and management systems. These changes will challenge today's managers and employees to restructure traditional adversarial labor-management relations along more cooperative and participatory lines. How well we manage this sea-change will largely determine the success of the technological revolution.

Marilyn Ferguson in *The Aquarian Conspiracy* views the coming changes in terms of a shift from one way of thinking to another. These ways of thinking, or paradigms, outline two contrasting realities for the 1980's:

Old Paradigm	*New Paradigm*
Strong central government ⟶	Decentralized government
Government rewards and ⟶ punishes	Government encourages cooperation and creativity
Change is imposed by ⟶ authority	Change grows out of consensus
Power is used for or ⟶ against others	Power is used with others
Win/lose orientation ⟶	Win/win orientation
Rational orientation ⟶	Rational and intuitive orientation
Vested interest, manipulation ⟶	Respect for autonomy of others
Services are institutionalized ⟶	Volunteerism, self-help and mutual-help are encouraged
Quick-fix programs ⟶	Emphasis on foresight
Emphasis on freedom from ⟶ certain interferences	Emphasis on freedom for positive, creative action
Humankind as conqueror of ⟶ nature	Humankind as partner with nature
Makes us choose between ⟶ individual and community interests	Promotes reciprocal interest between self and community

John Naisbitt expands on these projected changes in *Megatrends* by attempting to document the restructuring of America. He identifies 10 fundamental trends, transformations, or maga-shifts which will have a major impact on our futures. These include:

(1) shift from an industrial to an informational society
(2) respond to new technology with new human responses —
     high tech/high touch
(3) live in an increasingly interdependent world
(4) plan more for the long-term
(5) innovate from the bottom-up as well as decentralize
(6) move toward more self-reliance, self-help, and entrepre-
     neurship
(7) reshape representative democracy along more participatory
     lines
(8) move from hierarchical to network organizational struc-
     tures
(9) shift of population from the North and East to South and
     West
(10) develop a multiple-option society

The key trend, influencing all others, is the shift from an industrial society to an informational society.

The restructuring of America already has important implications for workers in Toffler's Second Wave industrial society. Many jobs and careers are becoming obsolete as new occupations are created in relation to high technology and service industries. More and more skilled workers will be displaced by structural unemployment in the future. Ten percent unemployment, therefore, may well become the norm for unemployment, unless workers are better prepared to function in today's changing job market. At the very least, they must learn how to *re-career in turbulent times.*

RE-CAREERING TODAY AND TOMORROW

The nature of work and the process of finding employment have changed dramatically during the past few decades. For those who lived through the Great Depression, a job — indeed, any job — was something you were lucky to have. A good job — one you enjoyed and earned a good living from — was something only a few people were lucky enough to have.

As white-collar employment expanded in the 1950's and 1960's, a new philosophy of work evolved. Work was to be enjoyed and based upon one's strongest skills. Individuals also were advised to change jobs and careers when they were no longer happy with their work.

Pioneered in the career planning methods of Bernard Haldane in the 1950's and 1960's and popularized in Richard Bolles' self-

directed *What Color is Your Parachute?* in the 1970's, job hunting
was itself a skill that could be learned and applied with considerable
success. Individuals were told to identify what they do well — their
strengths — and enjoy doing. Based on this primary knowledge, they
next were to seek employment outside the deceptive formal job
market of classified ads and employment agencies by engaging in
informational interviews, that is, asking people for information and
advice about jobs and employment. The key principles for successful
job hunting were prospecting and networking — methods for developing job contacts and acquiring job information, advice, and referrals. Changing careers primarily involved a strategy of identifying
and communicating transferable skills to employers rather than
acquiring new job-related skills.

The process identified by Haldane, Bolles, and other career
counselors for finding employment is what Adele Scheele calls
"successful careering." It requires the use of certain marketing skills
and strategies for selling yourself. According to Scheele, these skills
are (1) self-presentation, (2) positioning, and (3) connecting. Other
writers refer to these skills as (1) role playing, (2) risk taking, and
(3) networking — key skills, principles, or strategies applicable to
most sales and marketing situations.

The job search skills promoted in the 1960's and 1970's are
based on a business-sales analogy. According to many career counselors, finding a job is like selling — you sell yourself in exchange
for status, position, and money. Seldom, if ever, do these career
counselors advise individuals to acquire new skills which are more
responsive to the changing job market. Doing so requires a major
investment of time and effort which may seem beyond the immediate employment needs of many individuals.

As more and more jobs require technical skills, and as the job
market becomes restructured in response to the emerging high-tech
economy, the career planning approaches of the 1960's and 1970's
may well become obsolete. They are, at best, *incomplete* in today's
job market. Few individuals who market their "skills" — which
often are the soft functional skills of reading, writing, and interpersonal communication — by networking will be successful in finding employment with a promising future. As many displaced homemakers and liberal arts students are learning in the 1980's, such
strategies have limitations in a job market requiring specific technical
skills. Lacking technical skills, these individuals may become the displaced, underemployed, and discontented workers of tomorrow.

The process we call "re-careering" addresses present and future
job realities. Re-careering goes beyond the standard "careering" skills
popularized in the 1960's and 1970's, which were based upon an

understanding of a job market in an industrial-service economy. As the job market becomes restructured in the direction of high technology and communication, a new approach to job hunting, responsive to new economic realities, is required for the 1980's and 1990's.

We anticipate a very different job market in the future. The major dynamic for restructuring the job market is the emergence of Toffler's turbulent "Third Wave" society. This high-tech society demands highly *specialized* and skilled workers. But these workers should not be overly specialized or too narrow in their perception of the future demand for their skills. Instead, tomorrow's workers must be *flexible* in learning new skills, for their specialized jobs may become obsolete with the continuing advancement of technology. Furthermore, tomorrow's workers must be *adaptive* to new jobs and careers. Overall, success in tomorrow's job market will require a new breed of worker who *anticipates change*. This individual prepares for career transitions with a strategy of acquiring new skills and actively seeking new work environments by using effective job search strategies.

Re-careering is the process of repeatedly acquiring marketable skills and changing careers in response to the turbulent job market of the high-tech society. The standard *careering* process of the 1960's and 1970's, therefore, must be modified with three new *re-careering* emphases:

- acquiring new marketable skills through retraining on a regular basis
- changing careers several times during a lifetime
- utilizing more efficient communication networks for finding employment

ACHIEVING RESULTS

This book departs from the standard career planning and job search literature of the past two decades. Many of the standard works are extremely useful yet redundant, based upon the self-actualizing job hunting strategies of Haldane and Bolles. While this book incorporates much of this redundancy, it revises previous job search strategies in light of the new realities outlined by Toffler, Drucker, Naisbitt, and others. The result is a new synthesis and approach for career planning which should better prepare individuals for finding employment and changing careers in the years ahead.

The following chapters address the problems of jobs and careers in the turbulent 1980's as well as outline the necessary skills and strategies for finding employment in the challenging job markets of today and tomorrow. Written for every working individual in the decade ahead, the book gives practical advice on how to prepare for new jobs and careers as well as how to make career changes. Individual chapters outline ways to identify and acquire marketable skills, state goals, write resumes and letters, prospect, network, interview, negotiate salaries, and advance and change careers. Special chapters address the problems of job-keeping and job-revitalization, making community moves, starting your own business, and finding public sector employment in a cutback era.

Our goals in writing this book are concrete, specific, and oriented toward action and results. You should acquire certain knowledge and skills which will result in positive changes in your behavior. Upon completing this book you should be able to:

- better understand the changing nature of jobs and careers in the decades ahead
- assess your goals in relation to your values and the demands of the job market
- identify your present skills as well as the skills you can best transfer to other jobs and careers
- specify your need for skills training as well as know how to acquire the necessary training
- communicate your goals and skills to employers
- conduct research on alternative jobs, careers, organizations, and communities
- write different types of effective resumes and job search letters
- prospect for job leads and contacts
- network for job information, advice, and referrals
- conduct informational and job interviews
- negotiate salaries and the terms of employment
- keep and revitalize your job
- advance on the job
- make a cost-effective move to another community
- acquire employment with federal, state, or local governments
- start your own business
- implement your career goals

In the end, our goal is to lead you to action which will have a positive impact on your future.

Chapter Two

WORKING
IN THE FUTURE

Turbulent times require new strategies based on an understanding of new realities. But few people know how to plan for a turbulent future. Many, instead, deny new realities and thus continue to operate on old assumptions. Their adjustment to change is at best difficult.

How do you anticipate the future and plan accordingly? During turbulent times planning becomes a problem. Traditional planning,

> *assumes a high degree of continuity. Planning starts out, as a rule, with the trends of yesterday and projects them into the future — using a different "mix" perhaps, but with very much the same elements and the same configuration. This is no longer going to work. The most probable assumption in a period of turbulence is the unique event which changes the configuration — and unique events cannot, by definition, be "planned." But they can often be foreseen. This requires strategies for tomorrow, strategies that anticipate where the greatest changes are likely to occur and what they are likely to be, strategies that enable a business — or a hospital, a school, a university — to take advantage of new realities and to convert turbulence into opportunity* (Drucker: 4).

11

At the level of the individual, turbulent times also can be dangerous times for people who fail to adjust to new changes. Assuming continuity, or a return to a previous time, they engage in wishful thinking. Many of these people are today's victims of structural unemployment. For others, who take action based upon an understanding of new realities, turbulent times can offer new and exciting opportunities. These people anticipate and adapt to change and advance with the new jobs and careers of tomorrow.

LOOKING OUT FOR TRENDS

The economic transformation of American society has far reaching social and political implications which you should be aware of in planning your future. The projected changes are discussed at length in Toffler's *The Third Wave* and in Naisbitt's *Megatrends*. Our major concern here is with the implications of turbulent times for jobs, careers, and you.

The question we need to address is this: What future should you prepare for in the world of work? Based on an understanding of future changes in work, we believe you can better develop strategies for converting turbulence into new opportunities.

Two powerful currents — one demographic and another technical — are converging at present in the workplace and affecting the nature of work. Together they present a picture of new realities for the future of work in America. These changes, in turn, influence the emergence of 14 new trends for developing job strategies in the turbulent 1980's and 1990's.

DEMOGRAPHIC CURRENTS

The paradox of major labor shortages in the midst of high unemployment is partly due to the impact of demographic changes on today's labor market. For the structure of the American population is undergoing fundamental changes at the same time the economy shifts from an industrial to a high-tech base.

The major implication of these demographic changes for the high-tech society during the next two decades will be continuing labor shortages. However, the paradox of high unemployment may continue if millions of displaced workers are not retrained for new jobs.

Forces

Two major demographic changes took place in the post-World War II period to help shape the present labor force. The first change was the baby-boom. As birth rates increased nearly 50 percent between 1947 and 1949, a new labor force was created for the latter part of the twentieth century. American industry in the 1960's and 1970's absorbed some of this new labor force, but the rapidly growing service sector absorbed most of it. The U.S. economy, especially the service and high-tech sectors, was able to provide employment for 10 million new workers between 1963 and 1980 — a remarkable achievement for such a short time span.

The second major demographic change has been the rapid increase of women entering the labor force. This demographic current continues. For example, in 1980 over 50 percent of women worked outside the home. By 1990 more than 60 percent of women are projected to be in the labor force.

Implications

Declining birth rates in the 1960's and 1970's, with America now approaching a zero-population growth rate, have important implications for the future labor market. Assuming the American economy will continue to expand, stimulated by the high-tech and service industries, major labor shortages are likely to occur during the 1990's. The continuing entry of women into the labor force as well as the expansion of automation in the workplace will not significantly offset this labor deficiency.

Since birth rates declined in the 1960's and 1970 s, there are fewer young people available for entry-level and low wage positions. In addition, women, who used to take part-time, low paying sales positions, are fast leaving this labor scene for better paying full-time positions. Teenagers, who make up a disproportionate share of the labor forces of fast-food restaurants, are scarcer because there are fewer teenagers in the population as a whole than during the previous 20 years.

Adjustments in the changing labor force have already begun. Fast-food restaurants are employing older workers. Department stores are forced to recruit lower quality sales clerks — generally individuals who are less educated, skilled, stable, and responsible; training demands have increased accordingly. Many small businesses, especially the "Mom and Pop" stores with fewer than five employees, are experiencing difficulty recruiting the traditional young, low-salaried entry level workers. Instead, many businesses have begun to look toward the elderly, particularly retired individuals, for new recruits.

The changing population structure also has important implications for the quality of the labor force. While the private sector spends approximately $30 billion each year on training, much of this expenditure goes to training inexperienced entry-level personnel. Given the growing shortage of this traditional labor pool, high-tech industries will be forced to recruit and then *retrain* displaced workers. This will require a new emphasis on training — as well as a greater expenditure on retraining.

Other population dynamics have additional implications for the work force of tomorrow. Minorities, especially blacks and Hispanics, will enter the labor force at a faster rate because of their higher birth rates. As a result, minorities will disproportionately occupy entry-level positions. Furthermore, there will be greater pressure from minorities for advancement up the ranks, even though the upper ranks are becoming glutted with the young managers and executives who were rapidly promoted during the 1960's.

With the entry of more women into the labor force and the concomitant emergence of the two-career family, individuals have greater freedom of choice to change jobs or careers, take part-time positions, retire, or drop out of the labor force altogether. Job-hopping may increase accordingly. In addition, employee benefit programs, many of which are still based on the model of the traditional male head of household supporting a family, will change in response to the two-career family with one, two, or no children.

Re-careering is directly related to these demographic changes. As the work force ages, life expectancy lengthens, the social security system becomes modified, and labor shortages abound, fewer people will retire in their 60's or retire at all. An individual's worklife may well become one's total adult life. Re-careering will become a standard way of functioning within tomorrow's labor markets. Thus, it will not be unusual for individuals to change careers in their 40 s, 50's, and 60's. Mid-life crises may well disappear as more individuals experience *re-careering transitions*.

Responses

Population changes also will create a more heterogeneous work force. In addition to an increase of minorities in entry-level positions, more and more immigrants may come to the U.S. — both legally and illegally — to meet the expanding labor needs. At present nearly 400,000 immigrants enter the U.S. legally each year. Another 500,000 immigrants, mainly from Mexico and the Carribbean, probably enter the U.S. illegally each year. Most of these people take low-paying, manual and service jobs which non-minorities avoid. Hispanic-Americans, who now number about 15 million, are expected to constitute one-fifth of the population, or 50 million out of 250 million, in the year 2000.

Assuming continuing low birth rates among middle class white Americans which, in turn, may contribute to labor shortages in the future, the government may open the doors to immigrants in order to alleviate the coming labor shortages. If this happens, training and retraining programs will become a more urgent need for the future of the high-tech and service society.

Peter Drucker, however, outlines another scenario which is by far one of the most interesting organizational forms for coping with the coming labor shortages in developed countries and the explosive expansion of working-age people in the developing countries. Under a *production sharing system*, developing countries with surplus labor would be responsible for labor-intensive aspects of production. Developed countries, such as the United States, would provide the needed capital, technology, and managerial skills for operating transnational companies. Such an arrangement would fully employ the surplus educated and skilled people in the developed countries and the less educated and skilled people in the developing countries without experiencing the social, economic, and political dislocation attendant with large scale migration.

Production sharing forms of organization are already in place for various industries in the United States, Japan, Singapore, Hong Kong, Malaysia, Taiwan, Korea, and Brazil — the so-called First and Second World countries. As Drucker sees this system,

> *Production sharing is the best hope — perhaps the only hope — for most of the developing countries to survive without catastrophe the explosive expansion of working-age people in search of a job. . . for the standard of living of the developed world can also be maintained only if it succeeds in mobilizing the labor resources of the developing world. It has the technical resources, the entrepreneurial resources, the managerial resources — and the markets. But it lacks, and will increasingly lack, the labor resource to do the traditional stages of production* (Drucker: 99-100).

Whether or not production sharing becomes a predominate organizational form, the changing population dynamics over the next two decades provide further evidence of the need for major skills training and retraining of the American labor force. Population dynamics undoubtedly will be a major force affecting the turbulent employment environment.

TECHNOLOGICAL ADVANCES

The electronics revolution began in 1948 in Western Electric Company's Allentown, Pennsylvania manufacturing plant. There, the transistor was produced, and it began an electronics revolution which has continued to evolve into even more revolutionary forms since the invention and application of the microprocessor in the 1970's. The end of this revolution is nowhere in sight. Many experts believe we are just at the initial stages of a profound transformation which will sweep across our society during the next two decades.

Evidence of a coming transformation began in the 1950's as white-collar workers began to outnumber blue-collar workers. The electronics revolution, when applied, initiated an information and communication revolution. In 1950, for example, approximately 17 percent of the population worked in information-related jobs. Today this number has increased to over 60 percent. During the 1970's, when nearly 19 million new jobs were created, only 16 percent were in the manufacturing and goods-producing sector.

We have just begun to move into the second stage of technological development — the application of technology to old industrial tasks. The third stage — innovation, when new discoveries are made by using the new technology — lies in the not-too-distant future (Naisbitt).

The impact of the high-tech revolution is *structural* in nature. As computers, fiber optics, robotics, and genetic engineering generate new businesses and are adapted to everyday life, the economy and workplace will be fundamentally altered. For example, fiber optics, which makes copper wire obsolete, will further revolutionize communication. Genetic engineering will create major changes in agriculture and medicine. The main-frame computer, which was developed for practical use in 1945, in the form of today's micro computer is now a common tool in many workplaces. With the continuing impact of fiber optics and micro-processing chips — not to mention some still unknown technological breakthroughs — computers with vastly expanded capabilities will become a common tool in the home over the next few years.

The micro-processor has dramatically altered the workplace, from robots replacing assembly line workers to word processors replacing traditional typists. Office automation has transformed many secretaries into area managers, who are now in charge of coordinating work flows and managing equipment. Factory workers either become displaced or are retrained to deal with the new technology. Unfortunately, as documented in recent studies, many displaced workers, who have not been retrained, have become permanently displaced or have moved into lower paying, high turnover, unskilled service jobs — the negative unemployment and under-employment consequences of structural changes.

Toffler predicts an even more radical transformation of the workplace — the emergence of the electronic cottage. Computers and word processors will create a decentralized workplace where individuals can work from their homes on assignments received and processed via computer terminals. The electronic cottage, in turn, will alter family relationships, especially child rearing practices, and the structure of the central business district. Many workers no longer will need to commute to the office, face traffic jams, and experience the accompanying office stress. Such changes, however, do not bode well for owners of downtown office buildings, parking lots, and businesses frequented by the noontime employee-shopper. The communication revolution may be the final death blow for those cities hoping to revitalize their downtown areas in response to anticipated opportunities arising out of the energy crises of the 1970's.

These technological changes, coupled with the demographic currents, are transforming the nature of jobs. Yesterday's and today's workers are increasingly being displaced into an environment which is ill-equipped to help them gain advantages in tomorrow's high-tech society. Instead, a new class of individuals, skilled in the technology of previous decades, may become permanently displaced in the turbulent job market of tomorrow.

FOURTEEN COMING CHANGES

Several additional trends are evident, and they will affect both the work force and the workplace in years ahead. These trends are mainly stimulated by the larger demographic and technological changes taking place within society. Fourteen changes are emerging in the areas of job creation, youth, elderly, minorities, women, immigrants, part-time employment, white-collar and service jobs, education and training, unions and labor-management relations, urban-rural shifts, regionalism, small businesses and entrepreneurship, and advancement opportunities. Together these changes point to both new opportunities and dangers.

New Jobs

Although experts are uncertain whether automation creates more jobs than it eliminates, automation at least does create new jobs. As we will note in the next chapter, most of these jobs will have a high-tech information component in the production and service sectors.

Youth

Fewer young people will be available for entry-level positions. Businesses will either recruit and train more of the hard-core unemployed and the elderly, and/or they will automate. As a result, more stopgap job opportunities will be available for individuals losing their jobs or wishing to change jobs or careers.

Elderly and Retirement

More job and career choices will be available for the elderly. Forced retirement will end, and many people will never retire, preferring instead part-time or self-employment in their later years. Fewer social security benefits and higher costs of retirement will further promote the demise of retirement. Expect to see more elderly working in the McDonald's and 7-Eleven stores of tomorrow.

Minorities

More blacks and Hispanics, due to their disproportionately high birth rates and immigration, will enter the job market. For the most part, they will occupy the less skilled entry-level, service positions. Minorities may find their advancement blocked because of the glut of supervisors, managers, and executives already in most organizations.

Women

Women will continue to enter the labor market, with over 60 percent female participation predicted by 1990. From 1980 to 1995 women will account for two-thirds of the growth in all occupations. Women will continue to expand into non-traditional jobs, especially production and management positions. Both men and women in a growing number of two-career families will have the flexibility to change jobs and careers frequently.

Immigrants

More immigrants will enter the U.S. — both legally and illegally — to meet labor shortages at all levels. The brain drain of highly skilled scientific and technical workers from developing countries to the U.S. will accelerate. Unskilled immigrants will move into service positions vacated by upwardly mobile Americans.

Part-time Employment

With the increase in two-career families, the emergence of electronic cottages, and the smaller number of retirees, part-time employment will become a more normal pattern of employment. More women, who wish to enter the job market but not as full-time workers, will seek new part-time employment opportunities.

White-Collar Employment and Services

White-collar employment in an expanding service sector will continue to expand. Dramatic growth in clerical and service jobs will take place in response to the new information technology.

Education and Training

The need for a smart work force with specific technical skills will continue to impact on the traditional American educational system. Four-year colleges and universities will continue to face declining enrollments resulting from their inability to adjust to the educational and training requirements of the high-tech society as well as the demographics of fewer numbers in the student age population. Community colleges, as well as specialized private vocational-technical institutions, will adapt and flourish. More and more emphasis will be placed on providing efficient short-term, intensive skills training programs than on providing traditional degree programs — especially in the liberal arts. Re-careering will become a major emphasis in educational programs; a new emphasis will be placed on both specialization and flexibility in career preparation.

Unions and Labor-Management Relations

Union membership will continue to decline as more blue collar manufacturing jobs disappear. Initially however, as unions attempt to survive and adjust to the new society, labor-management relations will go through a turbulent period. In the long-run, labor-management relations will shift from the traditional adversarial relationship to one of greater cooperation and participation of labor and management in the decision-making process. Profit sharing, employee ownership, and quality circles will become prominent features of labor-management relations.

Urban-Rural Shifts

The population will continue to move into suburban and semi-rural communities as the new high-tech industries and services move in this direction. The large, older central cities, especially in the Northeast and North Central regions, will continue to decline as well as bear disproportionate welfare and tax burdens due to their declining industrial base and deteriorating infrastructure. Cutbacks in their city government programs will require the retraining of public employees for private sector jobs.

Regional Movement

The population, as well as wealth and economic activity, will continue to shift into the West, Southwest, and Florida at the expense of the Northeast and North Central regions. Florida, Texas, California, Arizona, New Mexico, Utah, and Colorado — the new energy and high-tech areas — will be the growth states of the 1980's and 1990's. Michigan, Ohio, Illinois, Indiana, Pennsylvania, Massachusetts, and Rhode Island are in for continuing bad times due to their declining industrial base and aging infrastructure. However, these same states may experience a strong recovery due to important linkages developing between their exceptionally well developed higher educational institutions and high-tech industries which depend on such institutions.

The growth regions also will experience turbulence as they see-saw between shortages of skilled labor, surpluses of unskilled labor, and urban growth problems. The problems of the declining regions are relatively predictable: they will become an economic drain on the nation's scarce resources; tax dollars from the growth areas will be increasingly transferred for nonproductive support payments. A new regionalism, characterized by numerous regional political conflicts, will likely arise centered around questions concerning the inequitable distribution of public costs and benefits.

Small Businesses and Entrepreneurship

The number of small businesses will continue to increase as

new opportunities for entrepreneurs arise in response to the high-tech revolution and as individuals experiment with re-careering. The number of business failures will increase accordingly. Increases in self-employment and small businesses will not provide great numbers of new opportunities for career advancement. The small promotion hierarchies of these businesses will help accelerate increased job-hopping and re-careering. This new entrepreneurship is likely to breed greater innovation, competition, and productivity.

Advancement Opportunities

Organizations will have difficulty providing career advancement for employees due to the growth of small businesses with short advancement hierarchies, the postponement of retirement, the continuing focus on nonhierarchical forms of organization, and the already glutted managerial ranks. In the future, many of today's managers will have to re-career for nonmanagerial positions. Job satisfaction will become less oriented toward advancement up the organizational ladder and more toward such organizational perks as club memberships, sabbaticals, vacations, retraining opportunities, flexible working hours, and family services.

At the same time, greater competition, few promotions, frustrated expectations, greater discontent, and job-hopping will arise in executive ranks due to limited opportunities for advancement. Managerial and executive turnover will increase accordingly. The problem will be especially pronounced for many women and minorities who are oriented toward traditional advancement to the top but who will be blocked by the glut of managers and executives from the baby-boom generation. Many of these frustrated individuals will become entrepreneurs and start their own businesses.

BEING REALISTIC

While many writers look toward the future with unquestioned optimism, there are reasons to be cautious and less than enthusiastic. In contrast to Naisbitt's conclusion that *"My God, what a fantastic time to be alive!"*, the 1980's and 1990's promise to be the worst of times for many people.

Although there is much to be said for having a positive attitude, there also is much to be said for being cautious. Take several examples which indicate a need to be cautiously optimistic. Factory workers who remain unemployed after five years will have received an industrial death sentence of continuing unemployment, underemployment, or socio-economic decline. Poor, unskilled minorities, with high birth rates, are destined to remain at the bottom of society; their children may fare no better. Large cities in the Northeast and North Central regions, and even small communities in these regions, will have terrible adjustment, if not survival, problems. And we should not forget that America has not solved its energy problems.

The best of times are when *you* are gainfully employed, enjoy *your* work, and look to *your* future with optimism. In the turbulent society, people experience both the best and worst of times at the same time. Those who are unprepared for the growing uncertainty and instability of the turbulent society may get hurt.

We lack a healthy sense of reality in facing change. Indeed, the future is seldom what we think it is. Only recently have we begun to take a second look at the high-tech revolution and raised some sobering questions about its impact on work and the workplace. We have not fully explored *unanticipated consequences* of the structural changes.

The 14 changes identified earlier will create dislocations for individuals, groups, organizations, communities, and regions. These dislocations will require some form of public-private intervention. For example, the question of renewable energy resources has not been adequately dealt with in relation to the high-tech revolution. Many of the key metals for fueling the high-tech economy are located in politically unstable regions of Africa as well as in the Soviet Union. Such resources must be secured or substitutions found in order for the revolution to proceed according to optimistic predictions. Capital formation, investment, and world markets must also be secure and stable. New management systems must evolve in response to the changes. In other words, these key factors are *variables* or "if's", and not the constants underlying most predictions of the future. As such, they are unpredictable.

The clearer picture of unanticipated consequences of the technological changes are already evident on the changing assembly lines, in the automated offices, and in the electronic cottages of today. While automation often creates more jobs as it displaces workers — usually at higher skill levels — the jobs may be psychologically and financially less rewarding. Supervising robots eight hours a day can be tedious and boring work with few on-the-job rewards. The same is true for the much touted "office of the future." Interacting at a work station with a computer terminal and screen eight hours a day is work that many may find tedious, tiring, and boring; and burnout may be accelerated.

The electronic cottage has similar unanticipated consequences.

Many people may miss the daily interaction with fellow workers — the gossip, the politics, the strokes. Instead of being rewarding, work at home can become druggery. It also may be low paying work, a twenty-first century version of the sweat shop.

The optimists often neglect the fact that the *nature of work itself* provides rewards. Many people intrinsically enjoy the particular job they perform. Furthermore, many rewards are tied to the *human dimension of work* — the interaction with others. Thus, the high-tech society will have to deal with serious management and motivational problems arising from the changing nature of work and the workplace.

Many workers may need to re-career in order to overcome the boredom and burnout accompanying many of the new jobs or work situations of tomorrow. And even if the high-tech society does not emerge in the form outlined by forecasters, the need to re-career will be a necessity in facing the job and career uncertainty of a turbulent society.

Chapter Three

IDENTIFYING TOMORROW'S JOBS

Where are the jobs? How do I get one? Many people ask these questions each day. However, another question now must precede these traditional questions: What are the jobs of tomorrow? For the nature of jobs is changing rapidly in response to new technology. The change is so rapid that skills learned today may become obsolete in another five to ten years. Knowing what the jobs are is a prerequisite to knowing how to prepare for them, find them, and change them in the future.

CHOOSING OCCUPATIONS

The information in this chapter should be used with caution. Normally individuals choose a career by first identifying their interests and abilities and then seeking occupations that best fit their interests and abilities. The next step is to acquire the necessary training before conducting a job search.

But during a period of turbulent change, occupational profiles may become quickly outdated. Training requirements change, and thus the individual encounters greater uncertainty in career choices. For example, based on trend analyses, individuals are being told that promising careers lie ahead for computer programmers. This may be true *if* thousands of newly trained individuals do not glut the job market with computer programming skills. Moreover, it may be true *if* computer technology remains stagnant and thus the coming generation of self-programmed computers does not make computer programmers — like their keypunch counterparts — obsolete. If either, let alone both, of these "if's" occur, many computer programming jobs may disappear and many newly trained computer programmers may have to re-career.

A similar situation arises for students getting the much publicized MBA degree or law degrees. Today, as more MBA's graduate and glut the job market, the glitter surrounding this degree has diminished, and the MBA may fast become an obsolete degree. While demand for lawyers is supposed to increase substantially over the next 10 years, the large number of law graduates will result in keen competition for legal positions. Furthermore, as lawyers become more competitive, promote more efficient legal services, and develop more do-it-yourself legal approaches, the demand for lawyers may actually decline as the legal profession undergoes substantial restructuring.

JOB GROWTH

The growth in jobs has been steady during the past three decades. From 1955 to 1980, the number of jobs increased from 68.7 million to 105.6 million. This represented an average annual increase of about 1.5 million new jobs. During the past decade the number of jobs increased by over 2 million per year. Projections for the period 1980 to 1985 are 2.2 to 2.7 million new jobs each year or an annual growth rate of from 1.6 to 2.4 percent. The rate of employment growth is expected to slow to 1.4 to 1.9 percent per year for the period 1985-1990. Hence, by 1990 the labor force should consist of 122 to 128 million workers — up 17 to 22 percent from 1980.

Highlighting these patterns of job growth are the following projections:

- Growth in state and local government employment will slow; it will decline in the case of secondary education.
- Service occupations will experience the greatest growth in jobs, accounting for 16 percent of all jobs in 1990.
- The largest total number of new jobs will be in the trade sector, reflecting its already large base. Approximately 5 to 7.2 million jobs will be created in the wholesale and retail trades.

- Manufacturing jobs will show little growth — 0.8 to 1.6 percent growth per year.
- Agricultural jobs will continue to decline.

However, one must be cautious about these projections made by the Bureau of Labor Statistics, U.S. Department of Labor. The assumptions underlying these projections tend to be conservative for a turbulent period. For example, the Department of Labor projected a high unemployment rate of 7.6 percent for 1982; but in 1982 unemployment actually stood at an unprecedented 10.8 percent. In addition, the deepening recession and the Reagan Administration's cuts in government programs were unanticipated developments which resulted in an actual decline in public employment for the first time since World War II. Thus, in 1982, there were 316,000 fewer public employees than in the year before.

Occupational projections, then, are nothing more than best guesses based upon a traditional planning model which assumes a certain degree of continuity. As Drucker has noted, such a planning model does not fare well in turbulent times!

OCCUPATIONAL PROFILES

Occupations normally are classified into four general categories. These consist of:

- white-collar workers — professional and technical, clerical, sales, and managerial jobs
- blue-collar workers — craft workers, operatives, and laborers
- service workers
- farm workers

Between 1978 and 1990 the U.S. Department of Labor anticipates the occupational growth and decline patterns as outlined in Table 1.

As expected, the greatest occupational growth will be among white-collar and service workers. Within the white-collar category, the greatest growth will take place among clerical workers — especially bank tellers, cashiers, and secretaries. However, a reordering of occupations within this category will take place due to information processing equipment. With the use of computers for storing information and billing, payroll, and other clerical calculations, employment opportunities during the 1980-1990 period will not grow as fast for file clerks (22.6 percent growth), office machine operators (26.2 percent growth), stock clerks (18.3 percent growth),

TABLE 1

PROJECTED CHANGE IN EMPLOYMENT AND JOB OPENINGS, BY MAJOR OCCUPATIONAL GROUP, 1978–90

(Numbers in thousands)

Projected Occupational group	1978 employment	Projected 1990 employment	Percent change 1978–90	Openings, 1978–90		
				Total	Growth	Replacement[1]
Total	94,373	114,000	20.8	66,400	19,600	46,800
White-collar workers	47,205	58,400	23.6	36,800	11,200	25,600
Professional and technical workers	14,245	16,900	18.3	8,300	2,600	5,700
Managers and administrators, except farm	10,105	12,200	20.8	7,100	2,100	5,000
Sales workers	5,951	7,600	27.7	4,800	1,700	3,100
Clerical workers	16,904	21,700	28.4	16,600	4,800	11,800
Blue-collar workers	31,531	36,600	16.1	16,200	5,100	11,100
Craft workers	12,386	14,900	20.0	7,000	2,500	4,500
Operatives, except transport	10,875	12,500	15.0	5,600	1,600	4,000
Transport operatives	3,541	4,100	16.2	1,700	1,600	1,100
Nonfarm laborers	4,729	5,100	8.1	2,000	400	1,600
Service workers	12,839	16,700	29.9	12,200	3,800	8,400
Private household workers	1,162	900	-23.2	500	-300	800
Other service workers	11,677	15,800	35.2	11,700	4,100	7,600
Farm workers	2,798	2,400	-15.9	1,300	-400	1,700

[1] Due to deaths, retirements, and other separations from the labor force. Does not include occupational transfers.

NOTE: Detail may not add to totals because of rounding.

SOURCE: *Occupational Projections and Training Data*, 1980 Edition, Bureau of Labor Statistics, U.S. Department of Labor.

and bookkeepers (11.8 percent growth) as for cashiers (49.7 percent growth) and secretaries and stenographers (45.4 percent growth). However, these projections may need to be revised in the light of prolonged recessions as well as the fact that banks may increasingly use new technology to replace the more labor intensive aspects of banking operations.

Computer-related occupations are generally expected to expand with the exception of keypunchers who will experience a -0.2 percent decline in the 1978-1990 period. This is indicative of how changing computer technology already is displacing computer-trained personnel. Computer programmers and systems analysts will experience occupational increases of 29.6 percent and 37.4 percent respectively — assuming new technological breakthroughs will not displace these specialties.

In recent years the number of service jobs has increased the greatest of any occupational category. The services will continue to experience the greatest growth in this decade, particularly among commercial cleaning, protective, food service, personal service, and leisure occupations.

Detailed statistics on occupational projections, compiled by the U.S. Department of Labor, for the 1978-1990 period are included in Appendix A.

TOMORROW'S JOBS

Industrial Profile

- *Service-producing industries:* Over two-thirds of the Nation's workers currently are employed in industries that provide services such as health care, trade, education, repair and maintenance, government, transportation, banking, and insurance. Employment in this sector has increased at a faster rate than employment in the goods-producing industries. Employment in service-producing industries is expected to increase from 65.7 million workers in 1980 to between 78.7 and 83.5 million in 1990, or by 20 to 27 percent.

- *Goods-producing industries:* Agriculture, mining, contract construction, and manufacturing make up this sector. Employment only rose 10 percent for this sector between 1970 and 1980. Between 1980 and 1990, employment in these industries is expected to increase from 29 million to between 32.5 and 35.5 million workers, or by 13 to 22 percent.

Occupational Profile

- *White-collar occupations:* White-collar workers now represent about half of the total labor force, up from 43 percent in 1960.

  - *Professional and technical workers:* This group includes many highly trained workers, such as scientists and engineers, medical practitioners, teachers, entertainers, pilots, and accountants. Between 1980 and 1990, employment is expected to grow from 16.4 million to between 19.7 and 20.7 million workers, or by 20 to 26 percent. The demand will be strong for scientists, engineers, technicians, medical professionals, system analysts, and programmers. Job prospects for secondary and college and university faculty are poor. Demand for lawyers and architects will grow but competition will be keen because of the glut of trained professionals in these occupations.

  - *Managers and administrators:* This group includes bank officers and managers, buyers, credit managers, and self-employed business operators. Between 1980 and 1990, this group is expected to grow from 9.4 million to between 10.6 and 11.3 million or by 13 to 21 percent.

  - *Clerical workers:* This group constitutes the largest occupational group and includes bank tellers, bookkeepers and accounting clerks, cashiers, secretaries, and typists. Between 1980 and 1990, employment in these occupations is expected to grow from 18.9 million to between 22.4 and 23.9 million workers, or by 19 to 27 percent. Although new developments in computers, office machines, and dictating equipment will enable clerical workers to do more work in less time and will change the skills needed in some jobs, continued growth is expected in most clerical occupations. Improved computer technology is reducing the need for keypunch operators, stenographers, and airline reservation and ticket agents, but the more extensive use of computers will greatly increase the employment of computer and peripheral equipment operators.

  - *Sales workers:* These workers are employed primarily by retail stores, manufacturing and wholesale firms, insurance companies, and real estate agencies. Employment in this group is expected to grow from 6.8 million to between 8.1 and 8.8 million workers, or by 19 to 28 percent. Much of this growth will be due to expansion in the retail trade industry which employs nearly one-half of these workers. The demand for both full- and part-time sales workers in the retail trade is expected to increase as the growing population, along with its geographic movement, requires more shopping centers and stores. Despite the use of labor-saving merchandising techniques, such as computerized checkout counters, more stores and longer operating hours will cause unemployment to increase.

- *Blue-collar occupations:* The blue-collar work force has grown slowly and farm workers have declined.

    - *Craft workers:* This group includes a wide variety of highly skilled workers, such as carpenters, tool-and-die makers, instrument makers, all-round machinists, electricians, and automobile mechanics. Between 1980 and 1990, employment in this group is expected to increase from 12.4 million to between 14.6 to 15.8 million, or by 18 to 27 percent. While there will be a growing demand for individuals in the construction trades, due to an expected increase in residential and commercial construction, employment declines are expected in the railroad industry, especially in the craft occupations of railroad and car shop repairers. Because of advances in printing technology, very little growth is anticipated in the printing crafts.

    - *Operatives except transport:* This group includes production workers such as assemblers, production painters, and welders. Between 1980 and 1990, employment is expected to rise from 10.7 million to between 12.2 and 13.2 million workers, or by 13 to 23 percent. Since the employment of operatives is tied closely to the production of goods, workers in this occupational area will be affected by the fate of various industries. Employment of textile operatives, for example, is expected to decline as more machinery is used in the textile industry.

    - *Transport operatives:* This group includes workers

who drive buses, trucks, taxis, and forklifts, as well as parking attendants and sailors. Employment in most of these occupations will increase because of greater use of most kinds of transportation equipment. Some occupations, such as bus driver and sailor, will grow only slowly. Between 1980 and 1990, employment of transport operatives is expected to rise from 3.5 million to between 4.2 and 4.4 million workers, or by 18 to 26 percent.

- *Laborers:* This group includes such workers as garbage collectors, construction laborers, and freight and stock handlers. Employment in this group is expected to grow slowly as machinery increasingly replaces manual labor. Between 1980 and 1990, employment of laborers is expected to increase from 5.9 million to between 6.7 and 7.1 million workers or by 14 to 22 percent.

- *Private household service workers:* These workers include housekeepers, child care workers, and maids and servants. Employment is not expected to increase for this group of workers.

- *Service workers:* This group includes a wide range of workers — firefighters, janitors, cosmetologists, bartenders, etc. These workers make up the fastest growing occupational group. Factors expected to increase the need for these workers are the rising demand for health services as the population becomes older and — as incomes rise — more frequent use of restaurants, beauty salons, and leisure services. Between 1980 and 1990, employment of service workers is expected to increase by about 24 to 32 percent, from 14.6 million to between 18.1 and 19.2 million workers.

- *Farm workers:* This group includes farmers and farm managers as well as farm laborers. Employment of these workers has declined for decades; farm productivity has increased as a result of fewer but larger farms, the use of more efficient machinery, and the development of new fertilizers and pesticides. Between 1980 and 1990 the number of farm workers is expected to decline from 2.7 million to between 2.4 and 2.2 million workers.

SOURCE: *Occupational Outlook Handbook,* 1982-83 Edition.

GROWING AND DECLINING OCCUPATIONS

The growing fields are computers, engineering, accounting, banking, economics, physics, and health care. The declining occupations include jobs for textile workers, domestics, farm laborers, assemblers, machine-tool operators, molders, and boiler tenders.

The patterns of growth and decline in industries and occupations for the 1978-1990 period generally follow the larger changes in the economy discussed earlier. The Bureau of Labor Statistics projects that the industries in Table 2 will experience the greatest growth and decline patterns for the period 1979-1990.

During the same period the following occupations will experience the greatest percentage decline in jobs:

Occupation	*Percent decline in employment*
— Shoemaking-machine operators	-19.2
— Farm laborers	-19.0
— Railroad-car repairers	-17.9
— Farm managers	-17.7
— Graduate assistants	-16.7
— Housekeepers, private households	-14.9
— Child-care workers, private household	-14.8
— Maids and servants, private household	-14.7
— Farm supervisors	-14.3
— Farmers, owners and tenants	-13.7
— Timber-cutting and logging workers	-13.6
— Secondary-school teachers	-13.1

On the other hand, the 20 fastest growing occupations during 1978-1980, by percentage, include the following:

Occupation	*Percent growth in employment*
— Data processing machine mechanics	+147.6
— Paralegal personnel	+132.4
— Computer systems analysts	+107.8
— Computer operators	+ 89.7
— Office machine and cash register servicers	+ 80.8
— Computer programmers	+ 73.6
— Aero-astronautic engineers	+ 70.4

TABLE 2
PROJECTED EMPLOYMENT CHANGES
FOR SELECT INDUSTRIES, 1979 -- 1990

Fastest growing	Average annual rate of job growth
— Other medical services	+4.6
— Typewriters and other office equipment	+4.5
— Computers and peripheral equipment	+4.2
— Coal mining	+4.1
— Hospitals	+3.8
— Crude petroleum and natural gas	+3.6
— Doctors' and dentists' services	+3.4
— Local government passenger transit	+3.3
— Other state and local government enterprises	+3.2
— Automobile repair	+3.1

Most rapidly declining	Average annual rate of job decline
— Dairy and poultry products	-3.3
— Alcoholic beverages	-3.1
— Leather tanning and industrial leather	-2.7
— Logging	-2.4
— Synthetic fibers	-2.1
— Other agricultural products	-1.8
— Railroad transportation	-1.7
— Wooden containers	-1.6
— Dairy products (processed)	-1.6
— Bakery products	-1.5

Largest job gains	Employment gain (in thousands)
— Eating and drinking places	1,912
— Retail trade, except eating and drinking places	1,878
— Hospitals	1,347
— Miscellaneous business services	1,171
— Other medical services	909
— New construction	892
— Wholesale trade	866
— Doctors' and dentists' services	580
— Banking	490
— Educational services (private)	416

SOURCE: *Economic Projections to 1990,* U.S. Department of Labor, Bureau of Labor Statistics, March 1982.

— Food preparation and service workers, fast food restaurants	+ 68.8
— Employment interviewers	+ 66.6
— Tax preparers	+ 64.5
— Correction officials and jailers	+ 60.3
— Architects	+ 60.2
— Dental hygienists	+ 57.9
— Physical therapists	+ 57.6
— Dental assistants	+ 57.5
— Peripheral EDP equipment operators	+ 57.3
— Child-care attendants	+ 56.3
— Veterinarians	+ 56.1
— Travel agents and accomodations appraisers	+ 55.6
— Nurses' aides and orderlies	+ 54.6

Not surprisingly, five of the six top growth occupations are in the information fields.

When examining the total number of new jobs created, the following 20 occupations come out on top as contributing to the largest number of additional jobs for the period 1978-1990:

Occupation	Employment growth (in thousands)
— Janitors and sextons	671.2
— Nurses' aides and orderlies	594.0
— Sales clerks	590.7
— Cashiers	545.5
— Waiters/waitresses	531.0
— General clerks, office	529.8
— Professional nurses	515.8
— Food preparation and service workers, fast food restaurants	491.9
— Secretaries	487.6
— Truckdrivers	437.6
— Kitchen helpers	300.6
— Elementary schoolteachers	272.8
— Typists	262.1
— Accountants and auditors	254.2
— Helpers, trades	232.5
— Blue-collar worker supervisors	221.1
— Licensed practical nurses	215.6
— Guards and doorkeepers	209.9
— Automotive mechanics	205.3

NEW OCCUPATIONS

In the early 1970's the auto and related industries – steel, rubber, glass, aluminum, railroads, and auto dealers – accounted for one-fifth of all employment in the United States. Today that percentage is declining. New occupations, centering around information and energy-related industries, are taking hold. They promise to create a new occupational structure and vocabulary in the future relating to computers, robotics, biotechnology, lasers, and fiber optics.

New occupations for the future, by number of new employees and occupational qualifications, are presented in Table 3.

TRENDS AND YOU

Most growth industries and occupations require skills training and experience. Moving into one of these fields will require knowledge of job qualifications, the nature of the work, and sources of employment. Fortunately, the Department of Labor publishes several useful sources of information to help you. These include the *Dictionary of Occupational Titles,* which identifies nearly 20,000 job titles. The *Occupational Outlook Handbook* provides an overview of current labor market conditions and projections as well as discusses various occupations according to several useful informational categories: nature of work; working conditions; employment; training, other qualifications, and achievement; job outlook; earnings; related occupations; and sources of additional information. Anyone seeking to enter the job market or change careers should consult these publications for initial information on trends and occupations.

However, remember that labor market statistics are for industries and occupations *as a whole.* They tell you nothing about the outlook of particular jobs for you, *the individual.* Therefore, be careful in how you interpret and use this information. If, for example, you want to become a high school teacher, and the data indeed tells you there will be a 10 percent decline in this occupation during the next 10 years, this does not mean you could not find employment as well as advance in this field. It merely means that, on the whole, competition may be keen for these jobs and that future advancement and mobility in this occupation may not be very good – on the whole. You, on the other hand, may do much better in this declining occupation than in a growing field, depending on your interests, motivation, and abilities.

TABLE 3

PROJECTIONS FOR FUTURE JOBS, 1980–1990

Occupational title	Employment growth	Qualifications required
Industrial Laser Process Technician	2,500,000 jobs	High-school, technical training, and retraining requirements will vary with levels of skill required under a severe system of job revolution.
Housing Rehabilitation Technician	1,750,000 jobs	Technicians, inspectors, and supervisors will require a high-school education and equivalent of two years of technical-college education plus appropriate experience (such as formal apprenticeship).
Energy Technician	1,500,000 jobs	Technicians, inspectors, and supervisory positions will require high-school education and the equivalent of two years of technical college.
Hazardous Waste Management Technician	1,500,000 jobs	Highly specialized technical training will be required for workers, supervisors, and managers in this very hazardous occupation.
Industrial Robot Production Technician	1,500,000 jobs	Knowledge and skills requirements will compare with present-day computer programmers and electronics technicians.
Materials Utilization Technician	500,000 jobs	An education level equivalent to that of an electronics technician, tool and die maker, nondestructive materials testing specialist, or industrial inspector will be required. Two years of technical college will be the minimum requirement.

TABLE 3 — *continued*

Occupational title	Employment growth	Qualifications required
Battery Technician	250,000 jobs	The processes within this occupation include potential hazards, but they can be safely performed by technicians with a vocational high school education.
Bionic-Electronic Technicians	200,000 jobs	These technicians will require appropriate technical knowledge of microprocessors and specialized accredited education in the respective anatomical, physiological, and psychiatric disciplines equivalent to a minimum of four years of college work. Medical professionals who establish a reputation will move into the higher six-figure levels of earnings.
Holographic Inspection Specialist	200,000 jobs	Specialist working in this new technology will require a minimum of two years of postsecondary technical education and training, with emphasis on optical fibers characteristics and transmission, photography, optical physics, and computer programming.
Genetic Engineering Technician	150,000 jobs	A bachelor's degree in chemistry, biology, or medicine will be helpful in the initial industrial production work, but production operations will be accomplished by "process technicians" with high-school and two-year postsecondary technical education and training.

SOURCE: *The Futurist*, June, 1982.

As we emphasized earlier, use this industrial and occupational data to expand your awareness of job and career options. By no means should you make occupational choices based upon this information *alone*. Such choices require an additional type of information — something which we will address shortly.

Chapter Four

ACQUIRING TRAINING AND SKILLS

The imbalance between skills workers possess and those employers need has widened in recent years. This imbalance and related structural unemployment are expected to continue, if not increase, during the next decade.

The skills imbalance is due to several training failures and failures to train on the part of both government and industry. Traditional educational institutions fail to teach the skills needed for the new jobs of today and tomorrow. Government policies, emphasizing redistributive subsidy and welfare programs, provide little incentive for individuals to seek retraining. And present training programs offered by the private sector tend to be oriented toward managers in the soft skill areas; training of production workers in the hard technical skill areas is relatively neglected.

In the meantime, a large segment of the workforce is still oriented to the job market with skills and expectations best suited for the 1950's and 1960's. Rather than take initiative to acquire new skills, many people do nothing; they remain unemployed, underemployed, or unhappy with their work. Others, unwilling to accept responsibility, seek scapegoats for their plight.

In this chapter we discuss the problem of training as well as outline how individuals can acquire the necessary education and training for the jobs and careers of tomorrow. This knowledge is essential information for re-careering in the decades ahead.

GOVERNMENT AND INDIVIDUALS

The structure of education and training in the United States is highly fragmented, and its scope, quality, and effectiveness varies greatly. As a result, many people have difficulty understanding and utilizing education and training opportunities.

Federal government-sponsored training programs consist of a maze of 22 programs ranging from Trade Adjustment Assistance to programs for redwood forest lumberjacks. The major federal program has been the controversial Comprehensive Employment and Training Act (CETA) program. It is now being replaced with the Jobs Training Partnership Act. This new program, like its predecessor, is of limited scope, mainly designed for the hardcore unemployed.

Pat Choate and Noel Epstein best characterize federal training programs for the public: they tend to be subject to *"confusion, fragmentation, bureaucracy and the political pork barrel"* (Choate and Epstein: D5). While much needed, programs of such limited scope will not have a great effect on the overall training and retraining needs of the nation.

But politicians, journalists, employment specialists, and many other "experts" continue to propose more government-sponsored training and retraining programs in order to "put America back to work." Such well-meaning proposals have limitations. They fail to take into account the capabilities of the government to develop and manage such programs. First, the costs of training and retraining are so massive that the government could not sustain them for long. Second, the intergovernmental system through which retraining must take place — state and local governments — is already too fragmented, decentralized, and political to allow for effective *implementation* of a government-sponsored program. Third, given these constraints, any realistic government-sponsored program would be small in scale; consequently, it would have little impact on the overall training and retraining needs of the country. These are real — not ideological or philosophical — constraints.

Despite its failures and limitations, government still has a major role to play. For instance, it would be ideal if both government and the private sector provided new *incentives* to encourage more people to re-career. These incentives might include tax breaks for individuals engaged in retraining and for corporations sponsoring training programs. Another incentive, by far the most innovative, would be to create an Individual Training Account (ITA), structured similarly to a pension fund (Choate and Epstein: D5). Jointly financed by employers and employees, the ITA would provide money for retraining displaced workers. The individual could use this money — perhaps in the form of a retraining voucher — to enroll in a specialized program of his or her own choosing. This problem of *financing retraining* will have to be addressed with these and other public policy options in the not-too-distant future.

The problem with most government policies and programs is that they are inevitably political. They are controversial, reflecting competing values in American society. They take time to develop and implement. And they often fail. In the meantime, *the individual must be responsible for his or her own employment fate* by taking appropriate actions to solve his or her own employment and career problems. Government is not likely to solve these problems.

The old cliche that *"there is no such thing as a free lunch"* should be reinforced with a new saying for the coming re-careering era: *"Times will be tough for those who don't get off their duff!"* At the very least, re-careering requires individuals to take risks, invest time and money, learn something new, and apply new knowledge and skills to changing employment situations.

RETRAINING PROBLEMS AND NEEDS

Retraining needs in the decade ahead are difficult to estimate. Indeed, conducting a survey on the present state of training is difficult, if not impossible, given the fragmented nature of organizations in America. Nonetheless, certain trends are evident in the workplace, and some statistics are available on the scope and depth of training in the United States. For example, during the past 30 years, blue-collar employment has fallen from the peaks outlined in Table 4:

		TABLE 4		
		DECLINES OF MAJOR INDUSTRIES		
Industry	*year*	*High* *employment*	*1982* *employment*	*percent* *decline*
Steel mills	1957	719,900	306,700	-57%
Textile mills	1952	1,073,200	633,900	-41%
Auto making	1978	760,500	533,800	-30%
Railroads	1952	1,399,800	448,400	-68%

SOURCE: U.S. Department of Labor, 1982.

Further declines are expected in these blue-collar occupations due to continuing technological changes in the workplace.

The changes have been evident during the past decade, and they will likely accelerate in the decade ahead. For example, Bluestone and Harrison found in their study, *The Deindustrialization of America*, that between 35 and 40 million Americans lost their jobs in the 1970's; many were forced to relocate as plants closed and industries moved South. A recent study by Carnegie-Mellon University predicts that robots will supplant 3 million factory workers by the year 2000. Many factories may be completely automated — requiring only a handful of technicians to supervise the robots. In fact, the Japanese are well on the way to completing the first totally automated factory; it should be operational by 1986.

Where will the displaced workers of today and tomorrow go? The fear — justifiably so — is that many workers will be permanently displaced by the new technology. For example, Harvard University economist James L. Medoff points to Commerce Department statistics; between 1969 and 1978 job-related training provided by employers for workers aged 25 to 49 only increased 6 percent from 5.2 percent. A further indication of a growing skills imbalance in the labor market since 1969 is found in Medoff's study of unemployment. Prior to 1969, when unemployment increased among 25 to 64 year old men, the number of help-wanted ads declined as employers hired from the excess pool of skilled unemployed workers. However, since 1969 the number of help-wanted ads has not declined proportionately during a period of high unemployment. Medoff believes this indicates there is now a decreasing demand for the skills of present unemployed workers, a clear sign of worsening structural unemployment (*Business Week*, July 19, 1982: 178)

On the other hand, the new technology promises to create new jobs. Many people hope it will create a sufficient number of new jobs to absorb displaced workers and that employers will retrain them for the new technology.

Both the fear and the hope will probably come true, but for different groups in the society. The fears are indeed real. For example, at present 23 million Americans are estimated to be functionally illiterate — they can't read or write. Add to this number the fact that nearly 1 million students drop out of high school each year. These realities, as Department of Education Secretary Terrel E. Bell told Congress, have alarming consequences for the future: *"up to 75 percent of the unemployed lack the basic skills of communication, personal relations, motivation, self-confidence, reading and computing that would enable employers to train them for the jobs that will open up in the next few years"* (*Washington Post,* November

27, 1982:1) Therefore, a large segment of the population will re-quire remedial training *prior to* receiving job skills training.

For poor inner city and rural people, the consequences of the new technology are frightening. Many of these people may become hopeless wards of the state, ill-equipped to function in a highly literate information society. Facing a vicious circle of circumstances which prevent them from taking initiative, they will constitute a major problem for society. In the end, government may be the only institution willing and able to provide basic training in functional skills for these individuals.

The worldwide problem of unemployment is even more fright-ening. Some forecasters predict that 35 million people — a third greater than today — will be unemployed in the major industrial nations by 1985. Third World nations, with 300 to 500 million un-employed at present, are expected to have around 900 million to 1 billion unemployed in the year 2000. Jobs are increasingly becoming the top priority problem for all nations (Merritt: 37).

MISPLACED PUBLIC EDUCATION

Public educational institutions have been slow in responding to the obvious training and retraining needs of employers. Despite billions of dollars expended on university education, the quality of reading, writing, and communication skills, as well as analytical and problem-solving abilities, seems to be declining compared to previous generations of graduates. The critical high-tech programs of engineer-ing and computer science are not producing enough graduates to meet the demands of private industry.The result is a mismatch of college and university educational programs with the employment needs of companies.

Colleges and universities continue to graduate students in fields where there are few job opportunities. For example, while most college graduates in the 1960's found jobs in their chosen occupations, more graduates in the 1970's were forced to seek employment outside their fields. The Department of Labor con-cludes:

> *Like college graduates in the 1970's, future graduates may be less likely to find jobs in the occupation of their choice than graduates during the 1960's. Many may be unemployed or have to move from job to job to find sat-isfying employment or compete with nongraduates for the most desirable jobs not previously filled by graduates. (Occupational Projections: 20).*

The transition for public education will be slow and difficult. Many public schools are too tradition-ladden as well as insulated from the realities of the labor market to place a major emphasis on vocational-skills training within their academic programs. Lacking accountability, public colleges and universities continue to teach a disproportionate number of subjects, courses, and disciplines which are favorites of the faculty, simply considered necessary for a "well-rounded" graduate, or at best "interesting" rather than emphasize skills for a turbulent job market.

On the other hand, community colleges, business colleges, vocational-technical schools, specialized training institutes, and university-sponsored conferences and workshops have been more responsive to training students in relation to job market needs. Many of these institutions provide practical, intensive skills training programs as well as placement services for their graduates. Over 25 million people participate in these programs each year. In 1980-81 the American Association of Continuing Education reported that 585,719 individuals enrolled in university-sponsored conferences and workshops which ran from 1 to 10 days at an enrollment cost of $150 to $800.

PRIVATE INITIATIVES

If public educational institutions fail to respond to real needs, the private sector will have to provide the bulk of the training and retraining necessary for the decades ahead. More private educational and professional training organizations will be required to provide short two to five-day workshops, four-week refresher courses, or 15-week intensive training programs.

The private sector is equipped to provide training alternatives. Thousands of private organizations already provide off-the-shelf, custom-designed, and generic training seminars. Most of these programs last one to five days and stress intensive training in particular subject and skill areas. However, all is not well. Many of these organizations have recently experienced financial difficulties. The lagging economy, the misplaced emphasis on soft skills training, and the highly competitive nature of these firms have all contributed to the recent financial problems. In 1980, for instance, public seminars were a $350-million-a-year business. Since then, two of the four major firms filed for Chapter 11 bankruptcy proceedings. The largest group — the American Management Associations (AMA) — lost $6 million in 1981.

A few companies are preparing for the future with their own in-house training programs. For example, Ford Motor Company and the United Auto Workers are working with a nationwide network of community colleges to provide retraining for displaced automakers. Polaroid Corporation conducts reading labs and math tutorials for 200 assembly line workers in order to prepare them for new technology in the workplace. AT&T maintains the largest number of in-house trainers — 10,000 trainers with a $1.25 billion annual budget for 1,042,000 employees or a trainer-to-employee ratio of 1:104. AT&T designs retraining programs six to nine months prior to putting new equipment in place. The U.S. Navy maintains the highest trainer-to-employee ratio: 26,000 full-time trainers for 565,000 enlisted personnel or a 1:21 ratio. Altogether, the private sector spends from $30 to $40 billion a year on training and retraining. This figure is likely to increase as the skills required in the workplace change in response to the changing technology.

Most training takes place within organizations as either on-the-job or classroom training. Most firms with 500 or more employees have at least one full-time trainer in their organization; many of these organizations also have training departments. Organizations with more than 25,000 employees have an average of 50 full-time trainers. Organizations with 100 or fewer employees normally use part-time trainers or contract with private firms to conduct specific training programs for their employees. The overall distribution of trainers in organizations is identified in Table 5:

TABLE 5

**Proportion of Organizations Reporting
No, Full- and Part-time Trainers**

Organization size by # of employees	% of Respondents Reporting:					
	No employee with training responsibility	At least 1 full-time trainer in organization	Full-time head office-based trainers	Full-time field-based trainers	Part-time head office trainers	Part-time field-based trainers
50-99	42.9	16.1	11.6	5.4	42.9	15.2
100-499	21.0	30.9	29.1	7.3	55.5	30.0
500-999	3.9	62.1	58.3	9.7	53.4	34.0
1,000-2,499	3.7	82.6	79.8	30.3	50.5	47.6
2,500-9,999	2.8	85.3	84.4	33.9	38.7	43.4
10,000-24,999	0.0	91.7	91.7	79.2	33.3	66.7
25,000+	0.0	94.1	94.1	94.1	41.2	70.6
Full sample	**92.2**	**57.7**	**55.1**	**22.1**	**37.3**	**35.8**

SOURCE: *Training*, October 1982: 22.

In a recent survey of training in the United States, 26 different categories of training were identified as most salient. These are listed in Table 6:

TABLE 6

TYPES OF TRAINING MOST FREQUENTLY PROVIDED

Type of Training	Sample Providing
1. Supervisory skills	77.1
2. New employee orientation	71.2
3. Management skills and development	67.3
4. Communication skills training (reading, writing, listening, etc.)	58.2
5. Technical skills/knowledge updating	58.2
6. Time management	51.2
7. Safety	50.4
8. New equipment orientation	47.4
9. Productivity improvement	46.0
10. New methods/procedures	46.0
11. Customer relations/customer service	46.6
12. Mandated programs (EEO, OSHA, etc.)	43.0
13. Clerical/secretarial skills	42.3
14. Personal growth	38.6
15. Employee (non-sales) motivation/ incentive/recognition programs	36.7
16. Sales skills	36.3
17. Labor relations	35.7
18. Information management (word processing, MIS, etc.)	35.0
19. Data processing	32.6
20. Team building	32.5
21. Disease prevention/health promotion (Stress, nutrition, exercise, etc.)	29.2
22. Organization development	28.5
23. Product knowledge	27.2
24. Career planning	22.8
25. Outplacement/retirement	17.2
26. Customer education	17.0
27. Foreign language/cross-cultural skills	8.5

SOURCE: *Training*, October 1982: 31.

According to this study, supervisors are the most likely to receive training. Furthermore, this type of training is of questionable value — the quick-fix, *"squishy, soft, and mushy stuff. . . the hard-to-do technical skills training"* has been sorely neglected (*Training*, October 1982: 70). Unfortunately, general office personnel (clerks, typists, etc.) and production workers — the two groups requiring the greatest amount of retraining — at present are the least likely to receive training. The study concludes on a note of alarm: *"In light of increasing demand for trained employees for both the office and factory of the future, this is an unsettling finding"* (*Training*, October 1982: 30).

Thus, while billions of dollars are spent each year on training and education, neither the public nor private sectors are adequately meeting the new retraining needs of society. From the perspective of training professionals, we are rapidly approaching a "human capital crisis!"

NEEDING GENERALIST-SPECIALISTS

As we noted earlier, individuals must take the initiative to acquire the training and retraining necessary for a turbulent job market. No longer will knowledge of job hunting techniques alone be sufficient to function in such a job market. Specific work-content skills — mostly technical in nature — must accompany well-defined job search strategies. And promising trends have begun. For example, in 1981 an estimated 2.5 million Americans enrolled in courses specifically designed to help them change careers (Hedberg: 45).

So where do you go for skills training in a highly fragmented, decentralized, and chaotic educational and training market? While many organizations provide their own in-service training and retraining programs, they assume one possesses a certain level of skill proficiency prior to being hired. In other words, they expect the employee is easily *trainable*. For many jobs, this means one needs a well-rounded educational background which develops basic reading, writing, and communication skills as well as interpersonal, analytical, organizational, and problem-solving abilities — the major thrust of a good generalist liberal arts education. Given the changing nature of the job market, such an educational background can best prepare you for the flexibility you will need in the future.

At the same time, while providing a good foundation, a generalist background is insufficient for functioning in today's job market. Individuals need a strong background in scientific-technical skills. These skills are in math, science, computers, and technical fields. In addition, individuals are expected to have developed basic work attitudes which translate into positive behaviors such as: coming to work, being on time, managing time, meeting deadlines, getting along with superiors and co-workers, and being courteous to the public.

The changing job market requires more generalist-specialists who are trainable and thus can adapt to rapidly changing work-places. For example, it is estimated that 35 million office workers will be using some type of electronic equipment in another 10 years — an increase of 30 million from today. Given the rapidly changing office technologies, employers may need to retrain the same workers five to ten times during a 20 year period. Therefore, regardless of what type of word processor an individual is trained on in a secretarial school today, the same individual can expect to operate one of a new generation of word processors five years from now. The important question for employers will be: "Is this individual, who is now a specialist on machine X, flexible enough to adapt to machine Y tomorrow?" The answers require a merging of the generalist and specialist traditions in individuals' educational and training programs.

TRAINING SOURCES

The Department of Labor identifies nine structured training programs individuals should familiarize themselves with prior to making educational and training choices:

- public vocational education
- private vocational education
- employer training
- apprenticeship programs
- federal employment and training programs
- Armed Forces training
- home study schools
- community and junior colleges
- colleges and universities

Most of these sources emphasize practical hands-on training. Private trade schools, for example, are flourishing at a time when university enrollments are declining — an indication of the shift to practical skills training in education.

Public vocational education is provided through secondary, postsecondary, and adult vocational and technical programs. The emphasis in many secondary schools is to give high school students vocational training in addition to the regular academic program. Postsecondary vocational education is provided for individuals who have left high school but who are not seeking a baccalaureate degree. Adult vocational and technical programs emphasize retraining or upgrading the skills of individuals in the labor force.

The traditional agricultural, trade, and industrial emphasis of vocational education has been vastly expanded to include training in distribution, health, home economics, office, and technical occupations. Most programs train individuals for specific occupations, which are outlined in the *Occupational Outlook Handbook*. In 1978 approximately 16.7 million people were enrolled in public vocational education programs.

Private vocational education institutions in 1978 numbered 6,813 with 14,600 programs. They enrolled 1,043,000 students in 165 different programs. The programs fell into seven areas, similar to the public vocational education programs: agribusiness, marketing/distribution, health, home economics, business/office, technical, and trades and industry. Two-thirds of these schools are specialized as cosmetology/barber, business/office, and flight schools. Most of these institutions are small, with fewer than 100 students, and specialized in only one or two skill areas such as real estate, nursing, auto work, commercial art, or apparel.

Employer training usually involves training new employees, improving employee performance, or preparing employees for new jobs. Skilled and semi-skilled workers are trained through apprenticeships, learning by doing, and structured on-the-job instruction. White-collar employees usually receive structured classroom training offered by in-house trainers, professional associations, private firms, or colleges and universities. Tuition-aid programs are used frequently among firms lacking in-house training resources.

Apprenticeship programs normally range from one to five years, depending on the particular organization. These programs are used most extensively in the trade occupations. For example, of the 50,464 apprenticeship completions registered with the Department of Labor in 1978, 60 percent were in construction trades, 12 percent in metalworking, 4 percent in personal services, 2 percent in printing, and 22 percent in miscellaneous areas. Nearly 300,000 individuals are involved in apprenticeships each year.

Federal employment and training programs largely function through state and local governments. Since 1973 the Comprehensive Employment and Training Act (CETA) has been the major federal government jobs training and employment program for the disadvantaged. The program serves about 3 million individuals as

well as another 1 million youth in subsidized summer jobs. When
the CETA program ends in October 1983 and is replaced by the Jobs
Training Partnership Act, greater emphasis will be placed on public-
private collaboration in identifying training needs and developing
training programs. Private industry councils (PIC's) will play the
major role in this highly decentralized jobs training program. Provisions of this Act also address the training needs of displaced workers.

The other federal programs — Work Incentive (WIN) Program
and Job Corps — also provide jobs training. However, like CETA,
these programs are geared primarily toward helping the hardcore
unemployed and the economically disadvantaged. Others in need of
training or retraining are largely left on their own to acquire education and training.

Armed Forces training focuses on five categories of training —
recruitment, specialized skills, officer acquisition, professional development, and flight. Specialized skills training is by far the most
important and extensive training conducted by the various services.
Within this category of training, enlisted personnel receive a great
amount of mechanical and technical training which may or may not
be transferable to the civilian work world.

Home study or correspondence schools provide a variety of
training options. Most programs concentrate on acquiring a single
skill; others will even offer a BA, MA, or Ph.D. by mail! Some
programs are of questionable quality. For many people, this is a
convenient, inexpensive, and effective way of acquiring new skills.
In 1978 approximately 3 million students were enrolled in home
study courses. About 1.2 million were enrolled in such programs
conducted by the federal government and the military.

Community and junior colleges in recent years have shifted
their emphasis from preparing individuals for university degree programs to preparing them for the job market. Accordingly, more of
their programs emphasize vocational or occupational curriculums,
such as data processing or dental hygiene, which are typically two-
year programs resulting in an associate degree. During the 1970's
degrees awarded by these programs increased more than 50 percent.
Community and junior colleges will probably continue to expand
their program offerings as they adjust to the employment needs of
communities.

Colleges and universities continue to provide the traditional
four-year and graduate degree programs in various subject fields.
While many of the fields are occupational-specific, such as engineering, law, medical, and business, many are not. The exact relationship
of the degree programs to the job market varies with different

disciplines. As noted earlier, in recent years, graduates of many programs have had difficulty finding employment in their chosen fields. This is particularly true for students who only have a generalist background in the liberal arts. More recently, however, many colleges and universities have adjusted to their declining enrollments by offering several nontraditional occupational-related courses and programs. Continuing education, special skills training courses, short courses, and workshops and seminars on job-related matters have become popular with nontraditional, older students who seek specific skills training rather than degrees. At the same time, traditional academic programs are placing greater emphasis on internships and cooperative education programs in order to give students work experience related to their academic programs.

Additional training programs may be sponsored by local governments, professional associations, women's centers, YWCA's, and religious and civic groups. As training and retraining becomes more acceptable to the general public, we can expect different forms and types of training programs to be sponsored by various groups.

We also can expect a revolution in the training field, closely related to high-tech developments. Computer-based training, similar in some respects to traditional home study programs, will become more prevalent as home computers and interactive video training packages are developed in response to the new technology and the rising demand for skills training. Training may well fall into Toffler's "prosumer" category: in a decentralized information market, individuals will choose what training they most desire as well as control when and where they will receive it. With the development of interactive video training programs, individuals will manage the training process in a more efficient and effective manner than with the more centralized, time consuming, and expensive use of traditional student-teacher classroom instruction. This type of training may eventually make many of the previously discussed categories of education and training obsolete.

MAKING CHOICES

Choosing a skills training program presupposes you know what you want to do. As we will see later, knowing what it is you want to do is the key to doing it. The fact that many organizations offer a multiplicity of training options gives you little comfort in choosing training and retraining options that are right for you.

Should you go to college to get a degree or go for a certificate program? Should you enroll in a public vocational school or the

Armed Forces for skills training? What about a home study course
or a two-year community college program? We cannot answer these
questions for you. You must first know what it is you want to do.
Perhaps you don't need to enter a structured program after all. Maybe you first need to get a job, using your present work-content
skills, and then take advantage of training opportunities provided
by the employer.

Whatever you do, you must engage in some soul searching
about yourself. As outlined in Chapter Seven, ask yourself what do
I want to do with my life? Chart a course, however vague, and begin
filling in the blanks by doing the research we outline in Chapter
Nine. Start by taking an inventory of your present skills, as outlined
in Chapter Six. What is it you do well and enjoy doing? What is it
you would like to do but you don't have sufficient skills to do?
Once you have answered these questions, you should be ready to
research your educational and training options.

Begin by consulting several published sources of information
on education and training. If you are contemplating a degree program, for a few words of caution, read Ivar Berg's *Education and
Jobs: The Great Training Robbery* (The Center for Urban Education,
105 Madison Avenue, New York, NY 10016, $7.50). If you are
more oriented toward acquiring a specific work-content skill, consult
various professional or trade associations; many of these can provide
you with a list of institutions that provide training in particular
fields. Check the "Sources of Additional Information" section of
the *Occupational Outlook Handbook* for useful names and addresses
relating to employment training in specific fields.

Other sources of published information on education and training opportunities include the reference section of the library, a career
planning center, or a guidance office. Most have collections of cata-
logues and directories listing educational and training opportunities.

For information on private trade and technical schools, write
the National Association of Trade and Technical Schools (NATTS)
for copies of these two publications:

- *Handbook of Trade and Technical Careers and Training*
- *How to Choose a Career and a Career School*

Their mailing address and telephone number are: NATTS, 2021 K
St. NW, Washington, DC 20006, Tel. 202/296-8892.

For information on apprenticeship programs, contact the
closest Apprenticeship Information Center (AIC). It is affiliated with
the U.S. Employment Service, and provides information, counseling,
aptitude testing, and referrals to union hiring halls and employers.

Also write to the U.S. Department of Labor's Bureau of Apprenticeship and Training for several pamphlets dealing with apprenticeships. Their address is: Office of Information, Inquiries Unit, Employment and Training Administration, U.S. Department of Labor, Rm. 10225, 601 K St. NW, Washington, DC 20213, Tel. 202/376-6730.

If you are interested in home study and correspondence courses, the National Home Study Council provides information in these publications:

- *Directory of Accredited Home Study Schools* (free)
- *There's a School in Your Mail Box* ($5.00 postpaid)

Their address is the National Home Study Council, 1601 18th St. NW, Washington, DC 20009, Tel. 202/234-5100. The National University Extension Association also publishes a useful guide entitled *Guide to Independent Study Through Correspondence Instruction* (Petersen's Guides, 228 Alexander St., Princeton, NJ 08540, $2.00, plus $1.00 for shipping).

In addition to familiarizing yourself with these options, you need to determine the quality of the programs and their suitability to your needs. When contacting a particular institution, ask to speak to former students and graduates, and write to the Council on Postsecondary Accreditation (One Dupont Circle, Suite 760, Washington, DC 20036) to inquire about the school's credentials. Focus your attention on the *results or outcomes* the institution achieves. Instead of asking how many faculty have Master or Ph.D. degrees or how many students are enrolled, ask:

- *What happened to last year's graduates?*
- *Where do they work?*
- *How much do they earn?*
- *How many were placed in jobs through this institution?*

If they can't answer these questions, they may not be doing an adequate job to meet your needs.

Most colleges and universities will provide assistance to adult learners. Contact student services, continuing education, academic advising, adult services, or women's offices at your local community college, college, or university. Be sure to talk to present and former students about the *expectations and results* of the programs for them. Always remember that educators are in the business of keeping themselves employed, and today, more than ever, educational institutions need students to keep their programs alive. Don't necessarily

expect professional educators to be objective about your future
vis-a-vis their skills and programs. At the very least, you must do a
critical evaluation of the programs.

If you need further assistance, contact a local branch of the
National Center for Educational Brokering. While there is no na-
tional clearinghouse to help you match your goals with appropriate
educational programs, NCEB can assist you nonetheless. NCEB
counselors will help you identify your goals and career alternatives.
For information on the center nearest you, write to the National
Center for Educational Brokering, National Institute for Work and
Learning, 1211 Connecticut Avenue N.W., Washington, DC 20036.

Other sources of information on educational and training programs are the Yellow Pages of your telephone directory and
employers. Look under "Schools" in the telephone book. Call the
schools and ask them to send you literature and application forms.
Ask them how best to acquire the necessary skills for particular
occupations. Most important, *thoroughly research alternatives before
you invest money, time, and effort.*

FINANCING YOUR FUTURE

Most people can take advantage of training opportunities in
order to better function in today's job market. Lack of information
and money are often excuses based upon ignorance of available
resources and costs. Education and training may not be cheap, but
neither need they be excessively expensive. It is best to view education and training as good investments in your future. There are
alternatives to expensive training. For example, adult education
programs sponsored by the public school system as well as community colleges are relatively inexpensive to attend. If you have the
will, you usually can find the way in the American educational and
training system.

Financial aid for education and training is somewhat bewilder-
ing and confusing. It requires research and perseverance on your
part. You should begin by contacting the financial aid officers at
various institutions that offer the training you desire for advice on
financial aid. The particular institutions as well as many other organizations provide scholarships, fellowships, grants, loans, and
work-study programs. The American Legion publishes a useful booklet — *Need a Lift?* — on careers and scholarships for undergraduate
and graduate students. Write to: American Legion, Attn: Emblem
Sales, P. O. Box 1055, Indianapolis, IN 46206, $1.00 postpaid. The
College Board publishes information on student financial aid. It is

free for the asking: College Board Publication Orders, Box 2815, Princeton, NJ 08541.

Information on Federal Government financial aid programs — grants, loans, work-study, and benefits — can be obtained by writing to the Department of Education for a pamphlet entitled *Five Federal Financial Aid Programs, 1981-82; A Student Consumer's Guide.* Revised yearly, this publication can be obtained by calling toll-free: 800/638-6700 (Maryland residents call 800/492-6602) or write to: Bureau of Student Financial Assistance, P. O. Box 84, Washington, DC 20044.

For information on financial assistance for specific groups, such as Hispanics, blacks, Native Americans, and women, write for a copy of the Department of Education's most current edition of *Selected List of Postsecondary Education Opportunities for Minorities and Women* (Superintendent of Documents, U.S. Government Printing Office, Washington, DC 20402, $6.00, GPO stock number 065-000-00118-7. Two other publications can be obtained by writing to Impact Publications, 10655 Big Oak Circle, Manassas, VA 22111, Tel. 703/361-7300:

- *Directory of Special Programs for Minority Group Members: Career Information Services, Employment Skills Banks, Financial Aid Sources,* $20.00 postpaid

- *Financial Aid for Minority Students* (Series of booklets on Allied Health, Business, Education, Engineering, Law, Journalism/Communications, Medicine, Science), $20.00 postpaid for set of 8.

Don't forget to compare the different costs of various educational and training programs. Many are inexpensive whereas others are extremely costly. Indeed, one of the major characteristics of the American educational and training system is the variety of *options* it offers individuals. These include different choices in terms of programs, quality, costs, and expected outcomes. Therefore, you must do your research in order to identify your options and make informed choices.

PART II

Developing
Re-Careering
Skills

Chapter Five
GETTING ORGANIZED

GETTING ORGANIZED

Knowing about future employment projections as well as identifying job and training opportunities are initial steps to building your re-careering skills. The next step is to examine job market myths which may prevent you from taking action or lead you into unproductive channels. Finally, you should organize yourself by developing an effective job search campaign based upon the realities of today's job market.

This chapter links our previous overview of re-careering to the practical planning and implementation aspects of conducting a job search. In this chapter we examine the basic prerequisites for launching a successful job search: overcoming myths; understanding the job market; focusing on the career development and job search processes; choosing from multiple job search options; organizing your time; developing a plan of action; following key principles for successful implementation; taking risks; handling rejections; developing a support group; and handling the IRS. Throughout this chapter we emphasize the importance of *organizing and implementing* for success. Your understanding of problems, approaches, and solutions must be translated into concrete action steps for achieving results.

YESTERDAY'S MYTHOLOGY

Most people have an image of how the job market works as well as how they should relate to it. This image is based upon a combination of facts, stereotypes, and myths learned from experience and from the advice of well-meaning individuals. Unfortunately, this image guides many people into unproductive job search channels and thus reconfirms the often-heard lament of the unsuccessful job searcher — *"What more can I do — there are no jobs out there for me."*

Myths about jobs, careers, and the job market must be addressed before proceeding to organize yourself for dealing with employment realities. Ten such myths most frequently affect the job search:

Myth 1: *Anyone can find a job; all you need to know is how to find a job.*

Reality: This is the "form versus substance" myth developed and perpetuated by career counselors in the 1960's and 1970's and preached by leading writers. It is probably a reality in an industrial society with low unemployment — a reality for the 1950's and 1960's. It is a myth for the post-industrial, high-tech society of the 1980's and 1990's. For example, in 1982 there were 12 million unemployed Americans, many of whom knew how to find a job. Reading the how-to books and knowing how to find a job were not enough. They encountered other harsh realities not addressed by the career counselors. Many of the unemployed were highly skilled in the technology of the industrial society, and they lived and owned homes in such depressed communities as Detroit. Unfortunately, these people lacked the necessary *skills and mobility* required for performing jobs which were in demand in other communities. While it is extremely important to learn job search skills, these skills are no substitute for acquiring concrete work-content skills. Many career counselors still believe it is often more difficult to find a job than to do a job, but this is only true if you are well qualified to do a job in areas where there are jobs. This myth is ideally suited for individuals in the job finding businesses — you pay them money to get a job in a hurry, without having to go back to school to get retraining. It results in finding stopgap jobs which may have little or no future or not finding a job at all.

Myth 2: *The best way to find a job is to respond to classified ads and announcements with employment agencies as well as submit applications to personnel offices.*

Reality: This is the most serious myth preventing an effective job search. These are the worst methods for finding jobs. They assume there is an organized, coherent, and centralized job market. Instead, the job market is highly decentralized, fragmented, and chaotic. Classified ads, employment agencies, and personnel offices are where the lowest level and most competitive jobs will be found. Avoid these unless you are desperate. The best jobs, with the least competition, are found on the hidden job market. Your most fruitful strategy will be to penetrate this hidden job market by conducting research and informational interviews. Chapters Nine and Ten show you how to do this.

Myth 3: *In a tight job market with high unemployment, few jobs are available for me.*

Reality: This may be true if you lack marketable skills and insist on applying for jobs listed in the newspapers, employment agencies or personnel offices. Competition in the advertised job market will increase during a period of high unemployment, but mainly for jobs requiring few skills. However, many jobs are available on the hidden job market during hard times. Jobs requiring advanced technical skills will go begging during such times. There may be less competition for many jobs during a high unemployment period because many people become discouraged and quit job hunting after a few weeks of disappointments with the advertised job market.

Myth 4: *I know how to find a job but opportunities are not available for me.*

Reality: Most people don't know how to find a job or they
           lack marketable work-content skills. They continue
           to use the most ineffective methods — responding
           to job listings, sending resumes, and contacting em-
           ployment agencies. Opportunities are readily avail-
           able for those who understand the structure and
           operation of the job market, have appropriate work-
           content skills, and use job search methods designed
           for the hidden job market.

Myth 5:   *Employers are in the driver's seat; they have the*
           upper hand with applicants.

Reality: Employers often do not know what they want; many
           make poor hiring decisions. Frequently they let the
           applicants define needs. If you can help employers
           define their needs as being your skills and talents,
           you will be in the driver's seat.

Myth 6:   *Employers hire the best qualified candidates. Without*
           a great deal of experience and numerous qualifica-
           tions, I don't have a chance.

Reality: Employers hire people for all kinds of reasons; ex-
           perience and qualifications tend to rank third or
           fourth in their pecking order of hiring criteria. For
           many jobs, they seldom hire the best qualified indi-
           vidual because "qualifications" are difficult to
           measure. Employers normally seek people who are
           competent, intelligent, honest, and likable. In ad-
           dition to your paper qualifications, you must com-
           municate to employers that you are the individual
           who is most competent, intelligent, honest, and
           likable. Since they are hiring your future and not
           your past, you must communicate your future
           value to employers. You must learn how to over-
           come employers' objections to any lack of experi-
           ence or qualifications. Don't confess your weak-
           nesses. In the end, the best qualified person is the
           one who knows how to get the job — convinces
           employers they will *like* him or her the most.

Myth 7:   *It is best to go into a growing field where jobs are*
           plentiful.

Reality: It depends on several factors. First, so-called growth fields can quickly become no-growth fields, such as aerospace engineering and nuclear energy. Second, by the time you acquire the necessary skills for entering a growth field, you may experience the "disappearing job" phenomenon: too many people did the same thing you did. Third, since many people may be leaving a no-growth field, you may see new opportunities arising for you. Fourth, going after a growth field is another way of trying to fit into a job rather than find one that is fit for you. You should first find out what it is you do well and enjoy doing (Chapter Six), what additional training you may need, and then find a job or career which is conducive to your skills and interests. You will be better off in the long run if you go after what *you* want to do.

Myth 8.   *People over 40 have difficulty finding a good job.*

Reality: Yes, if they apply for youth jobs. If they conduct a well organized job search, they should find their age no barrier to employment. Employers want experience, maturity, and stability. People over 40 have these qualities. In fact, as the population continues to age and birth rates decline, it should become easier for older individuals to change jobs and careers if they are willing to re-career.

Myth 9:   *You must be aggressive in order to find a job.*

Reality: Aggressive people tend to be offensive people (Germann and Arnold: 5-6). You must be *purposeful* and *persistent*.

Myth 10: *One should not change jobs and careers more than once or twice; job-hoppers are discriminated against in hiring.*

Reality: While this may have been true 30 years ago, it is not true today. America is a skills-based society where individuals market their skills to different organizations in exchange for money. Most organizations are small businesses with limited advancement opportunities. In such a society, often the only way to advance your career is to change jobs frequently. Job-hopping is okay as long as you don't make a bad habit of it. Most individuals entering the job market today will undergo several career and job changes during their lifetime.

You also should be aware of several other realities which will affect your job search or which you might use to develop your plan of action:

- There is less competition for high-level jobs than for middle and low-level jobs.
- Personnel offices seldom hire. They screen candidates for bosses who are found in operating units of organizations.
- Politics are both ubiquitous and dangerous in organizations. Don't think you are above politics. If so, you may well become a victim. Read DuBrin's *Winning In Office Politics* or Kennedy's *Office Politics* in order to learn how to play *positive* politics.
- It is best to narrow or "rifle" your job search on particular organizations and individuals rather than broaden or "shotgun" it to many alternatives.
- Beware of employment firms and personnel agencies. They work for employers and themselves rather than for applicants. They do not have your best interests at heart.
- Most people can make satisfying job and career changes. They should minimize efforts in the advertised job market and concentrate instead on planning and implementing a well organized job search tailored to the realities of the hidden job market.
- Since jobs and careers tend to be fluid and changing, you should concentrate on acquiring and marketing those skills, talents, and abilities which you can transfer from one job setting to another.
- You should use whatever "connections" or "pull" you have developed over the years and can mobilize to make a job or career change (see Chapter Ten on how to organize your "pull").
- Most people — 40 to 80 percent — are unhappy with their jobs or feel underemployed. Others retire or die. Therefore, you have millions of potential job possibilities available to you.
- Most people, regardless of their position or status, love to

talk about their work and give advice to both friends and strangers. You can learn the most about job opportunities and alternative careers by talking to such people.

As you conduct your job search, you will encounter many such myths and realities. Several people will give you advice. While much of this advice will be useful, a great deal of it will be useless and misleading. In the end, you should be skeptical of well-meaning individuals who most likely will reiterate the common job and career myths. You should be particularly leary of those who try to *sell* you their advice. Always remember that there is a disorganized job market with numerous job opportunities. Your task is to organize the chaos around your skills and interests. You must convince prospective employers that they will like you more than other "qualified" candidates.

FINDING JOBS AND CHANGING CAREERS

Many people change jobs and careers each year. Approximately 40 million individuals go through a work related transition at any given moment (Bolles, 1981:22). Such transitions include (1) trying to change jobs or careers due to dissatisfaction, (2) trying to keep a job which is being eliminated, or (3) trying to find a job due to unemployment. Indeed, 15 to 20 million adults experience unemployment each year (Aslanian and Brickell). And most people will make an average of 10 job changes and 13 moves during their lifetime (Hedberg:45); three to five career changes may be a normal lifetime pattern for individuals.

Most people make job or career transitions by accident. They do little other than take advantage of opportunities that may arise unexpectedly. While chance and luck play important roles in finding employment, we recommend planning for your future job and career changes so that you will experience even greater degrees of chance and luck!

Finding a job or changing a career in a systematic and well-planned manner is hard yet rewarding work. The task should first be based upon a clear understanding of the key ingredients that define jobs and careers. Starting with this understanding, you should next convert key concepts into action steps for implementing your job search.

A career is a series of related jobs which have common skill, interest, and motivational bases. You may change jobs several times without changing careers. But once you change skills, interests, and motivations, you change careers.

Finding a job is not an easy task. The job market is relatively disorganized, although it has an outward appearance of coherence. Comprehensive, accurate, and timely job information is difficult to locate. Employment services are fragmented and often disappointing. Job search methods are controversial and many are ineffective.

No system is organized to give people jobs. At best you will encounter a decentralized and fragmented system consisting of job listings in newspapers, magazines, employment offices, or computerized job data banks. Many people will try to sell you job information as well as questionable job search services. While efforts are underway to create a nationwide computerized job bank which would list available job vacancies on a daily basis, don't expect such data to become available soon nor to be very useful. Many of the listed jobs may be nonexistent, at a low skill and salary level, or represent only a few employers. In the end, most of the systems organized to help you find a job do not provide you with the information you need in order to land a job that is most related to your skills and interests.

Finding a job is both an art and a science; it encompasses a variety of facts, principles, and skills which can be learned but which also must be adapted to individual situations. Thus, *learning how to find a job* can be as important to career success as knowing how to perform a job. However, having marketable skills is essential to making job search strategies work effectively for you.

Our understanding of how to find jobs and change careers is illustrated in Figures 1 and 2. As outlined in Figure 1, you should involve yourself in a four-step career development process as you move from one job to another. Your first step should be to conduct a self-assessment of your skills, abilities, motivations, interests, values, temperament, experience, and accomplishments. Based upon this assessment process, your second step is an exploratory, research phase. You set goals, gather information about alternative jobs and careers by reading literature and talking to informed people, and then narrow your alternatives to specific job targets.

Your third career development step centers on acquiring specific skills which are critical to implementing a successful job search. These skills relate to the individual job search steps outlined in Figure 2: research; resume and letter writing; prospecting, networking, and informational/referral interviewing; and negotiating salary. The final career development step involves implementing the knowledge, skills, and abilities you acquired in steps 1, 2, and 3.

Figure 2 outlines seven job search steps that relate to your

FIGURE 1

CAREER DEVELOPMENT PROCESS

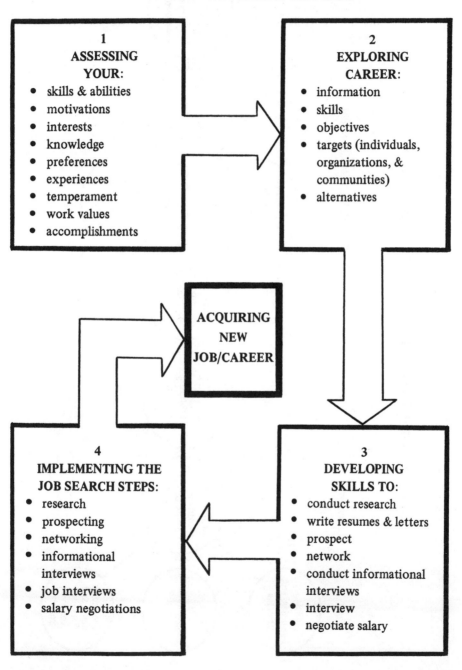

1
ASSESSING YOUR:
- skills & abilities
- motivations
- interests
- knowledge
- preferences
- experiences
- temperament
- work values
- accomplishments

2
EXPLORING CAREER:
- information
- skills
- objectives
- targets (individuals, organizations, & communities)
- alternatives

ACQUIRING NEW JOB/CAREER

4
IMPLEMENTING THE JOB SEARCH STEPS:
- research
- prospecting
- networking
- informational interviews
- job interviews
- salary negotiations

3
DEVELOPING SKILLS TO:
- conduct research
- write resumes & letters
- prospect
- network
- conduct informational interviews
- interview
- negotiate salary

FIGURE 2

RELATIONSHIPS OF ACTIVITIES IN JOB SEARCH CAMPAIGN

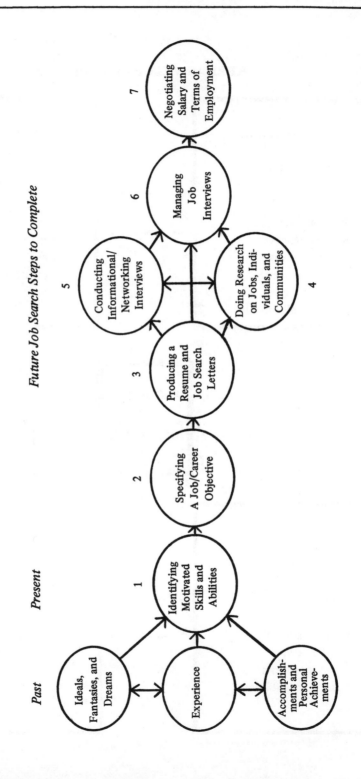

past, present, and future. Each step is examined in a separate chapter of this book (Chapters Six to Twelve). Notice that your past is well integrated into the process of finding a job or changing your career. Therefore, you should feel comfortable conducting your job search; it represents the best of what you are in terms of your past and present accomplishments as these relate to your present and future goals. When following this type of job search, you will communicate your *best self* to employers.

Since the individual job search steps are interrelated, they should be followed in sequence. If you fail to properly complete the initial steps, your job search may become haphazard, aimless, and costly. For example, you should never write a resume (Step # 3) before first conducting an assessment of your skills (Step # 1) and identifying your objective (Step # 2). The Steps # 1 and # 2 sequence is especially critical to the successful implementation of all other job search steps. You *must* complete Steps # 1 and # 2 *before* continuing on to the other steps. Since Steps # 3 through # 6 can be conducted simultaneously, they complement and reinforce one another. Try to sequence your job search as close to our steps as possible. The true value of this sequencing will become very apparent as you implement your plan.

The processes and steps identified in Figures 1 and 2 represent the careering process we and others have used successfully with thousands of clients during the past 25 years. They are equally applicable to the re-careering process as long as you recognize the importance of acquiring work-content skills as well as job search skills. Knowing only how to find a job will not be sufficient in the coming era of skills retraining. Once you have acquired the necessary skills through training and retraining, you will be ready to target your skills on particular jobs and careers that you do well and enjoy doing. You will be able to avoid the trap of trying to fit into jobs that are not conducive to your particular mix of skills, motivations, and abilities.

IDENTIFYING YOUR CAREERING COMPETENCIES

Just how prepared are you for planning and implementing an effective job search? Successful job seekers use a great deal of information and skills in getting the jobs they want. Test yourself to see what job search information and skills you currently possess and which ones you most need to concentrate upon improving. Identify your level of job search competence by responding to each of the statements in Table 7 on a scale of 1-5.

TABLE 7

TESTING YOUR CAREERING COMPETENCIES

SCALE: 1 = strongly agree
                    2 = agree
                    3 = maybe, not certain
                    4 = disagree
                    5 = strongly disagree

1. I know what skills I can offer employers in
   different occupations.   1 2 3 4 5

2. I know what skills employers most seek in
   candidates.   1 2 3 4 5

3. I can clearly explain to employers what
   I do well and enjoy doing.   1 2 3 4 5

4. I can specify why an employer should hire me.   1 2 3 4 5

5. I can gain support of family and friends for
   making a job or career change.   1 2 3 4 5

6. I can find 10 to 20 hours of time each week
   to conduct a part-time job search.   1 2 3 4 5

7. I have the financial ability to sustain a
   three-month job search.   1 2 3 4 5

8. I can conduct library and interview research
   on different occupations, employers,
   organizations, and communities.   1 2 3 4 5

9. I can write different types of effective
   resumes, job search letters, and
   thank-you notes.   1 2 3 4 5

10. I can produce and distribute resumes and
    letters to the right people.   1 2 3 4 5

11. I can list my major accomplishments in
    action terms.   1 2 3 4 5

12. I can identify and target employers I
    want to interview.   1 2 3 4 5

13. I can develop a job referral network.   1 2 3 4 5

14. I can persuade others to join in forming
a job search support group.   1 2 3 4 5

15. I can prospect for job leads.   1 2 3 4 5

16. I can use the telephone to develop
prospects and get referrals and
interviews.   1 2 3 4 5

17. I can plan and implement an
effective direct-mail job search
campaign.   1 2 3 4 5

18. I can generate one job interview for
every 10 job search contacts I make.   1 2 3 4 5

19. I can follow up on job interviews.   1 2 3 4 5

20. I can negotiate a salary 10-20% above
what an employer initially offers.   1 2 3 4 5

21. I can persuade an employer to
renegotiate my salary after six
months on the job.   1 2 3 4 5

22. I can create a position for myself
in an organization.   1 2 3 4 5

Add the numbers you circled for a total composite score. If your total score is more than 60 points, you need to work on developing your careering skills. If you score under 40 points, you don't need this book!

The following chapters focus on developing these careering competencies in order to better prepare you for planning and implementing your own re-careering campaign. By the time you finish this book, you should be able to score under 40 points on the exercise in Table 7.

SEEKING PROFESSIONAL HELP

This book is designed to be self-directed. If you use it as we suggest, you should be able to organize and implement your own re-careering plan. You need not pay someone to do this work for you.

However, we also are realistic. We know many people will purchase this book, read a few chapters, and do nothing. After a while they will seek professional assistance and pay good money to be told that they should do exactly what this book tells them to do. Some people need this type of expensive motivation.

At the same time, we recognize the value of professional assistance. Especially with the critical skills identification (Chapter Six) and objective setting (Chapter Seven) steps, some individuals may need more assistance than our advice and exercises can give them. If this is the case for you, by all means seek professional help.

But beware of the pitfalls in seeking such advice. There are excellent as well as useless and fraudulent services available. Career planning and job assistance are big businesses involving millions of dollars each year. Many people enter these businesses without expertise. Others are frauds and hucksters who will take your money in exchange for broken promises. You should know something about these professional services before you venture beyond this book.

If you look in the Yellow Pages of your telephone directory, you will find several career planning and employment services listed under the following headings: Management Consultants, Employment, Resumes, Career Planning, and Social Services. Some services help everyone regardless of occupational or skill specialties. Other services are highly specialized for groups such as oil riggers, computer specialists, or engineers. Most will tell you they can help. If they promise to find you a job, be careful. You should seek some very specific services you need, and these are outlined in subsequent chapters. If you read these chapters, you will know what questions to ask. Not surprisingly, you may discover you know more about finding a job than some of the so-called professionals! This is because there is a high turnover of personnel in the career planning field. Many counselors are in "training" when they meet you – and many may be reading this book as part of their "homework."

You will encounter at least 10 different career planning and employment services for assisting you with your job search. Again, approach them with caution. Don't sign a contract before reading the fine print, getting a second opinion, and talking to former clients about *results*. With these words of caution in mind, let's take a look at the variety of services available.

Public employment services usually consist of a state agency which provides employment assistance as well as dispenses unemployment compensation benefits. Employment assistance largely consists of job listings and counseling services. However, counseling services often are a front to screen individuals for employers who list with the public employment agency. If you are looking for entry-level jobs in the $7,000 to $15,000 range, contact this service. Most employers do not list with this service, especially for positions requiring skills in the $18,000 plus range. If you walk through one of these offices, you will find that most people are unemployed and look poor; they will likely remain so for some time. In fact, some experts believe we should abolish these offices altogether because they exacerbate unemployment; they take people away from the more productive channels for employment — personal contacts — and put them in a line with other hopeless individuals. We recommend avoiding these offices unless you are really down on your luck and want some company.

Private employment agencies work for money, either from applicants or employers. Approximately 8,000 such agencies operate nationwide. Many are highly specialized in technical, scientific, and financial fields. The majority of these firms serve the interests of employers since employers — not applicants — represent repeat business. While employers normally pay the placement fee, many agencies charge applicants 10 to 15 percent of their first year salary. These firms have one major advantage: job leads which you may have difficulty uncovering elsewhere. Especially in highly specialized fields, a good firm can be extremely helpful. The major disadvantages are that they can be costly and the quality of the firms varies. Be careful in how you deal with them. Make sure you understand the fee structure and what they will do for you before you sign anything.

College and university placement offices provide in-house career planning services for graduating students. While some give assistance to alumni, don't expect too much. Many of these offices are understaffed or provide only rudimentary services, such as maintaining a career planning library, coordinating on-campus interviews for graduating seniors, and conducting workshops on how to write resumes and interview. Nonetheless, check with your local campus to see what services you might use.

Private career and job search firms are organized to help individuals acquire job search skills. They do not find you a job. In other words, they teach you much — maybe more but possibly less — of what is outlined in this book. Expect to pay anywhere from $1,500 to $10,000 for this service. If you need a monetary incentive to conduct your job search, contract with one of these firms. The most highly respected and innovative firm is Haldane Associates. Many of their pioneering career planning and job search methods are incorporated in this book.

Executive search firms work for employers in finding employees to fill critical positions in the $25,000 plus salary range. They also are called "headhunters," "management consultants," and "executive recruiters." These firms play an important role in linking high level technical and managerial talent to organizations. Don't expect to contract for these services. Executive recruiters work for employers — not applicants. If a friend or relative is in this business or you have relevant skills, let them know you are available — and ask for their advice.

Marketing services represent an interesting combination of job search and executive search activities. They can cost $2,500 or more, and they work with individuals anticipating a starting salary of at least $20,000. These firms try to minimize the time and risk of applying for jobs. A typical operation begins with a client paying a $100 fee for developing psychological, skills, and interests profiles. Next, a marketing plan is outlined and a contract signed for specific services. Using word processing equipment, the firm normally develops a slick "professional" resume and mails it along with a cover letter, to hundreds — maybe thousands — of firms. Clients are then briefed and sent to interview with interested employers. While you can save money and achieve the same results on your own, these firms do have one major advantage. They save you *time* by doing most of the work for you. Again, approach these services with caution.

Women's Centers and special career services have been established to respond to the employment needs of special groups. Women's Centers are particularly active in sponsoring career planning workshops and job information networks. These centers tend to be geared toward elementary job search activities because their clientele largely consists of housewives who are entering or re-entering the workforce with little knowledge of the job market. Special career services arise at times for different categories of employees. Unemployed aerospace engineers, teachers, veterans, air traffic controllers, and government employees have formed special groups for developing job search skills and sharing job leads.

Testing and assessment centers provide assistance for identifying vocational skills, interests, and objectives. Usually staffed by trained professionals, these centers administer several types of tests and charge from $400 to $600 per person. You may wish to use some of these services if you feel our activities in Chapters Six and Seven do not give you enough information on your skills and interests to formulate your job objective. Try our exercises before you hire a psychologist.

Job fairs or career conferences are organized by employment agencies to link applicants to employers. Consisting of one or two day meetings in a hotel, employers meet with applicants as a group and on a one-to-one basis. Employers give presentations on their companies, resumes are circulated, and candidates are interviewed. Many of these conferences are organized around particular skill areas, such as engineering and computers. These are excellent sources for job leads and information, if you get invited to the meetings. Employers pay for this service – not applicants.

Professional associations often provide placement assistance. This usually consists of listing job vacancies and organizing a job information exchange at annual conferences. These meetings are good sources for making job contacts in different geographic locations within a particular professional field. But don't expect much from these services. Talking to people at professional conferences will probably yield better results than reading job listings and interviewing at conference placement centers.

Other types of career planning and employment services are growing and specializing in particular occupational fields. We recommend using these services as a supplement to this book. Again, proceed with caution and know exactly what you are getting. Remember, there is no such thing as a free lunch, and you often get less than what you pay for. After reading the next six chapters, you should be able to make intelligent decisions about what, when, where, and with what results you can use professional assistance. Shop around, compare services, ask questions, talk to former clients, and read the fine print with your lawyer before giving a professional a job!

USING TIME EFFECTIVELY

If you decide to conduct your own job search with minimum assistance from professionals, your major cost will be your time. Therefore, you must find sufficient time to devote to your job search. Ask yourself: How valuable is my time in relation to finding a job or changing my career? Assign a dollar value to your time; compare it to what you might pay a professional for doing much of the job search work for you. Figure on a $1,500 to $10,000 range if you hired a professional.

The time you devote to your job search will depend on whether you want to work at it on a full-time or part -time basis. If you are unemployed, by all means make this a full-time endeavor – 40 to 80 hours per week. If you are presently employed, we do not recommend quitting your job in order to look for employment. You will probably need the steady income and attendant health benefits during your transition period. Furthermore, it is easier to find new employment by appearing employed. Unemployed people project a negative image in the eyes of many employers — they appear to *need* a job. Your goal is to find a job based on your *strengths* rather than your needs.

However, if you go back to school for skills retraining, your present employment status may be less relevant to employers. Your major strength is the fact that you have acquired a skill the employer needs. If you quit your job and spend money retraining, you will communicate a certain degree of risk-taking, drive, responsibility, and dedication which employers readily seek, but seldom find, in candidates today.

Assuming you will be conducting a job search on a part-time basis — 15 to 25 hours per week — you will need to find the necessary time for these job activities. Unfortunately, most people are busy, having programmed every hour to "important" personal and professional activities. Thus, conducting a job search for 15 or more hours a week means that some things will have to go or receive low priority in relation to your job search.

This is easier said than done. The job search often gets low priority. It competes with other important daily routines, such as attending meetings, taking children to games, going shopping, and watching favorite TV programs. Rather than fight with your routines — and create family disharmony and stress — make your job search part of your daily routines by improving your overall management of time.

Certain time management techniques will help you make your job search a high priority activity in your daily schedule. These practices may actually lower your present stress level and thus enhance your overall effectiveness.

Time management experts estimate that most people waste their time on unimportant matters. Lacking priorities, people spend 80 percent of their time on trivia and 20 percent of their time on the important matters which should get most of their attention. If you reverse this emphasis, you could have a great deal of excess time — and probably experience less stress attendant with the common practice of crisis managing the critical 20 percent.

Before reorganizing your time, you must know how you normally utilize your time. Therefore, complete the statements in Table 8 for a preliminary assessment of your time management behavior. While many of these statements especially pertain to individuals in managerial positions, respond to those statements that are most relevant to your employment situation.

TABLE 8

YOUR TIME MANAGEMENT INVENTORY

Respond to each statement by circling "yes" or "no," depending on which response best represents your normal pattern of behavior.

1. I have a written set of long, intermediate, and short-range goals for myself (and my family). — Yes No
2. I have a clear idea of what I will do today at work and at home. — Yes No
3. I have a clear idea of what I want to accomplish at work this coming week and month. — Yes No
4. I set priorities and follow-through on the most important tasks first. — Yes No
5. I judge my success by the results I produce in relation to my goals. — Yes No
6. I use a daily, weekly, and monthly calendar for scheduling appointments and setting work targets. — Yes No
7. I delegate as much work as possible. — Yes No
8. I get my subordinates to organize their time in relation to mine. — Yes No
9. I file only those things which are essential to my work. When in doubt, I throw it out. — Yes No
10. I throw away junk mail. — Yes No
11. My briefcase is uncluttered, including only essential materials; it serves as my office away from the office. — Yes No
12. I minimize the number of meetings and concentrate on making decisions rather than discussing aimlessly. — Yes No
13. I make frequent use of the telephone and face-to-face encounters rather than written communication. — Yes No
14. I make minor decisions quickly. — Yes No
15. I concentrate on accomplishing one thing at a time. — Yes No
16. I handle each piece of paper once. — Yes No
17. I answer most letters on the letter I receive. — Yes No
18. I set deadlines for myself and others and follow-through in meeting them. — Yes No
19. I reserve time each week to plan. — Yes No
20. My desk and work area are well organized and clear. — Yes No
21. I know how to say "no" and do so. — Yes No

22. I first skim books, articles, and other forms of   Yes   No
    written communication for ideas before reading
    further.
23. I monitor my time use during the day by asking   Yes   No
    myself "How can I best use my time at pres-
    ent?"
24. I deal with the present by getting things done   Yes   No
    that need to be done.
25. I maintain a time log to monitor the best use   Yes   No
    of my time.
26. I place a dollar value on my time and behave   Yes   No
    accordingly.
27. I — not others — control my time.   Yes   No
28. My briefcase includes items I can work on   Yes   No
    during spare time in waiting rooms, lines, and
    airports.
29. I keep my door shut when I'm working.   Yes   No
30. I regularly evaluate to what degree I am achiev-   Yes   No
    ing my stated goals.

If you answered "no" to many of these statements, you should consider incorporating a few basic time management principles into your daily schedule.

Don't go to extremes by drastically restructuring your life around the "religion" of time management. If you followed all the advice of time management experts, you would probably alienate your family, friends, and colleagues with your narrow efficiency mentality! A realistic approach is to start monitoring your time use and then gradually re-organize your time according to goals and priorities. This is all you need to do. Forget the elaborate flow charts that are the stuff of expensive time management workshops and consultants. Start by developing a time management log. Keep daily records of how you use your time over a two week period. Identify who controls your time and the results of your time utilization. Within two weeks clear patterns will emerge. You may learn that you have an "open door" policy that enables others to control your time; you have little time to do your own work. Based on this information, you may need to close your door and be more selective about access. You may find from your analysis that most of your time is used for activities that have few if any important outcomes. If this is the case, then you may need to set goals and prioritize daily activities.

A simple yet effective technique for improving your time management practices is to complete a "to do" list for each day.

You can purchase tablets of these forms in many stationery and office supply stores, or you can develop your own "Things To Do Today" list. This list also should prioritize which activities are most important to accomplish each day. Include at the top of your list a particular job search activity or several activities that should be completed on each day. If you follow this simple time management practice, you will find the necessary time needed to include your job search in your daily routines. You can give your job search top priority, and accomplish more in less time, with better results.

If you want more information on time management, consult the following books which represent the major works in this field:

> Alan Lakein, *How to Get Control of Your Time and Life* (New York: Signet Books, 1973).
> Michael LeBoeuf, *Working Smart* (New York: Warner Books, 1979).
> R. Alex MacKenzie, *The Time Trap* (New York: AMACOM, 1972).
> Robert T. Riley, *How to Manage Your Time Successfully* (Dallas, Texas: The Drawing Board, Inc. 1978).

PLANNING FOR ACTION

While we recommend that you plan your job search, we want you to avoid the excesses of too much planning. Like time management, planning should not be all-consuming. Planning makes sense because it requires that you set goals and develop strategies for achieving the goals. However, too much planning can blind you to unexpected occurrences and opportunities. Be flexible enough to take advantage of new opportunities.

We outline a hypothetical plan for conducting an effective job search. This plan, as illustrated in Figure 3, incorporates the individual job search activities over a six month period. If you phase in the first five job search steps during the initial three to four weeks and continue the final four steps in subsequent weeks and months, you should begin receiving job offers within two to three months after initiating your job search. Interviews and job offers can come anytime — often unexpectedly — as you conduct your job search. An average time is three months, but it can occur within a week or take as long as five months. If you plan, prepare, and persist at the job search, the pay-off will be job interviews and offers.

FIGURE 3

ORGANIZATION OF JOB SEARCH ACTIVITIES

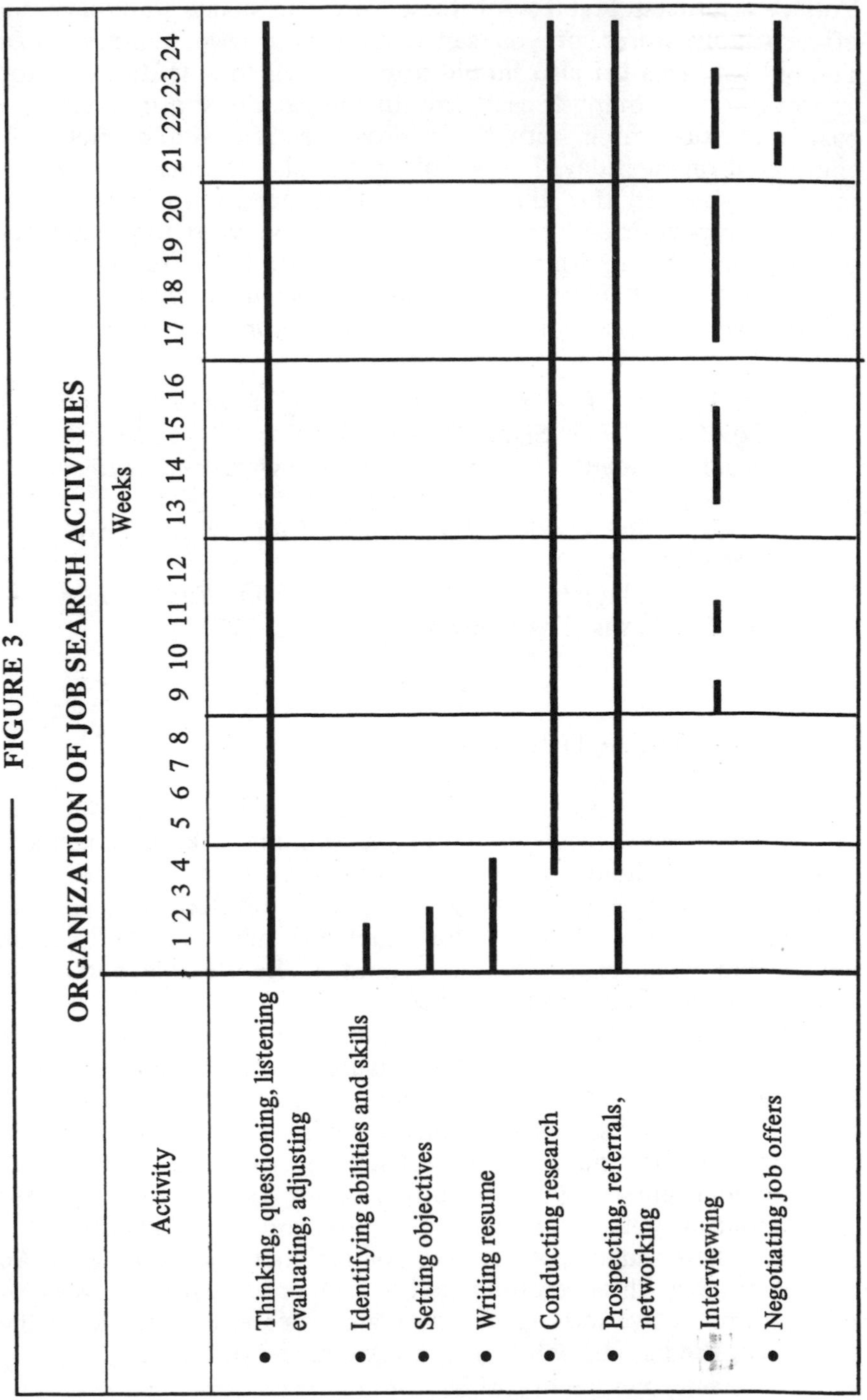

Activity	Weeks

Activity	1 2 3 4 5 6 7 8 9 10 11 12 13 14 15 16 17 18 19 20 21 22 23 24
● Thinking, questioning, listening evaluating, adjusting	
● Identifying abilities and skills	
● Setting objectives	
● Writing resume	
● Conducting research	
● Prospecting, referrals, networking	
● Interviewing	
● Negotiating job offers	

While three months may seem a long time, especially if you have just lost your job and you need work immediately, you can shorten your job search time by increasing the frequency of your individual job search activities. If you are job hunting on a full-time basis, you may be able to cut your job search time in half. But don't expect to get a job within a week or two. It requires time and hard work — perhaps the hardest work you will ever do — but it pays off with a job that is right for you.

FOLLOWING SUCCESS PRINCIPLES

Success is determined by more than just a good plan getting implemented. We know success is not determined primarily by intelligence, thinking big, time management, or luck. Based upon experience, theory, research, and common sense, we believe you will achieve success in re-careering if you follow many of these 20 principles:

1. *You should work hard at finding a job*: Make this a daily endeavor and involve your family.
2. *You should not be discouraged with set-backs*: You are playing the odds, so expect disappointments and handle them in stride. You will have many more "noes" before uncovering the one "yes" which is right for you.
3. *You should be patient and persevere*: Expect three months of hard work before you connect with the right job.
4. *You should be honest with yourself and others*: Honesty is always the best policy, but don't be naive and stupid by confessing your negatives and shortcomings to others.
5. *You should develop a positive attitude toward yourself*: Nobody wants to employ guilt-ridden people with inferiority complexes. Focus on your positive characteristics.
6. *You should associate with positive and successful people*: You are in the people-business, and your success will depend on how well you relate to others. Run with winners.
7. *You should set goals*: You should have a clear idea of what you want and where you are going. Without these, you will present a confusing and indecisive

image to others. Set high goals that make you work hard.

8. *You should plan*: Convert your goals into action steps that are organized as short, intermediate, and long-range plans.

9. *You should get organized*: Translate your plans into activities, targets, names, addresses, telephone numbers, and materials. Develop an efficient and effective filing system and use a large calendar for setting time targets and recording appointments and useful information.

10. *You should be a good communicator*: Take stock of your oral, written, and nonverbal communication skills. How well do you communicate? Since most aspects of your job search involve communicating with others, and communication skills are one of the most sought-after skills, always present yourself well both verbally and nonverbally.

11. *You should be energetic and enthusiastic*: Employers are attracted to positive people. They don't like negative and depressing people who toil at their work. Generate enthusiasm both verbally and nonverbally. Check on your telephone voice — it may be more unenthusiastic than your voice in face-to-face situations.

12. *You should ask questions*: Your best information comes from asking questions. Learn to develop intelligent questions that are non-aggressive, polite, and interesting to others. But don't ask too many questions.

13. *You should be a good listener*: Being a good listener is often more important than being a good questioner and talker. Learn to improve your face-to-face listening behavior (nonverbal cues) as well as remember and utilize information gained from others. Make others feel they enjoy talking with you because you appear to listen to what they say.

14. *You should be polite and courteous*: If rejected by others, thank them for the "opportunity" they gave you. After all, they may later have additional opportunities, and they should remember you in a positive manner. Treat gatekeepers, especially secretaries, as human beings. Don't be aggressive or too assertive. Being courteous to others won't hurt you. A thank-you note can go a long way.

15. *You should be tactful*: Watch what you say to others about other people and your background. Don't be a gossip, back-stabber, or confessor.

16. *You should maintain a professional stance*: Be neat in what you do and wear, and speak with the confidence, authority, and maturity of a professional.

17. *You should demonstrate your intelligence and competence*: Present yourself as someone who gets things done and achieves results — a producer. Employers generally seek people who are bright, hard working, responsible, can communicate well, have positive personalities, maintain good interpersonal relations, are likable, observe dress and social codes, take initiative, are talented, possess expertise in particular areas, use good judgment, are cooperative, trustworthy, and loyal, generate confidence and credibility, and are conventional. In other words, they like people who can score in the "excellent" to "outstanding" categories of the annual performance evaluation. Many want God!

18. *You should not overdo your job search*: Don't engage in overkill and bore everyone with your "job search" stories. Achieve balance in everything you do. Occasionally take a few days off to do nothing related to your job search. Develop a system of incentives and rewards — such as two non-job search days a week, if you accomplish targets A, B, C, and D.

19. *You should be open-minded and keep an eye open for "luck"*: Too much planning can blind you to unexpected and fruitful opportunities. Learn to re-evaluate your goals and strategies. Seize new opportunities if they appear appropriate.

20. *You should evaluate your progress and adjust*: Take two hours once every two weeks and evaluate what you are doing and accomplishing. If necessary, adjust your plans and reorganize your activities and priorities in light of new information. Don't become too routinized and therefore kill creativity and innovation.

These principles should provide you with an initial orientation for starting your job search. As you acquire job search experience, develop your own operating principles. As you immerse yourself in the task of structuring your career future, only you will know what works best for you.

TAKING RISKS AND HANDLING REJECTIONS

You can approach a job or career change in various ways. Some actions have higher pay-offs than others. Many people waste time by doing nothing, reconstructing the past, worrying about the future, and thinking about what they should have done. This negative approach impedes rather than advances careers.

A second approach is to do what most people do when looking for a job. They examine classified ads, respond to vacancy announcements, and complete applications in personnel offices. While this approach is better than doing nothing, it is relatively inefficient as well as ineffective. You compete with many others who are using the same approach. Furthermore, the vacancy announcements do not represent the true number of job vacancies nor do they offer the best opportunities. As we will see in Chapter Ten, you should use this approach to some degree, but it should not preoccupy your time. Responding to vacancy announcements is a game of chance, and the odds are usually against you. It makes you too dependent upon others to give you a job.

The third approach to making a job change requires *taking creative action* on your part. You must become a self-reliant risk-taker. You identify what it is you want to do, what you have acquired skills to do, and organize yourself accordingly by following the methods in subsequent chapters. You don't need to spend much time with classified ads, employment agencies, and personnel offices. And you don't need to worry about your future. You take charge of your future by initiating a job search which pays off with job offers. Your major investment is *time*. Your major risk is being turned down or rejected.

Job hunting is an ego-involving activity. You place your past, abilities, and self-image before strangers who don't know who you are or what you can do. Being rejected or having someone say "no" to you will probably be your *greatest job hunting difficulty*. We know most people can handle two or three "noes" before they get discouraged. If you approach your job search from a less ego-involved perspective, you can take "noes" in stride; they are a normal aspect of your job search experience. Be prepared to encounter 10, 20, or 50 "noes." Remember, the odds are in your favor. For every 20 "noes" you get, you also should uncover one or two "yeses." The more rejections you get, the more acceptances you also will get. Therefore, you must encounter rejections *before* you get acceptances.

This third approach is the approach of this book. Experience with thousands of clients shows that the most successful job seekers are those who develop a high degree of self-reliance, maintain a positive self-image, and are willing to risk being rejected time after time without becoming discouraged. This approach will work for you if you follow our advice on how to become a self-reliant risk-taker in today's job market.

FORMING A SUPPORT GROUP

We believe most people can conduct a successful job search on their own by following the step-by-step procedures of this book. We know they work because these methods have been used by thousands of successful job hunters. But we know it is difficult to become a risk-taker, especially in an area where few people have a base of experience and knowledge from which to begin. Therefore, we recommend that you share the risks with others.

Our self-directed methods work well when you team up with others in forming a job search group or club (Krannich, 1983). The group provides a certain degree of security which is often necessary when launching a new and unknown adventure. In addition, the group can provide important information on job leads. Members will critique your approach and progress. They will provide you with psychological supports as you experience the frustration of rejections and the joys of success. You also will be helping others who will be helping you. Some career counselors estimate that membership in such groups can cut one's job search time by as much as 50 percent!

You can form your own group by working with your spouse or by finding friends who are interested in looking for a new job. Your friends may know other friends or colleagues who are interested in doing the same. Some of your friends may surprise you by indicating they would like to join your group out of curiosity. If you are over 40 years of age, check to see if there is a chapter of the 40-Plus Club in your community. This group is organized as a job search club.

Your group should meet regularly — once a week. At the meetings discuss your experiences, critique each other's approaches and progress, and share information on what you are learning or what you feel you need to know more about and do more effectively. Include your spouse as part of this group. We will return to this subject in Chapter Ten when we discuss how to develop your networks for uncovering job leads.

One other aspect of this self-directed book should be clarified. While we do not urge you to seek professional assistance, such as a career counselor, this assistance can be useful at certain stages and depending on individual circumstances. For example, the next chapter focuses on skills identification. While we present the necessary information and exercises for you to identify your skills, some individuals may wish to enhance this step of their job search by seeking the assistance of a professional career counselor who may have more sophisticated testing instruments for meeting their needs.

On the other hand, if you bring to your job search certain health and psychological problems which affect your job performance, you should seek professional help rather than try to solve your problems with this book. This is especially true for those with alcohol or drug problems who really need some form of professional therapy before practicing this book. If you are in serious financial trouble or a separation or divorce is greatly troubling you, seek professional help. Only after you get yourself together physically and mentally will this book produce its intended results for you. Remember, no employer wants to hire alcohol, drug, financial, or marital problems. They want productive, job-centered individuals who are capable of handling their personal problems.

You must be honest with yourself before you can be honest with others. The whole philosophy underlying this book is one of personal honesty and integrity in everything you do related to your job search.

CHARGING IT TO UNCLE SAM

Among all the great American subsidies to both the rich and the poor, Uncle Sam also throws in the expenses incurred in finding a new job. According to the IRS, all job hunting expenses are tax deductible. But there is one catch. The IRS permits you to deduct your job search expenses as long as you are changing jobs in the same career field. If you change careers — go from one professional field to another — technically you cannot deduct your job search expenses.

We are not experts on the IRS. Check with your lawyer, accountant, or someone in the IRS for legal opinions. Keep a diary and all receipts relating to your job search regardless of whether it results in a career or job change. These expenses include the cost of this book, printing, stationery, typing services, long distance telephone calls, and travel, meals, and lodging relating to interviews and job research. If you hire yourself a professional, their services also are tax deductible. While the IRS may accept these expenses even if you change careers — after all, jobs are eliminated and skills do become obsolete — check with the experts on this particular point of interpretation.

Chapter Six
COMMUNICATING YOUR SKILLS

In Chapter Four we addressed the question of how to acquire skills training for re-careering in the years ahead. Learning new skills requires a major investment of time, money, and effort. Nonetheless, the long-term pay-off should more than justify the initial costs. Indeed, research continues to show that well selected education and training provide the best returns on individual and social investments.

FUNCTIONAL AND WORK-CONTENT SKILLS

In this chapter we assume you have already acquired certain technical and *work-content skills* necessary to function effectively in today's job market. At the same time, you have *functional skills* which also are marketable; many of these skills enable you to target your work-content skills on specific occupations. However, you must first be aware of your functional skills before you can adequately relate them to the job market.

Most people view the world of work in traditional occupational-job-skill terms. This is a *structural view* of occupational realities. Occupational fields are seen as consisting of separate and distinct jobs which, in turn, require specific work-content skills. From this perspective, occupations and jobs are relatively self-contained entities. Social work, for example, is seen as being different from paralegal work; social workers, therefore, are not "qualified" to seek paralegal work.

On the other hand, a *functional view* of occupations and jobs emphasizes similar characteristics among jobs as well as common linkages between different occupations. Although the structure of occupations and jobs may differ, they have similar functions. They involve working with people, data, and things. If you work with people, data, and things in one occupation, you can transfer that experience to other occupations which have similar functions. Once you understand how your skills relate to the functions as well as investigate the structure of different occupations, you should be prepared to make job changes from one occupational field to another. Whether you possess the necessary work-content skills to qualify for entry into another occupational field is another question altogether.

The skills we identify and help you organize in this chapter are the functional skills career counselors normally emphasize when advising clients to assess their *strengths*. In contrast to work-content skills, functional skills can be transferred from one job or career to another. They enable individuals to make some career changes without having to acquire additional education and training. They constitute an important bridge for re-careering from one occupation to another.

Therefore, before deciding on whether you need retraining, you should first assess both your functional and work-content skills to see how they can be transferred to other jobs and occupations. Once you do this, you should be better prepared to make re-careering decisions as well as relate your functional skills to your work-content skills.

Regardless of what combination of work-content and functional skills you possess, a job search must begin with identifying your strengths. Without knowing these, your job search will lack content and focus. Your goal should be to find a job that is fit for you rather than one you think you might be able to fit into. Of course, you also want to find a job for which there is a demand. This particular focus requires a well-defined approach to identifying and communicating your skills to others. You can best do this by asking the right questions about your strengths and then conducting a systematic self-assessment of *what you do best as well as enjoy doing*. This chapter gets you started with your job search by raising the key questions and outlining alternative self-assessment techniques.

QUESTIONING STRENGTHS AND WEAKNESSES

Knowing the right questions to ask will save you time and steer you into productive job search channels from the very beginning. Asking the wrong questions can cripple your job search efforts and leave you frustrated. The questions must be understood from the perspectives of both employers and applicants.

Two of the most humbling questions you will encounter in your job search are *"Why should I hire you?"* and *"What are your weaknesses?"* While employers may not directly ask these questions, feel assured they are asking them nonetheless. If these questions are not answered in a positive manner — directly, indirectly, verbally, or nonverbally — your job search will likely flounder and you will join the ranks of the unsuccessful and disillusioned job searchers who feel something is wrong with them. Individuals who have lost their jobs are particularly vulnerable to these questions since many lack a positive self-image and their self-esteem has been lowered by being terminated. Many such people focus on what is wrong rather than what is right about themselves. Such thinking creates self-fulfilling prophecies and is self-destructive in the job market. By all means avoid this fate!

Employers want to hire individuals who are *competent, intelligent, honest,* and *likable* (Stanat: 100). In other words, they want to hire your *value or strengths*. Since it is easier to identify and interpret weaknesses, employers look for indicators of your strengths by trying to identify your weaknesses. Your job is to make sure they learn about your strengths by identifying your strengths. The more successful you are doing this, the better off you will be in relation to both employers and fellow applicants.

Therefore, you should organize your questions around the concerns of employers. Above all, don't dwell on your weaknesses — past or present. Employers hire strengths — not weaknesses. Start from a position of strength by learning to communicate your strengths to others.

What do you do well and enjoy doing? Together, these key questions identify your strengths. They must be answered prior to deciding on alternative jobs and careers. The questions identify the skills, abilities, and talents you have to offer potential employers.

Unfortunately, many people work against their own best interests. Not knowing their strengths, they market their weaknesses by first identifying job vacancies and then trying to fit their "qualifications" in job descriptions. This approach often frustrates applicants; it presents a picture of a job market which is not interested in the applicant's strengths. This leads some people toward acquiring new skills which they hope will be marketable, even though they do not enjoy using them. Millions of individuals find themselves in such misplaced situations. Your task is to avoid joining the ranks of the misplaced and unhappy work force.

RE-CAREERING SKILLS

We know most people stumble into jobs by accident. Some are at the right place at the right time to take advantage of a job or career opportunity. Others work hard at trying to fit into jobs listed in classified ads, employment agencies, and personnel offices; identified through friends, acquaintances; or found by knocking on doors. After 15 to 20 years in the work world, many people wish they had better planned their careers from the very start. All of a sudden they are unhappily locked into jobs because of retirement benefits and the family responsibilities of raising children and meeting monthly mortgage payments. Re-careering is an option they fail to pursue because they lack knowledge of how to do it or they fear taking the risks of pursuing a new career.

After 10 or 20 years of work experience, most people have a good idea of what they don't like to do. While their values are more set than when they first began working, many people are still unclear as to what they do well and enjoy doing as well as how their skills fit into the job market. If they have the opportunity to change jobs or careers — either voluntarily or forced through termination — and find the time to plan the change, they *can* move into jobs and careers which fit their skills and motivational patterns.

The key to understanding your non-technical strengths is to identify your transferable or functional skills. You can use these skills in more than one job setting. These are re-careering skills which provide bridges from one career to another. While most people can only identify 5 or 10 work-related skills, research shows that the average individual possesses between 500 and 800 such skills.

Once you identify your particular mix of re-careering skills, you will be better prepared to identify what it is you want to do. Moreover, your self-image and self-esteem will improve and you will be prepared to *communicate* your strengths to others through a rich skills vocabulary. These outcomes are critically important for writing your resume and letters as well as for conducting interviews.

Let's illustrate the concept of transferable or re-careering skills by examining the case of educators. Many educators view their skills in strict work-content terms — knowledge of a particular subject matter such as math, history, English, physics, or music. When looking outside education for employment, many educators seek jobs which will utilize their subject matter skills. However, they soon discover that non-educational institutions are not a ready market for their "skills."

On the other hand, educators possess many other skills that are directly transferable to business and industry. Most educators are not aware of these skills and thus they fail to communicate their strengths to others. For example, research (Solomon, Ochsner, Hurwicz: 70-76) shows that graduate students in the humanities most frequently possess these transferable skills, in order of importance:

- critical thinking
- research techniques
- perseverance
- self-discipline
- insight
- writing

- general knowledge
- cultural perspective
- teaching ability
- self-confidence
- imagination
- leadership ability

Other studies (Wiant), based on research with employers, identify three general categories of transferable skills which most people possess: intellectual/aptitudinal, interpersonal, and attitudinal. These skills are acquired through experiences at home, school, and work. Specific skills associated with each category are:

Intellectual/Aptitudinal Skills

_____ Communicating
_____ Problem solving
_____ Analyzing/assessing
_____ Planning/layout
_____ Decision-making
_____ Creativity/imagination/
  innovation
_____ Problem identification/
  definition
_____ Managing one's own time
_____ Basic computation
_____ Logical thinking
_____ Evaluating
_____ Ability to relate common
  knowledge or transfer
  experiences
_____ Coping with the labor

_____ Trouble shooting
_____ Job awareness
_____ Mechanical aptitude
_____ Typing
_____ Accounting
_____ Implementing
_____ Self-understanding,
  awareness, actualization
_____ Situational analysis
_____ Assessing environments/
  situations
_____ Understanding human system
  interactions
_____ Organizational savvy
_____ Conceptualization
_____ Generalization
_____ Goal setting

_____ market and job movement
_____ Understanding others
_____ Synthesizing
_____ Marshaling resources
_____ Accommodating multiple
        demands
_____ Judgment
_____ Foresight

_____ Controlling
_____ Dealing with work
        situations
_____ Finance
_____ Tool usage
_____ Bookkeeping
_____ Artistic ability
_____ Business sense
_____ Tolerance of ambiguity

Interpersonal Skills

_____ Working with, getting
        along with, or relating
        to others
_____ Empathizing, or being
        sensitive to others
_____ Counseling
_____ Helping or cooperating
_____ Selling
_____ Delegating
_____ Team building

_____ Managing, directing, or
        supervising
_____ Teaching, training, or
        instructing
_____ Motivating
_____ Gaining acceptance, or
        building rapport
_____ Cultivating cooperation
_____ Accepting supervision
_____ Instilling confidence

Attitudinal Skills

_____ Diligence, or a positive
        attitude toward the value
        of work
_____ Acceptance/appreciation/
        concern for others
_____ Ambition/motivation
_____ Pride
_____ Patience
_____ Assertiveness
_____ Loyalty
_____ Risk taking

_____ Receptivity/flexibility/
        adaptability
_____ Determination/perseverance
_____ Responsibility
_____ Willingness to learn
_____ Self-confidence
_____ Enthusiasm
_____ Self-actualization
_____ Honesty
_____ Reliability
_____ Compromising
_____ Kindness

Crystal and Bolles identify several types of transferable skills, many of which you already possess but which you may have difficulty articulating to others:

___ organizing   ___ problem solving   ___ coordinating
___ making decisions   ___ public speaking   ___ managing

— counseling
— motivating
— leading
— selling
— assessing
— initiating
— updating
— communicating
— performing
— attaining

— advising
— coaching
— evaluating
— training
— supervising
— interpreting
— planning
— estimating
— achieving
— negotiating

— reporting
— administering
— persuading
— encouraging
— improving
— analyzing
— designing
— implementing
— reviewing
— maintaining
   responsibility

Other skills relate to your personality:

— dynamic
— imaginative
— innovative
— perceptive
— outstanding
— tactful
— reliable
— vigorous
— sensitive
— accurate
— trained
— expert
— astute
— calm

— unique
— versatile
— responsible
— concerned
— successful
— easy-going
— humanistic
— competent
— objective
— warm
— broad
— outgoing
— experienced
— democratic

— challenging
— sophisticated
— diplomatic
— discrete
— creative
— effective
— adept
— efficient
— honest
— aware
— self-starter
— strong
— talented
— empathic

And still other transferable skills relate to your relations with different objects and publics:

— data
— recommendations
— inefficiencies
— facts
— feelings
— procedures
— techniques
— project planning
— relations
— events
— processes
— statistics

— reports
— systems
— programs
— conclusions
— groups
— art
— methods
— objectives
— individuals
— information
— records
— handbooks

— designs
— unusual conditions
— research projects
— communication systems
— statistical analyses
— approaches
— presentations
— problems
— goals
— theories
— journals
— human resources

___ equipment	___ inputs	___ costs
___ living things	___ investigations	___ duties
___ tools	___ outputs	___ plants
___ training programs	___ charts	___ surveys
___ points of view	___ strategy	___ energy
___ prima donnas	___ growth	___ senior executives

Richard Bolles (1978: 142-150) classifies skills into self-management, functional, and work-content areas. The most important career transition skills — functional or transferable — relate to handling data (information), people, or things:

Self-management Skills

___ ability to choose, or make a decision	___ diplomacy	___ patience, persistence
___ alertness	___ easy-goingness	___ playfulness
___ assertiveness	___ emotional stability	___ performing well under stress
___ astuteness	___ empathy	___ poise, self-confidence
___ attention to details, awareness, thoroughness, conscientiousness	___ enthusiasm	___ politeness
	___ expressiveness	
	___ firmness	___ punctualness
	___ flexibility	___ reliability, dependability
___ authenticity	___ generosity	
___ calmness	___ good judgment	___ resourcefulness
___ candidness	___ high energy level, dynamicness	___ self-control
___ commitment to grow	___ honesty, integrity	___ self-reliance
___ concentration	___ initiative, drive	___ self-respect
___ cooperation	___ loyalty	___ sense of humor
___ courage, risk-taking, adventuresomeness	___ open-mindedness	___ sincerity
	___ optimism	___ spontaneity
___ curiosity	___ orderliness	___ tactfulness
		___ tidiness
		___ tolerance
		___ versatility

Functional Skills

data	*people*	*things*
___ synthesizing	___ mentoring	___ precision working
___ coordinating	___ negotiating	___ setting up
___ innovating	___ supervising	___ manipulating
___ analyzing	___ consulting	___ operating

__ computing	__ instructing	__ driving-controlling
__ compiling	__ treating	__ handling
__ copying	__ coaching	__ feeding-offbearing
__ comparing	__ persuading	__ tending
	__ diverting	
	__ exchanging information	
	__ taking instructions	
	__ helping, serving	

Work-content skills, the third skills category, are those peculiar to particular occupational specialties. Each occupation has its own skills vocabulary, jargon, and subject matter that help specify the technical qualifications for individuals entering and advancing in an occupation. These are the hard skills required for re-careering; they normally require retraining. While they do not transfer well from one occupation to another, they are critical for entering specific occupations.

Many terms on these lists of skills represent your strengths. In addition, they constitute a rich *skills vocabulary* you should learn to use when talking about what it is you do well and enjoy doing.

IDENTIFYING TRANSFERABLE SKILLS

If you are just graduating from high school or college and do not know what you want to do, you probably should take a battery of vocational tests and psychological inventories to identify your interests and skills. These tests are listed in Chapter Seven. If you don't fall into these categories of job seekers, chances are you don't need complex testing. You have experience, you have well defined values, and you know what you don't like in a job. Therefore, we outline several alternative skills identification exercises – from simple to complex – for assisting you at this stage.

If you feel the following exercises are inadequate for your needs, we recommend that you seek professional assistance from places such as testing and assessment centers staffed by licensed psychologists, as we noted in Chapter Five. These professionals have several in-depth testing instruments that go further than the activities we outline. For most people the following exercises will be sufficient.

1. *Checklist Method*

Your first skills identification alternative is the most simple.

Review the previous mentioned lists of skills. Place a "1" in front of the skills that *strongly* characterize you; a "2" before those that describe you to a *large extent*; and a "3" before those that describe you to *some extent*. After completing this exercise, review the lists and rank order the 10 characteristics that best describe you on each list.

2. Self-Directed Search

The second exercise also is relatively simple. Acquire a copy of John Holland's "The Self-Directed Search." You can find it in his book, *Making Vocational Choices: A Theory of Careers* or purchase it from ·Consulting Psychologists Press, 577 College Avenue, Palo Alto, California 94306. Most career counselors have copies of it. "The Self-Directed Search" is particularly good for quickly identifying what type of work environment you are motivated to seek — realistic, investigative, artistic, social, enterprising, or conventional — and aligns these work environments with lists of common, although somewhat dated, occupational titles. The exercise is extremely simple and gives you a quick overview of your general tendencies.

3. Skills Map

Richard N. Bolles has produced two useful exercises for identifying transferable skills. In his book, *The Three Boxes of Life* (1978: 158-175), he develops a checklist of 100 transferable skills which is compatible with Holland's self-directed search. They are organized into 12 categories or types of skills: using hands, body, words, senses, numbers, intuition, analytical thinking, creativity, helpfulness, artistic abilities, leadership, and follow-through. Bolles' second exercise, "The Quick Job Hunting Map," expands upon this first one. The "Map" is a checklist of 222 skills organized according to Holland's typology of skills. This exercise requires you to identify seven of your most satisfying accomplishments, achievements, jobs, or roles. After writing a page about each experience, you relate each experience to the checklist of 222 skills. After completing all this for the seven experiences, the "Map" gives you a comprehensive picture of what skills you (1) use most frequently, and (2) enjoy using in satisfying and successful settings. While this exercise may take you six hours to complete, it yields an enormous amount of data on your past strengths. In addition, the "Map" represents a rich skills vocabulary for communicating your skills to others. The "Map" is found in the appendix of Bolles' *What Color is Your Parachute?* or it can be purchased separately in either beginning or advanced versions from the publisher: Ten Speed Press, Box 7123, Berkeley, California 94707, $1.25.

4. *Career Analysis Worksheet*

Richard Lathrop has developed a useful "Career Analysis Worksheet" for identifying skills. With this exercise you identify your general, strongest, and specific abilities as well as assess and determine your ideal job, personal relationships, flexibility, working environment, pay goals, and fields of work. Lathrop outlines the procedure for developing a "Career Analysis Worksheet" in his book, *Who's Hiring Who* (1977:52-59). The worksheet also can be purchased separately by sending $2.00 to NCJMS-CAW, POB 3651, Washington, D.C. 20007.

5. *Autobiography of Accomplishments*

A fifth exercise consists of writing a lengthy essay about your accomplishments in life. This could range from 20 to 100 pages. After completing the essay, go through it page by page to identify what you most enjoyed doing (working with different kinds of information, people, and things) and what skills you used most frequently as well as enjoyed using. Finally, identify those skills you wish to continue using.

6. *Motivated Skills Exercise*

Our final exercise is the most complex and time consuming. However, it yields the best data on skills, and it is especially useful for those who feel they need a more thorough analysis of their skills than the previous exercises could give them. This particular exercise is variously referred to as "Success Factor Analysis" or "System to Identify Motivated Skills" (SIMS) and was developed by Haldane Associates (Germann and Arnold: 44-58). While you can use this technique on your own, it is best to work with someone else. Be prepared to devote from six to eight hours on this exercise. It is divided into six steps:

A. Take 15 to 20 sheets of paper and at the top of each sheet write one achievement. Your achievements consist of those things you enjoyed doing and felt a sense of accomplishment in doing. These include childhood experiences as well as educational, military, recreational, home, or work-related achievements. For example, at the top of the paper you might state:

"I learned to play the guitar and joined a rock group while in high school"

"I received an 'A' in physics from the toughest teacher in school"

"I reorganized the files of our office which improved the efficiency of operations"

"I competed in the marathon and finished in the upper third"

"I organized a committee to investigate reducing the number of customer complaints against our office"

"I sang a solo in our church choir"

B.   Select from among your achievements the seven most important ones and prioritize them. Examples of these success factors might include various aspects of managing, communicating, creating, analyzing, designing, supervising, coordinating and problem solving. On each page write the details of your achievements — how you got involved, what you did, how you did it, and what the outcome was.

C.   Further detail the "what" and "how" of your achievements by having your spouse or a friend interview you over a 60 minute period. Have them ask you to elaborate on each of your achievements and note the terminology you use to elaborate on your skills and abilities. Record your answers for each achievement on separate pieces of paper.

D.   Combine the self-generated and interview data on your achievements into a single master list of success factors. Group the factors into related categories beginning with the most important factor. For example, if "supervising" is your strongest achievement, "decision-making" and "delegating" may be related to this factor. Therefore, the factors would cluster as follows:

supervising	selling
decision-making	promoting
delegating	demonstrating

creating designing initiating		decision-making managing strategizing

E.   Try to synthesize the clusters into new combinations in order to project your past skills into the future. For example, the clusters "supervising, decision-making, delegating" and "creating, designing, initiating" may combine into a new skill category of "creative management." This is the key step in this exercise because it begins to relate your past strengths to your future goals. It thus functions as a bridge between skills and objectives.

USING REDUNDANCY

Knowing your strengths is the key to launching a successful job search. We recommend starting with the simple techniques for generating data on your transferable skills. If you don't feel comfortable with the results, try a more complex and thorough technique. Indeed, redundancy is a virtue at this stage; it will help reinforce understanding of your strengths. If our exercises still leave you uncertain about your strengths, by all means seek professional help.

Our self-assessment techniques stress your positives or strengths rather than dwell on your negatives or weaknesses. This is precisely the way you should communicate your "qualifications" to prospective employers. You should use the rich skills vocabulary from these exercises for communicating to employers that you have numerous skills which will produce concrete results for them.

As you complete these exercises, your self-image and self-esteem may well improve. You should be able to say *"Yes, that is me; I'm good at doing this, and I really enjoy it."* At the same time, you might note that you have been misplaced in previous jobs; you did things which you disliked as well as demonstrated your weaknesses. These exercises should put you on the right path for renewed career satisfaction and success.

But beware of one potential problem when completing these exercises. Don't expect them to outline a new future for you. These strength identification exercises are historical techniques. They examine your past experiences — from childhood to the present — in order to identify your past motivated patterns for success. They are compatible with most employers' assumptions: your past performance best predicts your future performance. You bridge your past and present when you integrate these motivated skills into your job and career objective — the subject of the next chapter.

ACHIEVING SUCCESS

Experience shows that individuals who know and can communicate their functional skills are better able to get jobs than those who don't view their capabilities in these terms. This is especially true for individuals seeking to change careers. Therefore, these skills play an important role for re-careering in the 1980's and 1990's.

However, as noted earlier, functional skills have their limitations in today's job market. These skills tend to have a general orientation; they lack specific work-content. While they are important skills to know and target, *functional skills will not substitute for specific work-content skills.* As jobs become more specialized and technical in nature, changing careers on the basis of functional skills alone will become increasingly difficult. More and more jobs require specialized knowledge and technical abilities which are beyond the scope of functional skills. Consequently, you may need to acquire new work-content skills *in addition* to learning how to best communicate your transferable skills to employers.

While retraining takes time, it is a wise investment in the long-run. In the meantime, if you find yourself suddenly unemployed or you need to change jobs and careers within a six to twelve month period, the best way to deal with the job market is to focus on your transferable skills in developing a job search campaign based upon your past and present strengths. But once you land a job, continue to develop new work-content skills as well as improve your functional skills for future re-careering. By stressing *both* functional and work-content skills, you will have an advantage over other job seekers who only emphasize functional or work-content skills.

Chapter Seven
DEVELOPING AND TARGETING OBJECTIVES

Once you identify your skills, you should be prepared to start developing a clear and purposeful objective for targeting your job search. Using your rich skills vocabulary, as outlined in Chapter Six, you can communicate to employers that you are a *purposeful* individual who *achieves results*. Your objective must tell employers what you will *do for them* rather than what you want from them. It targets your accomplishments around employers' needs. In other words, your objective should be other-directed rather than self-centered.

GIVING DIRECTION

Without a clear objective, your job search will most likely flounder. You will wander aimlessly in a highly decentralized, fragmented, and chaotic job market looking for interesting jobs you might fit into. Your goal, instead, should be to find a job or career that is compatible with your interests, motivations, skills, and talents.

Job hunters with clearly stated objectives have several advantages over those who do not. Their job search is much easier and enjoyable because they approach it with confidence and optimism. They gain greater control over the job market because they structure the job market around their goals. They communicate a reassuring sense of purpose and self-confidence to employers who worry about hiring individuals who don't know what they want. They write well designed resumes and letters that help employers make clear choices. For employers lacking basic hiring criteria, such applicants help them better define their "needs" as the applicant's job objective.

Therefore, if you want to achieve the best results, you must have an objective *before* conducting your job search. With a clear objective, you can target your job search at specific high pay-offs in the job market. A clear objective will help you organize your job search into a coherent and manageable whole.

TARGETING EMPLOYERS' NEEDS

Knowing the advantages and importance of a job objective does not tell you what an objective is. "Objective" is another one of those elusive terms which has as many definitions as definers. In its simplist form, an objective is a statement of *what you want to do.* However, this self-centered view of an objective may not impress employers who are mainly looking for *what you will do for them.*

Souerwine (39-54) develops one of the more complex and exhaustive definitions. He sees career objectives as having four major components:

1. What you *might* do. This requires identifying job and career opportunities.

2. What you *can* do. You did this already in Chapter Six when you identified your strengths or competencies.

3. What you *want* to do. This relates to your values and priorities.

4. What you *should* do. This is your sense of obligation to various individuals and groups within society regardless of their expectations.

The components in this definition require you to conduct an extensive self-assessment of your past, present, and future.

We have no problems with these differing definitions. Their usefulness depends on your needs and purposes. Our preference, however, is to orient a job or career objective toward its intended audience — employers. Therefore, we prefer defining an objective as a statement of *what you can and will do for employers* at present and in the future. Such a statement synthesizes as well as gives direction to what you might do, can do, and should do.

MOVING INTO THE FUTURE

The problem of historical determinism — your past determining your future — often arises when identifying objectives. Many people know their past strengths but they want to do other things in the future. For example, the secretary who makes $12,000 a year and enjoys her work, may have other goals which cannot be met by remaining a secretary. Those goals may be life-long dreams, such as acquiring a vacation home in the mountains, traveling to exciting places, owning a Mercedes-Benz, or receiving media recognition. Meeting these goals requires a healthy income from a new type of occupation.

At the same time, your ideals and fantasies may be unrealistic and thus you must temper them with a heavy dose of reality. For example, going directly from a $12,000 a year secretarial job to a $60,000 a year corporate management position is unrealistic. It may be realistic for the long term if you target your job search initially for an entry-level management position which leads to such advancement.

Many career changers have unrealistic goals such as doubling their salaries and moving into executive positions overnight. Government employees are a case in point. Contrary to public perceptions, many public employees feel underpaid and thus anticipate making a major salary jump by leaving government for the private sector. But reality tells them a different story. For example, a GS-14 federal government employee making $50,000 a year as a grants specialist may have to initially lower his or her monetary expectations in order to change jobs or careers. This may mean taking a $20,000 a year job in order to begin a new career. The same is true for the postal worker making $30,000 a year. The job market does not have many high salary opportunities for people with their experience. Therefore, these individuals should be prepared to take salary cuts in order to learn new skills for reinvesting in their future. If all goes well, they may meet and surpass their previous salaries within three to five years. But they should not expect to substantially advance their careers over a few months or in a single year. They must be realistic in relation to the job market and honest with themselves. Only then can they direct their job search in a purposeful, positive, and enthusiastic manner.

When developing your objective, keep in mind that you can state it over different time periods. Objectives can reflect your immediate, intermediate, and long-range goals. For example, if you have been terminated, your immediate goal will be to find a job in order to generate sufficient cash flow to pay bills and maintain a certain life style. This may require a stopgap job search strategy — take a part-time or full-time position which normally has high employee turnover with few expectations concerning employee loyalty. If you do this, try to find a job which permits spare time to conduct your job search. Many sales positions or jobs with evening shifts will give you enough flexibility to conduct your job search during the day. Avoid stopgap jobs which will lock you into an 8 a.m. to 5:00 p.m. work routine; you need some of this time frame for conducting your job search. If not, such jobs may turn into new and most unpromising careers!

You also should set intermediate and long-range goals. Your intermediate goal should state what you want to be doing or have achieved 5 to 10 years from today. Your long-range goals address the same consideration for 10 to 20 years from now.

GENERATING AND ANALYZING DATA

Some people know what they want to do and thus need little or no assistance in identifying their work objective. For others, identifying and stating an objective can be the most difficult and frustrating task in the whole job search process.

You have several alternatives in developing a clearly stated job objective. Most of these are self-directed exercises which require you to generate and analyze data about yourself. You should begin by thinking of your objective as a function of several ingredients relating to your work values, skills, and knowledge of work environments. Five steps are involved in generating a complete set of data for the final statement of your objective.

The first step is to identify your work and career values. This can be done by completing several of these exercises:

1. List 10 things you would like to achieve before you die. Alternatively, write your own obituary for the year 2010 which stresses the highlights or achievements of your career and life.
2. Fantasize by listing 10 answers to the question: *"If I had $1,000,000, I would . . ."*

3. List 10 things you prefer and enjoy doing. Prioritize each item.
4. List 10 working conditions which you view as negative. Prioritize each item.
5. List 10 working conditions which you view as positive. Prioritize each item.
6. Check as many as you wish of the following work values which you desire in your employment:

____ contribute to society	____ be creative
____ have contact with people	____ supervise others
____ work alone	____ work with details
____ work with a team	____ gain recognition
____ compete with others	____ acquire security
____ make decisions	____ make a lot of money
____ work under pressure	____ help others
____ use power and authority	____ solve problems
____ acquire new knowledge	____ take risks
____ be a recognized expert	____ work at my own pace

7. Write an essay on your ideal job. Include a weekly calendar of daily activities divided into one-hour segments. Specify your duties, responsibilities, authority, salary, working conditions, and opportunities.

Second, gather information on how others see you and your goals. Ask your spouse and/or two or three close friends to honestly critique both your strengths and weaknesses. You want them to answer these questions:

- *What are your strengths and weaknesses?*
- *How can they be improved?*
- *What working conditions do you enjoy?*
- *What are your career goals?*

Third, examine the data you generated in Chapter Six on your strengths. Include it with the information you just generated yourself and received from your spouse and friends. Rank order which skills you most and least prefer to use in your job or career.

Fourth, if you think you need more information on your work values, interests, and skills, take one or two psychological, aptitude, or vocational tests. These include:

- Strong-Campbell Interest Inventory

- Career Assessment Inventory
- The Self-Directed Search
- Temperament and Values Inventory
- Sixteen Personality Factor Questionnaire
- Edwards Personal Preference Schedule
- Myers-Briggs Type Indicators
- The Occupational View Deck
- Self-Description Inventory
- Kuder Occupational Interest Survey

The information from these tests should reinforce and validate the information you gathered from the self-assessment exercises. See a career counselor or a licensed psychologist for these tests.

Fifth, test the information on developing your objective against reality by asking yourself these questions:

- *Is my objective realistic?*
- *Can it be achieved within the next year, 5 years, or 10 years?*
- *Who needs my skills?*
- *What factors might help me or hinder me in achieving my objective?*

Further clarify your objective by conducting library research on various jobs and careers as outlined in Chapter Nine. Continue to clarify your objective when you talk to people about your skills, different jobs, and career opportunities during informational interviews as outlined in Chapter Ten.

EMPHASIZING SKILLS AND OUTCOMES

At this stage you should be prepared to develop a one sentence objective statement. This statement should be initially formulated at a general level as you clarify your goals. It should be stated at a more specific level for your resume.

We prefer following the advice of Haldane Associates in developing functional job objective statements (Germann and Arnold: 54-55). A functional job objective includes *skills* and *outcomes*. At a general level, it should be phased in the following skills-outcomes framework:

> *"I would like a job where I can use my ability to (a primary skill) which will result in (an outcome)."*

If you wish to write grant and research proposals, you might state the general objective like this:

> *"I would like a job where my technical research and writing experience will result in new and expanded programs."*

The same objective should be re-written at a more specific level for your resume:

> *"A management consulting position where strong grantsmanship, research, and writing abilities will be used for expanding human resource development operations."*

This objective includes both skills and outcomes; it is targeted toward particular employers.

While you have certain goals you wish to achieve for *you* and your family, employers want to know how you will achieve *their* goals. Therefore, always remember to develop a work-related objective which responds to the needs of your audience. Above all, tell employers what you have to offer — strengths, skills, or competencies — and what you will do for them. Emphasize that you produce concrete results or outcomes for employers.

Employers are less interested in what they can do for you. As many employees quickly learn, employees are expendible commodities. Employers feel no need to love them, take care of them, and become sensitive to their personal and professional needs.

"You're fired!" are two words which stress that the employer did not get what he or she wanted — your value for their money. Communicate that value loud and clear from the very beginning.

REFORMULATING YOUR OBJECTIVE

While you initially develop a job objective for orienting your job search and organizing your resume, your objective may be reformulated. Your objective continually will be reality-tested as you conduct various phases of your job search. Your library research will be one important component; conversations, informational interviews, and job interviews will be other important sources for refining your objective. By all means do not expect to live and die with this objective! Be flexible and open to changing it as you absorb more useful job and career information.

Chapter Eight
PRODUCING EFFECTIVE RESUMES AND LETTERS

Once you know what you do well, what you enjoy doing, and what you want to do in the future — the subjects of Chapters Six and Seven — you have the basic information necessary for targeting employers. But how will you communicate this information — by telephone, letter, or in face-to-face meetings? You have several options for communicating with employers. This and subsequent chapters are designed to assist you in perfecting your re-careering communications.

Resumes and letters are traditional means of communicating with employers. Most resumes and job search letters, however, are ineffective because they fail to relate work objectives and skills to the needs of employers. Upon completing this chapter you should be able to develop, target, and distribute effective resumes and job search letters that clearly communicate your *purpose* and *capabilities* to prospective employers.

This chapter is a primer for developing essential communication tools to probe the job market. Examples of resumes and letters are included in Appendices B and C. A more extensive and complementary treatment of this subject and chapter, including worksheets and examples, is found in Ronald L. Krannich and William J. Banis, *High Impact Resumes and Letters* (1982).

GETTING INTERVIEWED BY MAIL

Resumes and letters are greatly misunderstood. Many people overrate their purpose and effectiveness. Concentrating most of their efforts on mailing resumes and letters to numerous employers, they waste valuable job search time which should be devoted to other higher pay-off activities.

While few jobs can be acquired through the mail, it is difficult to pursue job opportunities without utilizing the mail. Therefore, you need to know when, where, and how to send resumes and letters for maximum effectiveness.

Much misunderstanding of resumes relates to the definition and purpose of resumes. Many people still believe a resume should summarize their history. Others believe it will get them a job. *A resume advertises your qualifications to prospective employers. It is your calling card for getting interviews.* If you equate resumes with anything else, you will probably produce an ineffective resume.

AVOIDING COMMON PROBLEMS

Perhaps 80 percent of all resumes in circulation are ineffective because people misunderstand their definition and purpose, as well as make numerous mistakes commonly associated with resumes. Most resumes lack an objective, include unrelated categories of information, are too long, and appear unattractive. Other common resume problems identified by employers include:

- poor layout
- misspellings, punctuation errors, and poor grammar
- unclear purpose
- too much jargon
- include irrelevant data
- too long or too short
- poorly typed and reproduced
- unexplained time gaps
- too boastful
- deceptive or dishonest
- difficult to understand or interpret

In avoiding these problems, you should develop a resume that has enough impact to open the doors of prospective employers for interviews. Consequently, your resume should:

- clearly communicate your purpose and competencies in relation to employers' needs
- be concise and easy to read
- immediately motivate the reader to read it in-depth
- tell employers that you are a responsible and purposeful individual − a doer who can solve their problems.

Knowing how to strengthen your resume is extremely important. Since many employers only glance at resumes, your resume must first be attractive or eye pleasing in order to motivate employers to spend more than the average 20 or 30 seconds reading it. Above all, the resume must be directed toward employers' needs. It should answer a major question asked by employers: why should I read this or contact this person for an interview? Always remember your audience; you are communicating to employers − not yourself, your mother, or your spouse. Once you know these critical points, you will be on the right road to developing an effective resume.

SELECTING APPROPRIATE RESUME FORMATS

Resumes normally are produced in one of four different formats: chronological, functional, combination, or resume letter. Each format has advantages and disadvantages depending on your background and purpose. For example, someone first entering the job market or making a major career change should use a functional resume. On the other hand, a person who wants to target a particular job but doesn't want to rewrite the resume, may want to use a resume letter. Examples of these different types of resumes are included in Appendix B; they should be referred to as we outline the various characteristics of the different resumes.

Chronological Resumes

The chronological resume typifies 80 percent of all resumes. Among resume writing experts, this is the most controversial type of resume. It can be written as either a traditional or an improved chronological resume.

Some call the *traditional chronological resume* the "obituary resume" because it both "kills" your chances of getting a job and is a good source for writing a newspaper obituary. This resume summarizes your work history. It often lacks a job objective, lists dates and names first and duties and responsibilities second, and includes extraneous information such as height, weight, age, marital status, sex, and hobbies. While relatively easy to write, the traditional chronological resume is the most ineffective resume you can write. It has no purpose other than to inform people of what you have done in the past as well as where, when, and with whom. It tells employers little or nothing about what you want to do, can do, and will do for them.

The *improved chronological resume* avoids these problems and communicates directly to employers your purpose, past achievements, and probable future performance. You should use this type of resume when you have extensive experience directly related to a position. This resume should include a work objective which reflects both your work experience and professional goals. The work experience section should include the names and addresses of former employers followed by a brief description of your accomplishments, skills, and responsibilities; inclusive employment dates should appear at the end. Do not begin with the dates, since they are the least significant element in the descriptions. Be sure to stress your *accomplishments* and *skills* rather than your formal duties and responsibilities. You want to inform your audience that you are a productive and responsible person who gets things done.

However, a chronological resume may not be for you. If you are changing careers or have an unstable employment history, avoid the chronological resume. It communicates the wrong messages — you lack direct work experience, you are an unstable worker, or you have not advanced in your career. If you have such a career background, consider writing a functional or combination resume.

Functional Resumes

Functional resumes are designed to inform employers of applicants' work objectives and skills — especially their transferable skills. This type of resume should be used by individuals making a significant career change, entering the workforce for the first time, or re-entering the job market after a lengthy absence. When using this resume, you should stress your accomplishments and skills regardless of your work settings. This could include accomplishments as a housewife or house husband, volunteer worker, or Sunday school teacher. Do not include names of employers or dates of employment since they will not strengthen your objective.

However, be careful with functional resumes. While they are important bridges for the inexperienced and for those making a career change, some employers have difficulty with these resumes. Like it or not, employers still look for names, dates, and direct experience; this resume doesn't meet these expectations. You should use a functional resume only if your past work experience does not strengthen your objective when making a major career change.

Combination Resumes

The combination resume is a good compromise between the chronological and functional resumes. This resume has more advantages than disadvantages, and it may be exactly what you need if you are making a career change with related experience from one career to another.

Combination resumes both *meet* and *raise* the expectations of employers. When writing this resume, you stress your accomplishments and skills as well as include work history. Your work history should appear as a separate section immediately following your presentation of accomplishments and skills in the "Areas of Effectiveness" or "Experience" section. It is not necessary to include dates unless they enhance your resume. This is the perfect resume for someone with work experience who wishes to change to a job in a related career field.

Resume Letters

The resume letter substitutes for a standard resume. Appearing as a job inquiry or application letter, a resume letter highlights one or two sections of what would normally appear in the body of your resume — work history, experience, areas of effectiveness, objective, or education. The resume letter should especially stress your objective, accomplishments and skills in relation to the employer's needs. This type of letter can be used at anytime. It is an ideal way to target a particular position for which you do not wish to send your more general resume. A resume letter has one major weakness: it may give some employers insufficient information and thus prematurely eliminate you from consideration.

After selecting an appropriate resume format, your next tasks are to generate and coordinate data, write drafts, produce the final copy, and distribute your resume into fruitful channels. Each stage requires particular knowledge and skills which you can develop.

STRUCTURING RESUME CONTENT

You should start by developing as much work-related information on yourself as possible. You generated much of this information in Chapters Six and Seven when you identified your strengths and specified your work objective. Now you need to round out this information with data for specific sections on your resume. Take several sheets of paper and include the following information categories and corresponding data on each sheet:

Contact information: name, address, telephone number.

Work objective: refer to Chapter Seven.

Education: degrees, schools, dates, highlights, special training.

Work experience: paid, unpaid, civilian, military, and part-time employment. Include job titles, employers, locations, dates, skills, accomplishments, duties, and responsibilities. Use the functional language of Chapter Six.

Other experiences: volunteer, civic, and professional organizations. Include your contributions, demonstrated skills, offices held, names, and dates.

Special skills or   foreign languages, teaching, para-
licenses/certificates: medical, etc. relevant to your objective.

Miscellaneous   references, expected salary, willing-
information: ness to relocate and travel, availability dates.

WRITING DRAFTS

Having organized the key information, your next task is to write two or three drafts of your resume. Assuming you will write a combination resume, the internal organization of the resume should be as follows:

- contact information
- work objective
- qualifications or functional experience
- work history or employment
- education

You may want to include a personal statement at the end. However, we discourage including extraneous information, such as height, weight, age, marital status, state of health, sex, hobbies, references. Also avoid any negative information, such as being divorced, fired, or having medical problems, or a criminal record. While you should never lie, you need not be naive or stupid by volunteering your negatives. Such categories do not enhance your resume. As for references, do not list them on the resume; omit this category or simply state "References available upon request." Refer to the examples in Appendix B for illustrations of how these categories are organized.

While your first draft may run two or more pages, as you rewrite try to get all the information on one page. The single page resume is still the best even though some people are now recommending longer resumes (Gray). Employers lose interest after one page. If you choose a longer resume, make sure to design the additional pages or attached supplemental materials so they are sufficiently eye catching to maintain the attention of the reader.

In completing your final draft, keep these "don'ts" in mind:

- *Don't* use abbreviations except for your middle initial.
- *Don't* make the resume cramped and crowded; it should be pleasing to the eyes.
- *Don't* make statements you can't document.
- *Don't* use the passive voice.
- *Don't* change tense of verbs.
- *Don't* use lengthy sentences and descriptions.
- *Don't* refer to yourself as "I".
- *Don't* include negative information.
- *Don't* include extraneous information.

At the same time, try to include these "does" in your resume:

- *Do* use action verbs and the active voice.
- *Do* be direct, succinct, and expressive with your language.
- *Do* appear neat, well organized, and professional.
- *Do* use ample spacing and highlighting (all caps or underlining) for different emphases.
- *Do* maintain an eye pleasing balance. Try centering your contact information at the top, keeping information categories on the left in all caps, and describing the categories in the center and on the right.
- *Do* check carefully your spelling, grammar, and punctuation.

- *Do* clearly communicate your purpose and value to employers.
- *Do* communicate your strongest points first.

EVALUATING THE PRODUCT

After completing one or two drafts, you should conduct both internal and external evaluations. The *internal evaluation* consists of reviewing our lists of "does" and "don'ts". The *external evaluation* involves circulating your resume to three or more individuals whom you believe will give you frank, objective, and useful feedback. Avoid people who tend to flatter you or make everyone feel good. The best evaluator would be someone in a hiring position similar to one you will encounter. Ask these people to critique your draft resume and suggest improvements in both form and content. This type of evaluation will serve as a dry-run for the final resume and will be your most important evaluation. In the end, the only evaluation that counts is the one that helps get you an interview. Asking someone to critique your resume is one way to spread the word that you are job hunting; you may even get invited to an interview in the process!

REPRODUCING QUALITY RESUMES

There are several alternative ways to produce your final resume. You can type it or have it typeset. If you type it, be sure it looks professional. This can be done by using an electric typewriter with interchangeable elements and a carbon ribbon. Varying the typing elements produces attractice copy. Do not use a portable typewriter with a nylon ribbon; it does not produce professional copy. Many typists will do your resume on a typewriter with a carbon ribbon for about $5.

Alternatively, you can have a printer typeset your resume. This may cost anywhere from $20 to $50. The final product should look first-class. However, it may look *too* professional or *too* slick; some employers may think you had someone else write the resume for you.

Whichever method you use, be sure to proofread the final copy. It is disheartening to spend good money on typing and copying, and later find a typing error. Have two other people also proofread.

In reproducing the resume, you need to consider the quality

and color of paper as well as the number of copies you need. By all means use good quality paper. You should use watermarked 20-pound or heavier bond paper. It costs 2¢ to 6¢ per sheet and can be purchased through stationery stores and printers. Don't cut corners at this stage by using cheap paper or copy machine paper. You may save $5 on 100 copies but you also will communicate to employers that you are not particularly professional. Remember, your major objective is to get an interview for a job — not to save $5.

In selecting paper color, use one of the following: off-white, light tan, light gray, or light blue. Avoid white, blue, yellow, green, pink, orange, red, or any other bright colors. Conservative, light muted colors are the best. Any of these colors can be complemented with black ink. In the case of light gray — our first choice — a navy blue ink looks best. Dark brown ink is especially attractive on light tan paper.

Your choices of paper quality and color say something about your personality and professional style. They are nonverbal cues to your strengths and weaknesses. Employers will use these as indicators for screening you in or out of an interview. At the same time, these choices may make your resume stand out from the crowd of standard black on white resumes.

You have two choices in reproducing your resume: a copy machine or an offset process. Most copy machines do not give good reproductions on the quality of paper you need. But there are a few exceptions, especially the large Kodak and Xerox machines. The offset process produces the best quality because it uses a printing plate. It also is relatively inexpensive — 2¢ to 5¢ per copy with a minimum run of 100 copies. The cost per copy decreases with larger runs of 300, 500, or 1000. In the end, you should be able to have your resume typed and 100 copies reproduced on high quality colored bond paper for about $12. If you have it typeset, the same number of copies may cost you $40.

Whatever you do, don't try to cut costs with your resume. It simply is not worth it. Your resume is your calling card. You are putting your best foot forward at this stage. Go in style by spending a few dollars for producing a first-class resume.

WRITING DIFFERENT JOB SEARCH LETTERS

A resume is normally accompanied by a cover letter. In addition, you will write other job search letters — especially approach and thank-you letters. Examples of the different types of letters are found in Appendix C.

Your letter writing should follow the principles of good resume and business writing. Job hunting letters are like resumes — they advertise you for interviews. As good advertisements these letters should (1) catch the reader's attention, (2) persuade the reader of your benefits or value, (3) convince the reader with more evidence, and (4) move the reader to acquire the product.

Before you write a letter, ask yourself several questions in order to clarify the content of your letters:

- What is the *purpose* of the letter?
- What are the *needs* of my audience?
- What *benefits* will my audience gain from me?
- What is a good opening sentence or paragraph for grabbing the *attention* of my audience?
- How can I maintain the *interests* of my audience?
- How can I best end the letter so that the audience will be *persuaded* to contact me?
- If a resume is enclosed, how can my letter best *advertise the resume*?
- Have I spent enough *time* revising and proofreading the letter?
- Does the letter represent my *best professional effort*?

As a form of business communication, your letters should conform to the rules of good business correspondence:

- Plan and organize what you will say by outlining the content of your letter.
- Know your purpose and plan the elements of the letter accordingly.
- Communicate your message in a logical and sequential manner.
- State your purpose immediately in the first sentence and paragraph; main ideas always go first.
- End your letter by stating what your reader can expect next from you.
- Use short paragraphs and sentences; avoid overly complex sentences.
- Punctuate properly and use correct grammar and spelling.
- Use simple and straight forward language; avoid jargon.
- Communicate your message as directly and briefly as possible.

These rules stress how to both *organize and communicate* your message with impact. At the same time, you should always have a specific purpose in mind as well as know the needs of your audience.

Cover letters provide cover for your resume. Therefore, do no overwhelm your one-page resume with a two-page letter or repeat the contents of the resume in the letter. A short and succinct one-page letter which highlights one or two points in your resume is sufficient. Three paragraphs will suffice. The first paragraph should state your interests and purposes for writing. The second paragraph should highlight your possible value to the employer. The third paragraph should state that you will call the individual at a particular time to schedule an interview.

Don't expect much from cover letters. As many professional job search firms, using high speed word processing equipment, flood the job market with resumes and cover letters, employers are becoming increasingly suspicious of them.

Approach letters are written for the purpose of developing job contacts, leads, or information as well as for organizing networks (Chapter Ten) and getting interviews (Chapter Eleven). Your primary purposes should be to get employers to (1) read your resume, (2) give you information and advice, (3) refer you to others, and (4) remember you. These letters provide access to the hidden job market.

Approach letters can be sent out en masse to uncover job leads or they can be targeted on particular individuals or organizations. It is best to target these letters since they have maximum impact when personalized in reference to particular positions.

The organization of approach letters is similar to other letters. The first paragraph states your purpose. In so doing, you may want to use a personal statement for openers, such as *"John Everts recommended that I write to you. . ."* or *"I am familiar with your. . ."* State your purpose, but do not suggest that you are asking for a job – only career advice or information. In your final paragraph request a meeting and indicate you will call to schedule such a meeting at a mutually convenient time.

Thank-you letters may well become your most effective job search letters. They especially communicate that you are a thoughtful individual. Being remembered as thoughtful is something you should frequently communicate to employers.

Thank-you letters come in different forms and are written for various occasions. The most common thank-you letter is written after receiving assistance, such as job search information or a critique of your resume. One of the most effective letters is sent immediately following an interview – thanking someone for the opportunity to interview. This letter also should reiterate your interest in the position and request a second interview. If you don't receive a job offer or if you reject a job offer, send a thank-you letter. If you terminate employment for any reason, try to send a thank-you letter. Once you begin a new job, send a thank-you letter to your new employer for giving you an opportunity which you feel will be mutually beneficial. This letter will be remembered by most employers since they rarely receive such thoughtful letters from new employees.

HANDLING WANT ADS

While most of your writing activities should focus on the hidden job market, you will occcasionally respond to job listings in newspapers and magazines. While this is largely a numbers game, you can increase your odds by the way you respond to the ads.

You should be selective in your responses. Since you know what you want to do, you will be looking for only certain types of positions. Once you identify them, your response entails little expenditure of time and effort — an envelope, letter, stamp, resume, and maybe 20 minutes of your time. Therefore, you have little to lose. While you have the potential to gain by sending a letter and resume in response to an ad, the odds are still against you.

It is difficult to interpret job listings. Some employers place blind ads with P. O. Box numbers in order to collect resumes for future reference. Others wish to avoid aggressive applicants who telephone or "drop-in" for interviews. Many employers work through professional recruiters who place these ads. While you may try to second guess the rationale behind such ads, respond to them as you would to ads which include the employer's name, address, or telephone number. Assume there is a real job behind the ad.

Most ads request a copy of your resume. You should respond with a cover letter and resume as soon as you see the ad. Depending on how much information on the position is revealed in the ad, your letter should be tailored to emphasize your qualifications vis-a-vis the ad. Examine the ad carefully. Underline any words or phrases which relate to your qualifications. In your cover letter you should use similar terminology in emphasizing your qualifications. Keep the letter brief and to the point.

If the ad asks you to state your salary history or salary requirements, state *"negotiable"* or include it by stating a salary range. For example, if you are making $25,000 a year, you can state this as *"in the $25,000 to $30,000 range."* You should address the salary question if this information is requested in the ad because some employers may screen you out if you "forget" to include it. By stating a salary range which goes above your present base salary, you establish some flexibility for future salary negotiations.

You may be able to increase your odds by sending a second copy of your letter and resume two or three weeks after your initial response. Ordinarily most applicants reply to an ad during the seven day period immediately after it appears in print. Since employers often are swamped with responses, your letter and resume may get lost in the crowd. If you send a second copy of your application two or three weeks later, the employer will have more time to give you special attention. By then, he also will have a better basis on which to compare you to the others.

Keep in mind that your cover letter and resume may be screened among 400 other resumes and letters. Thus, you want your cover letter to be eye catching and easy to read. Keep it brief and concise and highlight your qualifications as stated in the employer's ad. Above all, don't spend a great deal of time responding to an ad or waiting anxiously at your mailbox or telephone for a reply. The rule to follow is: *"Go on to the next and keep moving"* (Breitmayer: 16).

MANAGING YOUR COMMUNICATION

Your letters and resumes can be distributed and managed in various ways. Many people shotgun hundreds of cover letters and resumes to prospective employers. This is a form of gambling where the odds are against you. For every 100 people you contact in this manner, expect one or two who might be interested in you. After all, direct-mail experts only expect a 2 percent return on their mass mailings.

If you choose to use the shotgun method, you can increase your odds by *telephoning* a prospective employer within a week after he or she receives your letter. This technique will probably increase your effectiveness rate from 1 to 5 percent. However, many people are shotgunning their resumes today. As more resumes and letters descend on employers with the increased use of word processing equipment, the effectiveness rates may be even lower. This also can be an expensive marketing method.

Another generally ineffective distribution method, as noted previously, is to send resumes and letters in response to job listings. You will probably get better responses on your direct-mail efforts than in response to classified ads. The reasons are numerous. Many of the ads are blind ads. Competition is stiff; too many other people are applying in the same manner. Many positions are already filled with a friend or relative, but the job is listed to meet equal opportunity and affirmative action requirements.

Your best distribution strategy will be to (1) selectively identify whom you would be interested in working for, (2) send an approach letter, and (3) follow up with a telephone call seeking an appointment for an interview. In more than 50 percent of the cases, you will get an interview. However, do not include your resume with the approach letter. Keep your resume for the interview; present it near the end of the interview. Chapter Ten on networking outlines the procedures for conducting this interview.

Once you begin distributing letters and resumes, you also will need to keep good records for managing your job search writing campaign. Purchase file folders for your correspondence and notes. Be sure to make copies of all letters you write since you may need to refer to them over the telephone or before interviews. Also, record your activities with each employer — letters, resumes, telephone calls, interviews — on a 4 x 6 card and file it according to the name of the organization or individual. These files will help you quickly access information and enable you to evaluate your job search progress.

Always remember the purpose of resumes and letters — advertisements for interviews. They do not get jobs. You are a stranger; most employers know nothing about you. Therefore, *you must effectively communicate your value in writing prior to the critical interview*. While you should not overestimate the importance of this written communication, neither should you underestimate it.

Chapter Nine

CONDUCTING
JOB RESEARCH

A job search can be both a frustrating and exhilarating experience. Frustrations come when unrealistic expectations are dashed
by reality or job search progress is slow to nonexistent. Exhilaration
comes when your realistic expectations lead to an enjoyable and
successful job search. You will experience both feelings as you seek
to uncover re-careering opportunities.

In this chapter we point you in fruitful directions for mini-
mizing job search frustrations and maximizing successes. Research
is the key to starting off in the right direction. We recommend conducting research at three different levels: individuals, organizations,
and communities. This chapter focuses primarily on how to do
research on individuals and organizations; Chapter Fourteen is devoted to community research.

DOING RESEARCH

After identifying your skills, outlining your objective, and
writing your resume, what comes next? It depends on how well
prepared you are for entering the job market. A *strong knowledge
base* is required before taking the next critical steps — contacting
individuals and interviewing.

Throughout the job search you should be flexible and open to

123

new information. As you acquire more information, weigh it in light of your previous experience; modify your job search if it seems appropriate. Doing this will help you stay on target and utilize your time efficiently.

Research, the process of uncovering information, lies at the heart of your job search. It should be a continuous process which concentrates on developing two general areas of information. First, you must understand the structure and operation of the job market — advertised and hidden. Second, you must develop specialized knowledge on the key elements in the job market — individuals and organizations. You acquire this information by conducting research in libraries, by mail and telephone, and through face-to-face conversations. As an on-going process, this research begins the first day of your job search and continues until the last day and beyond.

Many people are reluctant to do research. Using a library intimidates some. Initiating contacts with strangers frightens others. But you do research every day as you acquire new information. If you want to become successful, you must overcome any reluctance to use unfamiliar sections of the library or initiate contacts with strangers. The best way to accomplish this is to *do it*! Get started immediately by going to the library and by talking to friends, acquaintances, and strangers about your career plans.

ADVERTISED AND HIDDEN JOB MARKETS

Research should first concentrate on better understanding the structure of the job market. As we noted in our earlier discussion of job myths (Chapter Five), you must be aware of two job markets — one advertised and another hidden. Both are characterized by a high degree of decentralization, fragmentation, and chaos. Neither should be underestimated nor overestimated.

The *advertised job market* consists of job vacancy announcements in newspapers, professional and trade journals, newsletters, employment agencies, and personnel offices. Most people focus on this market because it is relatively easy to find and because they believe it accurately reflects available job vacancies. In reality, however, the advertised job market probably represents no more than 25 percent of job opportunities at any given moment. For the most part, the positions represent extremes — low paid unskilled or high paid highly skilled jobs. The majority of positions, which lie between these two extremes, are not well represented. Competition often is great for the low and middle level positions. Worst of all, many of these advertised jobs are either nonexistent or are filled prior to being advertised.

We recommend spending a minimum amount of time looking for employment in the advertised job markets. Monitor this market, but don't assume it represents the entire spectrum of job opportunities. Your job search time and money are better spent elsewhere. When, as we noted in Chapter Eight, you identify an advertised position that is right for you, send a cover letter and resume — and move on.

There are exceptions to this general rule of avoiding the advertised job market. Each occupational specialty has its own internal recruitment and job finding structure. Some occupations are represented more by professional listing and recruitment services than others. Indeed, as we move into the high-tech society, greater efforts will be made to increase the efficiency of employment communication by centralizing job listings and recruitment services for particular occupational specialties. These services will be designed to reduce the *lag time* between when a job becomes vacant and is filled. Computerized job banks may increasingly be used by employers to locate qualified candidates, and vice versa. Employers in the high-tech society need to reduce lag time as much as possible given the increasing interdependency of positions in high-tech industries. If and when such employment services and job banks become available for your occupational specialty, you should at least investigate them. In the meantime, since the job market will remain relatively disorganized in the foreseeable future, do your research and follow our re-careering strategies.

Your research should center on one of the key dynamics to finding employment — helping employers solve their hiring problems. Many employers turn to the advertised job market *after* they fail to recruit candidates by other, less formal and public, means. The lag time between when a position becomes vacant, is listed, and then filled is a critical period for your attention and *intervention*. Your goal should be to locate high quality job vacancies before they are listed.

The *hidden job market* is where the action is. It is this job market that should occupy most of your attention. Although this job market lacks a formal structure, 75 percent or more of all job opportunities are found here. Your task is to give this market some semblance of structure and coherence so that you can effectively penetrate it. If you can do this, the hidden job market will yield numerous job interviews and offers that should be right for you.

Research is the key to penetrating the hidden job market. Consider, for example, the hiring problems of employers by putting yourself in their place. Suppose one of your employees suddenly gives you a two week notice or you terminate someone. Now you must hire a new employee. It takes time and it is a risky business you would prefer to avoid. After hours of reading resumes and interviewing, you still will be hiring an unknown who might create new problems for you. Like many other employers, you want to *minimize your time and risks*. You can do this by calling your friends and acquaintances and letting them know you are looking for someone; you would appreciate it if they could refer some good candidates to you. Based on these contacts, you should receive referrals. At the same time, you want to hedge your bets or fulfill affirmative action and equal opportunity requirements by listing the job vacancy in the newspaper or with your personnel office. While 300 people respond by mail to your want ad, you also get referrals from the trusted individuals in your network. In the end, you conduct 10 telephone interviews and three face-to-face interviews. You hire the *best* candidate — the one your former classmate recommended to you on the first day you informed her of your need to fill the vacancy. You are satisfied with your excellent choice of candidates; you are relatively certain this new employee will be a good addition to your organization.

This scenario is played out regularly in many organizations. It demonstrates the importance of getting into the hidden job market and devoting most of your time and energy there. If you let people know you are looking for employment, chances are they will keep you in mind and refer you to others who may have an unexpected vacancy. Your research will help you enter and maneuver within this job market of interpersonal networks and highly personalized information exchanges. Chapter Ten will show you how to do this with the maximum amount of impact.

WORKING THE LIBRARY

Libraries are filled with useful job and career relevant information. Reference and documents rooms of libraries have some of the best career resources. Career planning offices at colleges and universities have a wealth of job and career information in their specialized libraries — a wider selection than in most general libraries.

Do seek out library personnel for assistance. Reference librarians know what indexes and reference books are available. Tell them you are doing research on job and career alternatives; you would appreciate their assistance in locating information, such as lists of names and addresses of employers. Most librarians will be happy to share their knowledge with you. Some may even overwhelm you with assistance!

Your goal should be to acquire as much written information as possible on individuals and organizations relating to your job objective. Normally this means examining directories, books, magazines, and reports. These publications will provide general surveys of occupational fields, information on particular individuals and organizations, as well as names, addresses, and telephone numbers of key individuals within organizations. At this stage you need to understand the organizations and collect many names, addresses, and telephone numbers for initiating your writing and telephoning activities. Use 4 x 6 cards to record this information to develop your data files.

You should start your research by examining several of the following resources normally found in the reference or documents sections of libraries:

Directories of Reference Materials:	• *Ayer Directory of Publications* • *Applied Science and Technology* • *Business Periodicals Index* • *Directory of Directories* • *Guide to American Directories* (Bernard Klein) • *Readers' Guide to Periodical Literature* • *Standard Periodical Directory* • *Ulrich's International Periodicals Directory* • *Working Press of the Nation*
Career and Job Alternatives:	• *Ad Search* • *Advance Job Listings* • *Affirmative Action Register* • *The College Placement Annual* • *Dictionary of Occupational Titles* • *Encyclopedia of Careers and Vocational Guidance*, William E. Hopke (ed.) • *Guide for Occupational Exploration* • *Occupational Outlook Handbook* • *Occupational Outlook Quarterly* • *Work Related Abstracts*
Business Sources:	• *American Encyclopedia of International Information* • *Career Guide to Professional Associations* • *Directory of American Firms Operating in Foreign Countries*

- *The Directory of Corporate Affiliations: Who Owns Whom*
- *Dun & Bradstreet's Middle Market Directory*
- *Dun & Bradstreet's Million Dollar Directory*
- *Dun & Bradstreet's Reference Book of Corporate Managements*
- *Encyclopedia of Business Information Services*
- *Fitch's Corporation Reports*
- *Geographical Index*
- *Job Prospector*
- *MacRae's Blue Book — Corporate Index*
- *Moody's Manuals* (for various business fields)
- *The Multinational Marketing and Employment Directory*
- *Standard Directory of Advertisers*
- *The Standard Periodical Directory*
- *Standard & Poor's Industrial Index*
- *Standard Rate and Data Business Publications Directory*
- *Thomas' Register of American Manufacturers*

Associations:
- *Directory of Professional and Trade Organizations*
- *Encyclopedia of Associations*

Individuals:
- *American Men and Women in Science*
- *Standard & Poor's Register of Corporations, Directors, and Executives*
- *Who's Who in America*
- *Who's Who in Commerce and Industry*
- *Who's Who in the East*
- *Who's Who in the West*
- *Who's Who in the South*
- Directories of any professional or trade association

Government:
- *The Book of the States*
- *Congressional Directory*
- *Congressional Staff Directory*

- *Congressional Yellow Book*
- *Federal Directory*
- *Federal Yellow Book*
- *Municipal Yearbook*
- *Taylor's Encyclopedia of Government Officials*
- *United Nations Yearbook*
- *United States Government Manual*
- *Washington Information Directory*
- Other sources listed in Chapter Sixteen

Newspapers:
- *The Wall Street Journal*
- *The New York Times*
- *USA Today*
- *The Los Angeles Times*
- *The Houston Chronicle*
- *National Business Employment Weekly*
- *Washington Report*
- Trade newspapers
- Any newspaper – especially the Sunday edition for the area you are targeting

Business Publications:
Barron's, Business Week, Business World, Forbes, Fortune, Harvard Business Review, Money, Newsweek, Nation's Business, Time, U.S. News and World Report

Other Resources:
- Trade journals (the *Directory of Libraries and Information Centers* and *Subject Collections: A Guide to Special Book Collections in Libraries* compiles information on specialized business, government, and association libraries)
- Publications of chambers of commerce; state manufacturing associations; federal, state and local government agencies
- Telephone books – especially the Yellow Pages (if not in library, contact your local telephone company which may have a telephone book collection)
- Trade books on "how to get a job"

As you accumulate names and addresses, write or call for further information. Many companies have annual reports which they freely distribute to interested individuals. Your local stock broker also may be able to get some reports for you or suggest other information sources.

If you plan to move from a nonbusiness occupation to one in business, you should read business publications in order to familiarize yourself with various fields as well as the concepts and terminology business people use. The more you read in a field related to your job objective, the more you will be able to intelligently ask and answer questions in the language of employers.

Libraries have several other publications you may wish to consult concerning various occupational fields as well as job search strategies and techniques. Many of these are listed according to subject categories in the resource section of Appendix D.

TALKING TO PEOPLE

Reading and writing can take you only so far in your job search. Beware of becoming *too* preoccupied with library research. It never seems to end. Stop when you feel you have enough information to begin other types of research or start other job search steps. Two weeks or 40 hours in the library should get you off to a good start. If you are examining a highly specialized field where there are few names and addresses, you may achieve a high degree of redundancy within 10 hours. If you get carried away and are on your third week in the library, stop immediately and go on to more productive activities.

Your most productive research activity will be talking to people. Informal, word-of-mouth communication is still the most effective channel of job search information. In contrast to reading books, people have more current, and probably more accurate, information. In addition, most people are flattered to be asked for advice. They freely give it and will be happy to assist you with referrals to others. Don't hide the fact you are looking for a job, but don't ask for a job. Ask people about:

- occupational fields
- job requirements and training
- interpersonal environments
- performance expectations
- their problems
- salaries
- advancement opportunities
- future growth potential of the organization

- how best to acquire more information and contacts in a particular field
- how you can improve your resume

You may be surprised how willingly friends, acquaintances, and strangers will give you useful information. But before you talk to people, do your library research so that you are better able to ask thoughtful questions.

ACQUIRING AND USING POWER

Knowledge is power. Research will help increase your power in the job market. You should always collect new information, revise previous conceptions, and adjust your job search efforts to new realities uncovered through your research. As you do this, your research will affect your original objective and resume as well as guide you in accomplishing the other job search steps. Your power to give some structure and coherence to the hidden job market in your particular area of interest should increase accordingly.

Chapter Ten

PROSPECTING AND NETWORKING FOR INTERVIEWS

From your job research you will acquire useful names and addresses as well as meet people who will assist you in getting job interviews. The information and contacts will become the key building blocks for generating job interviews and job offers.

Since we know the greatest number as well as the best jobs are found in the hidden job market, you need job search methods to function effectively within the hidden job market. Research and experience clearly show the most effective means of communication are face-to-face and word-of-mouth. The informal, interpersonal system of communication constitutes the central nervous system of the hidden job market. Your task, as outlined in this chapter, is to penetrate this nervous system and utilize it to your advantage. You do this by prospecting, networking, and conducting informational and referral interviews.

MYTHS, EQUALITY, AND PULL

In Chapter Five we examined 10 job search myths that often prevent individuals from taking appropriate actions. Two additional myths function as obstacles to conducting an effective job search:

Myth 11: People who work hard and put in long hours get ahead.

Reality: People who are honest, work hard, and put in long hours also get fired, have ulcers, and die young. Other people get ahead by being dishonest and lazy and by having good luck or a helpful patron. Moderation in both work and play will probably get you just as far as the extremes.

Myth 12: You should not try to use contacts or connections in trying to get a job. Apply through the front door like everyone else. If you're the best qualified, you'll get the job.

Reality: While you may wish to stand in line for tickets, bank deposits, and loans because you have no clout, standing in line for a job is dumb. Every employer has a front door as well as a back door. It is best to go in the back door if you can.

While most people stand in lines for equal treatment, not everyone is treated equally. Furthermore, it is not desirable to do so when dealing with large numbers of applicants. After all, employers must limit candidates to a manageable number. This means discriminating against many people who expect equal treatment.

It is a time to dispell the myth of equal treatment. Instead, concentrate on how not to be discriminated against. You want to be *remembered and referred* to prospective employers. It is difficult to do if you are trying to get in the front door with the masses.

In the job search, you can best avoid discrimination by using prospecting, networking, and informational and referral interviewing strategies. This means sharpening your interpersonal communication skills and targeting them toward individuals and groups you may be reluctant to approach: the old boy network, connections, patrons, or debtors. These contacts may be relatives, friends, acquaintances, or strangers who will give you assistance in finding a job. There is nothing wrong, dishonest, or unethical in using your contacts. People do it all the time without realizing what they are doing. These people-resources or "pull" will play a key role in your job search success. As Stanat notes,

> Use pull. It gets big parts for marginal movie stars. It gets laws through Congress. It helps put multi-million dollar business deals across. And it can help you get a job. Pull is any force you can exert on the hiring process from inside the organization. . .

There are six kinds of pull:

- *Pull based on blood relationship.*
- *Pull based on business obligation.*
- *Pull based on friendship.*
- *Pull based on professional respect.*
- *Pull based on common bond.*
- *The pull of casual acquaintance.*

CAUTION: When you use pull, be absolutely certain that you can do the job. And if you get the job, you must work extra hard to produce. The professional credibility of a friend or another connection is riding on your performance. So you must deliver (Stanat: 94-98).

"Pull" helps you overcome one major problem in the job market: *communicating your qualifications to employers.* Without this "pull," your job search may become ineffective or take more time to complete; you will stand in line with all the other believers in equal treatment.

HELPING EMPLOYERS CHOOSE

Employers also prefer the informal system. Many are swamped with 400 or 500 resumes for a single position. In addition, many employers are uncertain what type of employee they need. By contacting employers through the informal system, you help them make decisions and thereby save them time.

At the same time, employers want to know more about candidates than just their paper qualifications. Indeed, studies show that employers seek candidates who have these skills: communication, problem solving, analytical, assessment, and planning (Stump: 55). Technical expertise, or knowledge of a particular job area, ranks third or fourth in employers' lists of most desired skills. These findings support what many people already know: employers' major problems with employees relate to communication, problem solving, and analysis. Furthermore, employers often fire employees because of political and interpersonal conflicts, rather than incompetence. Employers seek individuals they can get along with. In other words, they want to hire people they *like* both personally and professionally.

Communicating your qualifications to employers entails more

than just informing them of your technical competence. It requires communicating that you have the necessary mix of personal and professional skills for performing the job. The informal prospecting, networking, and informational and referral interviewing activities are the best way to communicate this information to employers.

CREATING AND LINKING NETWORKS

Networking is the process of developing relationships with others. Your interpersonal network consists of you interacting with other individuals. The concept is nothing new, but many people are unfamiliar with its use in the job search. It means developing your *connections* for conducting an effective job search.

Central to a successful job search is your ability to develop, maintain, and expand your networks for the purpose of finding a job. It is not difficult to do this, but it requires an awareness of networks and a knowledge of strategies for handling networks.

Your network is your interpersonal world. While you interact with hundreds of people over a lengthy period of time, on a day-to-day basis you probably meet with no more than 20 people. Figure 4, for example, outlines a hypothetical network for you. In this example you contact most people in face-to-face situations. Some people are more *important* to you than others. You *like* some more than others. And some will be more *helpful* to you in your job search than others. Therefore, you may want to contact several of these people for advice relating to your job search.

You can expand this basic network to include individuals you know and have interacted with over the past 5, 10, or 20 years. Begin by making a list of at least 200 people you know and who might be helpful to you in your job search. Include friends and relatives on your Christmas card list, past and present neighbors, former classmates, politicians, businesspersons, previous employers, professional associates, ministers, insurance agents, lawyers, bankers, doctors, dentists, accountants, and social acquaintances.

Since people in your network also have networks, you should try to link your network with theirs. Figure 5 illustrates this linkage principle. While the people in your network can give you job information, the people in these other networks also can assist you. Therefore, your goal should be to seek assistance from individuals in your immediate network as well as link your network to the networks of others for similar assistance.

So far we have examined how to identify and expand your network. At the same time, you want to create new networks with-

FIGURE 4

YOUR NETWORK OF RELATIONSHIPS

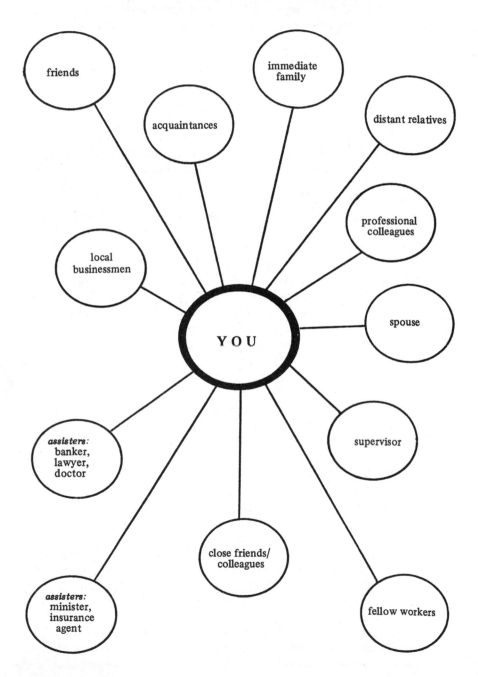

FIGURE 5

LINKING OF NETWORKS

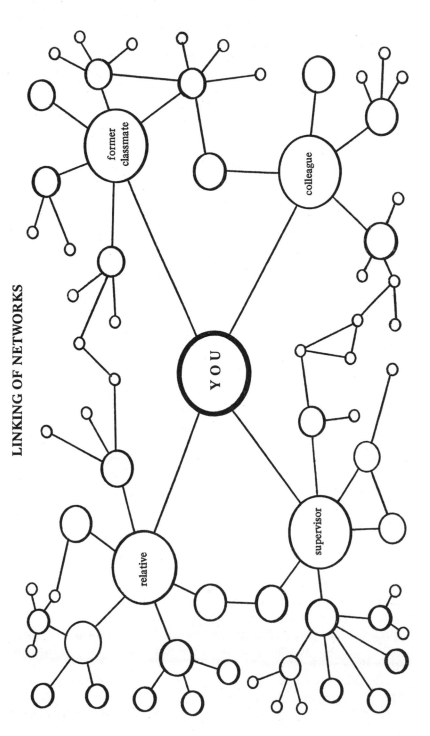

out the assistance of others in your network. For example, if you are interested in a public relations position with a firm in Chicago but no one in your network has a contact for you, try the "cold turkey" approach. Develop a new network by introducing yourself to a public relations specialist in your community; ask for advice and referrals. Chances are he or she will know someone who can refer you to the public relations community and networks in Chicago.

PROSPECTING FOR ACCEPTANCES

At the heart of your networking should be an active *prospecting campaign*. Salespersons in insurance, real estate, Amway, Shaklee, and other direct-sales businesses understand the importance and principles of prospecting. In order to generate enough interest in your product as well as make sufficient sales, you must continuously contact new people. Expect 9 out of 10 people to reject your product. But 1 out of 10 will accept it. Therefore, the more people you contact, the more acceptances you will receive. If you want to be successful, you must collect many more "noes" than "yeses." For example, in a 1 to 9 ratio of "yeses" to "noes," you need to contact 100 people in order to get 10 "yeses."

Most people have difficulty handling rejections. They take a "no" personally as a sign of failure — and quit. This works against them. If they had a positive outlook and persisted, they would achieve success after a few more "noes." This is precisely what you want to do. You must go out and prospect for job contacts. As you do, you will encounter rejections. Don't take them personally. Continue prospecting for those "yeses" which translate into job interviews and offers.

A good prospecting pace to begin with is two new contacts each day. At first you should contact people in your immediate network, as outlined in Figure 4. Tell them you are doing job research and would appreciate a few moments of their time to discuss your plans. You are seeking *information and advice* at this time, and you thought they could give you some valuable advice. By approaching them in this manner, you flatter them. In essence, you are saying to them *"I respect your opinions, evaluations, and advice."* This approach does not put them on the spot of having to help you find a job. You will seldom get "noes" when asking for job information rather than a job.

It will take approximately 20 minutes to make a contact by letter or telephone. Making two contacts a day only takes 40 minutes of your time. By the end of the first week you will have initiated

10 contacts. By that time you may want to increase your prospecting pace to four new contacts each day or 20 each week. The more contacts you make, the more useful information, advice, and job leads you will receive. If your job search seems to bog down, you probably need to increase your prospecting activities. Just think how many interviews and job offers you might receive if you contacted 200 people — perhaps 20 interviews and five job offers!

Your number of contacts should multiply considerably because each individual you contact will know other people they can refer you to. Expect each person to refer you to two or three others who, in turn, will refer you to another two or three people.

These prospecting methods are effective. While they are responsible for building, maintaining, and expanding multi-million dollar businesses, they work similarly for job hunters. But don't kid yourself. They only work if you are patient and persist. *The key to success is learning how to handle rejections.* Learn from them, forget them, and go on to more productive activities. The major reason direct-sales people fail is because they don't persist. The reason they don't persist is because they either can't take, or get tired of taking, rejections.

Rejections are no fun, but you will, and you must, get them as you travel on the road toward job success. And the road to job search success is strewn with individuals who quit prematurely — after being rejected only four or five times. Don't be one of them!

BEING SUBTLE, HONEST, AND PROFESSIONAL

Our prospecting and networking techniques minimize the number of rejections you will receive. If handled properly, at least 50 percent — maybe as many as 90 percent — of your prospects will turn into "yeses" rather than "noes." The reason for such a high acceptance rate is how you introduce and handle yourself while you are networking. Insurance agents and direct distributors may get a 90 percent rejection rate because they are trying to sell something to the prospect. People don't like to be put on the spot, especially in their home or office, with a pitch to buy a product.

The principles of selling yourself in the job market are similar. People don't want to be put on the spot of having to give you a job or being responsible for your livelihood. Therefore, you should never introduce yourself to a prospect by asking them for a job or a job lead.

Your approach to prospects must be subtle, honest, and professional. You are seeking *information, advice, and referrals* pertinent to several topics: job opportunities, your job search approach, your resume, others who may have similar information, advice, and referrals. Most people will gladly volunteer this and more information. They generally like to talk about themselves, their careers, and others. They especially like to give advice. Accordingly, you should be successful in getting a great deal of information, advice, and referrals from your prospects. As you do this, people remember you. If they hear of job opportunities for someone with your qualifications, they will probably contact you with job leads. After contacting 100 prospects, you will, in effect, have 100 sets of eyes and ears looking after your job and career future.

The guiding principle behind prospecting, networking, and informational and referral interviews is: *the best way to get a job is to ask for job information, advice, and referrals; never ask for a job.* If you follow this principle, you will join the ranks of thousands of successful individuals who practiced it; they, however, paid hundreds and thousands of dollars to learn the same principle from the professionals (Germann and Arnold: 79-80).

TELEPHONING FOR JOB LEADS

How do you best approach a prospective contact? Some people recommend writing a letter and waiting for a reply. Others suggest writing a letter and following it up with a telephone call (Irish: 101). Still others believe that telephone calls are the only way to go (Azrin and Besalel: 56-61). This may be another one of those proverbial *"six one way, half a dozen another"* situations. However, beware of the possible pitfalls of using the telephone excessively and aggressively.

There is much to be said for using the telephone in your job search. But using the telephone alone is a technique used by highly formalized job clubs which operate like phone banks. They normally take a client for two or three weeks and put him or her at the telephone in the morning. Using the Yellow Pages as their principal guide to employers, they call hundreds of employers and ask them for interviews. The telephone dialogue goes something like this:

- *"Hello, my name is Jim Baker. I would like to speak to the head of the training department. By the way, what is the name of the training director?"*

- *"You want to talk to Ms. Stevens. Her number is 723-8191 or I can connect you directly."*

- *"Hello Ms. Stevens. My name is Jim Baker. I have several years of training experience as both a trainer and developer of training materials. I would like to meet with you to discuss possible openings in your department for someone with my qualifications. Would it be possible to see you on Friday at 2:00 p.m.?"*

This telephone approach will result in many "noes." In fact, it is a good way to practice getting "noes" if you are somewhat reluctant to approach people. The principle behind this approach is *probability*. For every 25 telephone 'noes" you get, you will probably get one or two "yeses." Therefore, if you start calling prospective employers at 9:00 a.m. and finish your 25 calls by 12:00 noon, chances are you will have generated one or two interviews. That's not bad for three hours of job search work!

The telephone is more efficient than writing letters. But you are basically asking for a job. There is nothing subtle or particularly professional about this approach. And it works in uncovering job leads from individuals who are willing to be put on the spot and commit themselves over the telephone to strangers. Some people will do this, but many will not.

We neither discourage nor encourage this approach. You must follow your own judgment based upon your goals and needs. There is a time and place for it; perhaps you should at least try it to see if it produces results for you.

We prefer the more conventional approach of writing a letter and following it up with a telephone call. Don't wait for the individual to contact you. *You must take the initiative in contacting the individual for an appointment.* In this case, you do not put him or her on the spot because you are not asking for a job. This low-keyed approach has a higher probability of paying off with interviews than the aggressive telephone request. However, it takes more time to write a letter and follow it up with a telephone call than to sit down with the Yellow Pages and randomly call employers. But then, long distance calls can get expensive. While the results of these two methods may be the same, we believe the quality of the results will be different. You should be trying to uncover jobs that are right for you rather than any job that happens to pop up from a telephone blitz.

CONTACTING BUSY PEOPLE

Whom should you contact in an organization for conducting an informational and referral interview? Here, again, you will receive conflicting advice. Some career counselors advise you to aim at the top on the theory that individuals at the top have the most information and clout to assist you (Lin, Dayton, Greenwald: 3-7). Others feel people at the top are too busy to see you, so aim your sights lower. And still others believe you should target the person who has the power to hire (Bolles, 1980: 158-179). In any case, people in personnel departments are the least likely to have influence or assist you with the hidden job market.

We recommend contacting a variety of people. It is preferable to contact the person who has the power to hire. In many cases, this will be the head of an operating unit. But there are problems with this strategy. It is not always possible to find out who has the power to hire. Furthermore, it may be difficult to get an appointment with this key individual. People at the top may appear to be informed and powerful, but many times these people lack information on day-to-day personnel changes or their influence is limited in the hiring process.

From a practical standpoint, you may aim at the top as well as toward those who appear to have the power to hire, but you may have to settle for less. Secretaries, receptionists, and the individual you may want to meet with will refer you to others. While you may persist in trying to get in to see the influential person, you may have to take whomever you can schedule an appointment with. At the same time, we agree with Haldane Associates' guiding principle in this matter: *"The best kind of interviewer is a very busy person. Busy people are active, involved, and usually knowledgeable. You can get more information from such a person than from a dozen others"* (Germann and Arnold: 118). Aim for such busy people, but be prepared to take less. And sometimes people who are not busy can be helpful. Talk to a secretary or receptionist sometime about their boss or working in the office or company. You may be surprised with what you learn!

GETTING INFORMATION, ADVICE, AND REFERRALS

Your informational and referral interviews will be conducted with two audiences: individuals in your immediate and extended network and prospective employers. In some cases the two audiences will be one and the same — your professional colleague or former boss offers you a job.

With the first audience you can use more informal and personal approaches. For example, call your friend at home and meet at your house for dinner. The second audience is the most critical and thus it must be approached more deliberately than your friends and acquaintances.

The best way to initiate a contact with a prospective employer, who also may be a busy person, is to *send an approach letter*. As we noted in Chapter Eight, begin your letter with a personal statement: *"Mary Atkins suggested that I contact you. . ."* Briefly state your purpose — seek information and advice — and mention you will call at a certain time — perhaps Monday at 10:00 a.m. — to schedule a meeting. Do not enclose a resume with this letter. Again, your purpose is to get information and advice which will lead to referrals and being remembered; this is not a formal interview but it may well lead to one. Be sure to follow up with the phone call at your designated time.

Most people will meet with you. However, if you telephone the individual and he or she tries to put you off, clearly state your purpose and emphasize that you are not looking for a job with this person — only information and advice. If the person insists on putting you off, make the best of the situation by writing a nice thank-you letter in which you again state your intended purpose, mention your disappointment in not being able to learn from the person's experiences, and ask to be remembered for future reference. This time enclose your resume with the letter.

In most cases you will be able to schedule a meeting. While you are ostensibly seeking information and advice, treat this meeting as an important preliminary interview. In this meeting you will be communicating your qualifications — that you are competent, intelligent, honest, and likable. These are the same qualities you should communicate in a formal job interview. Therefore, the same advice we give in Chapter Eleven on interviewing, especially the "does" and "don'ts," should be followed in the informational and referral interview.

An informational and referral interview will be relatively unstructured compared to the formal interview. You want the interviewer to advise you; thus, you reverse roles by asking key questions which will yield useful information for you. You, in effect, become the interviewer.

Even though this interview is somewhat unstructured, you should be prepared with questions and the interview should follow a general pattern of questioning and answering. Most questions should be open-ended; they require the individual to give specific answers based on his or her experiences. You want to create an atmosphere wherein you are saying to the individual that *"I value your experience, opinions, and advice; please share those with me so that*

I can better improve my life." Such an orientation is extremely flattering to most people who will willingly assist you with your job search. In some cases, individuals take a personal interest in your job search by regularly keeping you informed of job leads.

MANAGING THE DIALOGUE

The procedure and dialogue for informational and referral interviews might go something like this. You plan to take no more than 45 minutes for this interview. The first three to five minutes of the interview will be devoted to small talk — the weather, traffic, the office, mutual acquaintances, or an interesting or humorous observation. Begin your interview by stating your appreciation for the individual's time:

> *"I want to thank you again for scheduling this meeting with me. I know you're busy. I appreciate your making special arrangements to see me on a subject which is very important to my future."*

Your next question is a statement in which you reiterate your purpose as stated in your letter:

> *"As you know, I am exploring job and career alternatives. I know what I do well and what I want to do. At this stage, I need to do sufficient research on job and career alternatives before I commit myself and my family to a new job. I thought you would be able to give me some advice about career opportunities, job requirements, and possible problems or promising directions in the field of _____."*

This statement normally will get a reaction from your interviewer who may want to know more about what it is you want to do. Therefore, be able to clearly communicate what your job objective is; don't fumble at this point by appearing lost, indecisive, or uncertain about yourself. If you do, the person may feel you are wasting his or her time. Moreover, you want to communicate that you are competent, intelligent, honest, and likable.

Your next line of questioning will probe several concerns. Since individuals usually like to talk about themselves, you may want to focus on the interviewer's own job or career or jobs he or she is most familiar with. These should be "how" and "what" questions centering on (1) specific jobs and (2) the job search process. Ask about various aspects of jobs:

- duties and responsibilities
- knowledge, skills, and abilities required
- work environment relating to fellow employees, work flows, deadlines, stress, initiative
- advantages and disadvantages
- advancement opportunities and outlook
- salary ranges

The interviewer will probably take a great deal of time talking about his or her experiences in each area. Be a good listener but try to move along with the questions.

Your second line of questioning should focus on your job search activities. You want to learn as much as possible about how to:

- acquire the necessary skills
- best find a job in this field
- overcome any objections employers may have to your background
- uncover job vacancies which may not be advertised
- develop job leads
- approach prospective employers

Your final line of questioning should focus on your resume. While the person may request to see it at the beginning of the interview, try to keep it for your last set of questions pertaining to the content of your resume. Your purpose here is threefold: (1) get the individual to read your resume in-depth, (2) acquire useful suggestions on how to improve your resume, and (3) refer your resume to other interested individuals who may be prospective employers. Show your resume and ask the following questions:

- *Is this an appropriate type of resume for the jobs I have outlined?*
- *If an employer received this resume in the mail, how do you think he or she would react to it?*
- *What do you see as possible weaknesses or areas that need to be improved?*
- *What should I do with this resume? Shotgun it to hundreds of employers with a cover letter? Use resume letters instead?*
- *What about the length, paper quality and color, layout, and*

typing? Are they appropriate?
- *How might I best improve the form and content of this resume?*

While you asked some of these questions before when you conducted your external resume evaluation (Chapter Eight), ask these questions again because you will receive useful advice for future revisions. Most important, such questions make the individual *read* your resume which, in turn, may be *remembered* for future reference.

Your last question is especially important in this interview. In addition to being remembered, you want to be *referred*. Therefore, ask the following question:

> *"I really appreciate all this advice. It is very helpful and it should improve my job search considerably. Could I ask you one more favor? Do you know two or three other people who could help me with my job search? I want to conduct as much research as possible, and their advice might be helpful also."*

As you get up to leave, mention one more important item:

> *"During the next few months, should you hear of any job opportunities for someone with my interests and qualifications, I would appreciate being kept in mind. And please feel free to pass my name on to others."*

Be sure to leave a copy of your resume behind.

Within 48 hours of completing this interview, send a nice thank-you letter in which you express your genuine gratitude for the interviewer's time and advice. Reiterate your interests and ask to be remembered and referred to others. Keep notes of your interview in a file.

Do follow up on any useful advice you receive, particularly names of referrals. Begin the same way with new referrals. Write a letter requesting a meeting. You begin the letter by mentioning that your previous interviewer suggested they would be a good person to contact in regard to your career research.

If you continue following up on referrals, within a short period of time you will be busy conducting interviews. These interviews will pay off in the end. If you conduct 100 informational and referral interviews over a two month period, these will probably lead to several formal job interviews and offers. However, the pay-offs are unpredictable because job vacancies are unpredictable. You may get lucky with your first referral interview. The first individual may have just heard on the grapevine about a job opportunity with a friend. He refers you to his friend and you conduct another informational and referral interview which becomes a job interview and a job offer. While this may not happen immediately in your case, it will happen to you if you conduct many such interviews.

THE JOB CLUB ALTERNATIVE

So far we have outlined job search techniques designed for individuals to conduct their own job search. One important alternative is to form a job club.

There are several types of job clubs ranging from an informal group of three people who meet regularly to share job search information to a highly formalized group of 12 individuals led by a trained counselor and supported with telephones, copying machines, and reference materials.

The basic principle behind the job club concept is that individuals can conduct a more effective job search if they join with others in sharing job information and job leads. In practice, this means individuals join together for developing mutual supports, creating a job search structure, and accomplishing specific job search tasks.

The highly formalized job clubs, such as the 40-Plus Club and groups led by professional counselors, organize job search activities aimed at both the advertised and hidden job markets. These activities involve:

- signing commitment agreements to achieve specific job search goals and targets
- contacting friends, relatives, and acquaintances for job leads
- completing activity forms
- using telephones, typewriters, photocopy machines, postage, and other supplies and equipment
- meeting with fellow participants to discuss job search progress
- telephoning to uncover job leads
- researching newspapers, telephone books, and directories
- developing research, telephone, interview, and social skills
- writing letters and resumes
- responding to want ads
- completing employment applications (Azrin and Besalel)

In other words, the job club is a highly structured way to formalize many of the prospecting, networking, and informational and referral interview activities within a group context.

One of the major emphases of such job clubs is on using the telephone. Job club members spend a great deal of time calling prospective employers and asking about job openings. The Yellow Pages of the telephone book become the job hunting bible. Over a two week period, a job club member might spend most of his or her morning telephoning hundreds of employers for the purpose of uncovering job leads and scheduling interviews. The afternoons are devoted to job interviewing. For an examination of such job club procedures, see Nathan H. Azrin and Victoria A. Besalel, *Job Club Counselor's Manual.*

We do not recommend joining such job clubs. Their job search methods are designed for the hardcore unemployed or for individuals who need a job – any job - in a hurry. The basic approach of these job clubs is to uncover job leads and schedule interviews by telephone. In essence, the job hunter asks employers *"Do you have a job for me."* If you need any job in a hurry, this is one of the most efficient ways of finding employment. It sure beats standing in line at the state employment office! However, if you are more concerned with making a job or career change that is right for you – that is, find a job you will do well and enjoy doing – these job club methods are not for you. Instead, turn your attention to conducting your own job search or to forming a support group which will utilize the job search methods outlined in this book (Krannich, 1983).

As we noted in Chapter Five, support groups can cut your job search time in half. These groups are actually small, informal job clubs. Forming one of these groups will help direct as well as enhance your individual job search activities.

Your support group can consist of three or more individuals who are job hunting. Try to schedule regular meetings with specific purposes in mind. While the group may be highly social, especially if it involves close friends, it also should be *task-oriented*. Meet at least once a week and include your spouse. At each meeting set *performance goals* for the week. For example, your goal can be to make 20 new contacts and conduct five informational and referral interviews. The contacts can be made by telephone, letter, or in person. Share your experiences and job information with each other. *Critique* each other's progress, make suggestions for improving the job search, and develop new strategies together. By doing this, you will be gaining valuable information and feedback. This group will provide important psychological supports to help you through your job search. After all, job hunting can be a lonely, frustrating, and exasperating experience. By sharing your experiences with others, you will find you are not alone. Indeed, the group will encourage you, and you will feel good about helping others achieve their goals.

Whatever strategy you choose, remember that millions of other people are going through the same experience of looking for a job. Most people will go about it haphazardly. You have the opportunity to put your best foot forward by developing your own job search campaign as well as joining others in forming a job search network. Putting your best foot forward requires you to prospect, network, and conduct informational and referral interviews on a regular basis. This requires a great deal of work, moreso than sitting behind a desk writing letters or telephoning in response to job listings in newspapers. It also is one of the most rewarding personal experiences you will encounter. You will uncover a world of concerned people who understand your needs and want to help you be successful. In the end, you may discover that finding a job may be more enjoyable than doing a job!

Chapter Eleven

INTERVIEWING FOR JOB OFFERS

A job interview is a prerequisite to receiving a job offer. Indeed, approximately 95 percent of all organizations interview candidates before offering them jobs. One study of 255 businesses hiring recent college graduates found that employers considered an effective interview to be the most important hiring criteria — outranking grade point average, related work experience, and recommendations (Einhorn, Bradley, Baird: 72).

While resumes are designed to get interviews, interviews are supposed to result in job offers. Therefore, if you want to receive job offers, you must develop effective interview skills. The more interviews you conduct, the higher the probability you will receive job offers.

This chapter outlines the basic interview skills you should acquire prior to meeting prospective employers. These involve written, telephone, and face-to-face verbal and nonverbal communication. A more extended treatment of this subject is found in Caryl Rae Krannich's *Interview for Success*.

EXPERIENCING STRESS

The job interview is the most important yet stressful step to getting a job. While your resume and letters got you the interview, the interview is where you must sell yourself in order to receive a job offer. Knowing the stakes are high, most people face interviews with dry throats and sweaty palms; it is a time of great stress. You will be on stage. How well you perform may determine your career future.

But how do you best prepare for the job interview? Unfortunately, you will receive a great deal of conflicting advice on how to conduct an effective job interview. "Experts" will tell you everything from how you should shake hands to when you should visit the restroom. Such advice is based on a combination of folklore, fads, common sense, experience, and research. You need to cut through this advice and get to what is most useful for you.

PLAYING ROLES

Most people view the job interview from one of two perspectives. The first perspective advises you to play a *role*. Your role is that of the interviewee who is seeking a job by interacting with an interviewer. Hence, you need to identify the expectations of the interviewer and adjust your behavior accordingly. Your task is to manage the interview encounter to your advantage by behaving in certain prescribed manners.

This interviewer-interviewee perspective is the predominate view of most career counselors. Having somehow discovered the expectations of interviewers, they advise you on how you can best persuade the interviewer to give you a job offer. The College Placement Council, for example, identifies sixteen traits employers expect in candidates:

EXPECTATIONS OF EMPLOYERS

1. *Ability to Communicate.* Do you have the ability to organize your thoughts and ideas effectively? Can you express them clearly when speaking or writing? Can you present your ideas to others in a persuasive way?

2. *Intelligence.* Do you have the ability to understand the assignment? Learn the details of operation? Contribute original ideas to your work?

3. *Self-Confidence.* Do you demonstrate a sense of

maturity that enables you to deal positively and effectively with situations and people?

4. *Willingness to Accept Responsibility.* Are you someone who recognizes what needs to be done and is willing to do it?

5. *Initiative.* Do you have the ability to identify the purpose for work and to take action?

6. *Leadership.* Can you guide and direct others to obtain the recognized objectives?

7. *Energy Level.* Do you demonstrate a forcefulness and capacity to make things move ahead? Can you maintain your work effort at an above-average rate?

8. *Imagination.* Can you confront and deal with problems that may not have standard solutions?

9. *Flexibility.* Are you capable of changing and being receptive to new situations and ideas?

10. *Interpersonal Skills.* Can you bring out the best efforts of individuals so they become effective, enthusiastic members of a team?

11. *Self-Knowledge.* Can you realistically assess your own capabilities? See yourself as others see you? Clearly recognize your strengths and weaknesses?

12. *Ability to Handle Conflict.* Can you successfully contend with stress situations and antagonism?

13. *Competitiveness.* Do you have the capacity to compete with others and the willingness to be measured by your performance in relation to that of others?

14. *Goal Achievement.* Do you have the ability to identify and work toward specific goals? Do such goals challenge your abilities?

15. *Vocational Skills.* Do you possess the positive combination of education and skills required for the

position you are seeking?

16. *Direction.* Have you defined your basic personal needs? Have you determined what type of position will satisfy your knowledge, skills and goals? (Rogers: 96)

When applying this role perspective, many writers view the interviewer as particularly sensitive to the "laws" of verbal and non-verbal communication. Some interviewers appear naive; they can be manipulated by clever interviewers who know how to meet their expectations.

This role perspective is responsible for most interview success formulas and checklists of "dos" and "don'ts." Komar (40), for example, tells you the key to successful interviewing is his formula of "presence":

PRESENCE = grooming and clothing +
nonverbal communication

According to this formula, how you communicate is an important part of what you communicate. You should package your image more than your job-related competencies; form outranks content.

Other experts include some content with their emphasis on form. Accordingly, your interview behavior should include:

- proper attire
- good grooming
- a firm handshake
- the appearance of control and confidence
- smiling and displaying appropriate humor
- showing interest in the employer and listening attentively
- being positive about past performance
- empathizing with the employer and appearing willing to help him or her
- communicating solid ideas
- taking control if the employer has difficulty interviewing

Furthermore, you should prepare for the job interview by doing these things:

- Research the organization and the interviewer ahead of time.
- Think about what it is you want to contribute to the inter-

viewer and his or her organization, such as increase quality and productivity. Be prepared to communicate this information in the interview.
- Learn to ask intelligent questions about job duties and personal qualities desired in employees. Be prepared to demonstrate how you meet or exceed the employer's expectations.
- Avoid questions about pay, vacations, and other benefits until later.
- Be prepared to ask questions and discuss problems facing the interviewer's employees in order to stress your qualifications in relation to the problems.
- Be well groomed. Wear attire appropriate to the job you will be interviewing for. Avoid faddish clothing and hair styles as well as heavy perfumes.
- Take to the interview extra copies of your resume, a list of references, and a sample of your work if design or writing skills are required.
- Confirm your appointment time and arrive five minutes early.
- Communicate energy, self-confidence, sincerity, and friendliness. Smile, have a firm hand shake, be relaxed, and maintain eye contact (Lathrop, 1977: 181-182).

Bolles (1978: 121-150; 156) agrees with this advice, but he goes one step further. He advises you to identify employers' problems and suggest solutions to them. While this novel approach makes sense, it is somewhat presumptuous, especially when you discover the so-called problem is the employer's pet project!

Most of this interview advice can be condensed into a handy list of "dos" and "don'ts," many of which remind you of Grandma's admonitions! Stanat (102-107) provides one of the most comprehensive such checklists:

"DOS"

___ *Do* have attractive hands — clean and nails trimmed.
___ *Do* comb your hair and wear it in a conservative style.
___ *Do* use a *moderate* amount of perfume or cologne.
___ *Do* use the restroom before the interview.
___ *Do* get a good night's sleep.
___ *Do* maintain eye contact since interviewers place a great deal of emphasis on it.
___ *Do* appear enthusiastic. Use gestures but make them smooth.

—— *Do* smile.

—— *Do* learn the name of the interviewer and use it occasionally during the interview.

—— *Do* take enough money with you, just in case you have an emergency of some kind.

—— *Do* research the organization ahead of time. Observe the dress modes and working environment.

—— *Do* take notes during the interview since the interviewer will be doing the same. Jot down some of your questions before the interview.

—— *Do* defer to the interviewer in setting the interview pace.

—— *Do* let the interviewer close the interview.

—— *Do* inquire about when you might expect to hear from the interviewer next.

"DON'TS"

—— *Don't* be late to the interview.

—— *Don't* wear an overcoat, topcoat, or rubber boots into an interview — you look anxious to leave.

—— *Don't* sit down or dash to your chair until the interviewer gives some indication to be seated; otherwise, you look forward.

—— *Don't* have a mouthful of anything except your teeth.

—— *Don't* lean on the interviewer's desk. Sit erect in your chair.

—— *Don't* wear dark glasses.

—— *Don't* carry a large handbag.

—— *Don't* have extremely long fingernails.

—— *Don't* demonstrate your nervousness by tapping your fingers, swinging your leg, or playing with your hands.

—— *Don't* fidget with your clothes.

—— *Don't* play with your hair.

—— *Don't* compare this interviewer with others.

—— *Don't* pick up items on the interviewer's desk unless invited to do so.

—— *Don't* appear to eavesdrop on any phone calls the interviewer receives in your presence.

—— *Don't* stand if someone enters the office during the interview.

—— *Don't* read materials on the interviewer's desk.

—— *Don't* refer to the interviewer as "sir" or "Ma'am".

—— *Don't* use the interviewer's name too much.

—— *Don't* over-extend your jokes and humor.

___ *Don't* answer questions with one and two word remarks.
___ *Don't* dominate the conversation. Answer the questions without lingering.
___ *Don't* interrupt the interviewer.
___ *Don't* swear, even though the interviewer may.
___ *Don't* use slang.
___ *Don't* gush or be syrupy.
___ *Don't* punctuate your conversation with "you know."
___ *Don't* use the interviewer's first name.
___ *Don't* be preachy.
___ *Don't* mumble.
___ *Don't* interpret your resume unless asked to.
___ *Don't* try to impress the interviewer by bragging.
___ *Don't* lie.
___ *Don't* criticize your employer.
___ *Don't* get angry or irritated during the interview.
___ *Don't* answer questions you consider too personal – but explain your reason for doing so.
___ *Don't* glance at your watch.
___ *Don't* ask if you can have the job. Instead, indicate your interest in the job.
___ *Don't* mention salary in the initial interview.

Richard Irish (124-125) rounds out this list with a few of his own "dos" and "don'ts":

___ Women should take the initiative in extending the handshake when meeting the interviewer.
___ Don't smoke, chew gum, tobacco, or your fingernails.
___ Maintain eye contact, but don't stare at the interviewer.
___ Occasionally glance off into another direction.
___ If the interviewer seems to run out of questions, ask him or her if you are giving them the information they want.
___ If a question sounds irrelevant, unprincipled, or unimportant, ask why the interviewer feels it's important.
___ Don't be "cool" and laid-back in the interview, unless you want to let the interviewer know you are a con-artist.

Since John Molloy became a popular wardrobe and image consultant, "dress for success" has become another important "interview for success" role theme. Molloy tells you exactly what to wear in terms of style, color, and quality of clothes. Women, for example, should wear a navy blue or gray skirted suit, light make-up, and little jewelry. Men should wear a dark blue or gray suit and a good quality white or light blue shirt; they should shine their shoes and have no facial hair. This upper class look of success should put you in a good light with interviewers.

Still others are more sophisticated with color shades and combinations. For them, just what does Molloy mean when navy blues and grays come in hundreds of shades? Some shades of blue and gray are inappropriate for many people. And these image and color consultants disagree among themselves as to whether everyone fits into a standard set of seasonal colors (Jackson) or whether you possess a unique color spectrum (Lewis and Nicholson). The increasing sophistication of the image and color consultants appears to raise questions about Molloy's research and simplistic advice!

BEING HONEST AND INSIGHTFUL

Contrasting with the role perspective is another perspective perhaps best termed "just be yourself." It stresses the importance of being honest and straightforward when interviewing for a position. Don't try to be something you are not because you will be discovered in the end. Therefore, just be your natural self in the interview. Playing a role is seen as being less than honest.

Both perspectives will pose problems for you. Learning to play the role of interviewee assumes we know the expectations of interviewers and that those expectations are similar for all interviewers. Furthermore, it assumes it is best to *meet* the expectations of others. The problem is twofold. Since interviewers differ, so do expectations. Some interviewers know how to interview effectively whereas others do not. As for meeting expectations, there is no evidence you should do this. It is probably better for you to *exceed* in a positive manner the expectations of the interviewer. For example, without being threatening, you want to communicate to the interviewer that you will be more productive than he or she originally anticipated. This will put you in a better position relative to other candidates who are trying to meet the interviewer's expectations.

The "just be yourself" perspective can pose difficulties too. Honest, frank, and straightforward people sometimes are inconsiderate, insensitive, and unprofessional with others. While employers want interviewees to be honest, they also want them to observe social graces, be considerate and sensitive to others, and play a professional role. Therefore, just being yourself is not as readily valued by employers as one might think.

In the end, there are few hard and fast rules in the interview game. Therefore, you must take much of the advice on how to interview with reservations. Our approach is to combine the "role" and "just be yourself" perspectives into a useful set of interviewing prescriptions. Using a contingency approach, we believe it is best to *know your situation and behave accordingly*. You need to develop your own insights and prescriptions based upon your unique experiences. This means you may have to create your own "dos" and "don'ts" as you become more knowledgeable about your own job search situation.

EXCHANGING CRITICAL INFORMATION

An interview is a two-way communication exchange between an interviewer and an interviewee. They exchange important information about each other. It is a complex communication situation:

> *During the employment interview, you communicate by what you say, what you do not say, what you do, and what you do not do. Thus, you need to become more sensitive to what you communicate through your answers, questions, and nonverbal behaviors* (Einhorn, Bradley, and Baird: 73)

You communicate both verbally and nonverbally. While we tend to concentrate on the content of what we say, research shows that approximately 65 percent of all communication is nonverbal. Furthermore, we tend to give more credibility to nonverbal than to verbal messages. Regardless of what you say, how you sit, stand, use your hands, move your head and eyes, and listen communicate both positive and negative messages.

Job interviews entail various communication mediums and situations. You will write job interview letters, schedule interviews over the telephone, be interviewed by telephone, and encounter one-on-one as well as panel and group interviews. Each situation requires a different set of communication behaviors. For example, while telephone communication is efficient, it may be ineffective for interview purposes. Only certain types of information can be effectively communicated over the telephone because this medium limits your nonverbal behavior. Honesty, intelligence, and likability – three of the most important values you want to communicate to employers – are primarily communicated nonverbally. Therefore, you should be very careful of telephone interviews – whether giving or receiving them.

Job interviews have different purposes and can be negative in many ways. From the perspective of the applicant, the purpose of most initial job interviews is to get a second interview, and the purpose of the second interview is to get a job offer. However, from the perspective of employers, the purpose of the interview is to eliminate you from a second interview or job offer. The interviewer wants to know why he or she should *not* hire you. Thus, the interviewer has a negative goal — to identify your weaknesses in order to eliminate you from further consideration. These differing purposes create an adversarial relationship and contribute to a great deal of interviewing stress for both the applicant and the interviewer.

Knowing this, you must *communicate your strengths* to the interviewer in order to lessen his or her fears of hiring you. After all, you are a risk which may cost the organization $25,000 or more a year. If the interviewer shows poor judgment, he or she may be threatened with a job loss. Your job is to help the interviewer overcome negative expectations by stressing your positives and by raising expectations.

PREPARING TO ANSWER QUESTIONS

Assume your networking has paid off with an invitation to interview with a company. What do you do next? Prepare for the interview as if it were a $500,000 prize. After all, this company may give you that much in income over the next 15 to 20 years.

The invitation to interview will most likely come by telephone. It may consist of a telephone interview or a request to meet for an interview at a certain time. The telephone interview is used frequently because employers may want to shorten their list of candidates from 10 to 3. By calling each candidate by telephone, the employer can make quick decisions on marginal candidates or update the job status of each candidate. When you get such a telephone call, you have no time to prepare. You may be dripping wet from just getting out of the shower or you may have a splitting headache. It always seems to come at the wrong time. Whatever your situation, put your best foot forward based upon your thorough preparation for an interview. We will examine this special case of the telephone interview shortly.

Once you have confirmed a job interview time and place, you should do as much research on the organization and employer as possible as well as learn to lessen your anxiety and stress levels by practicing the interview situation. *Preparation and practice* are the keys to doing your best.

During the interview, you want to impress upon the interviewer your knowledge of his or her organization by asking intelligent questions and giving intelligent answers. You can do this by going back to your library and consulting several sources on the organization and its key people. The sources are listed in Chapter Nine; the directories, reports, and articles will be especially helpful. Be sure to talk to people who know about the employer and the organization. This can include the competition, the chamber of commerce, the Better Business Bureau, suppliers, or clients. This research will establish a common ground of information for conducting the interview.

You should also do a "dry run" of the interview with your spouse or friend. Anticipate several questions which employers most frequently ask about your educational background, work experience, career goals, personality, and other concerns. Practice with these four categories of questions:

YOUR EDUCATION

- *Describe your educational background.*
- *Why did you attend _____ University (or College)?*
- *Why did you major in _____?*
- *What was your grade point average?*
- *What subjects did you enjoy the most? The least? Why?*
- *What leadership positions did you hold?*
- *How did you finance your education?*
- *If you started all over, what would you change about your education?*
- *Why were your grades so low? So high?*
- *Did you do the best you could in school? If not, why not?*

YOUR WORK EXPERIENCE

- *What were your major achievements in each of your past jobs?*
- *Why did you change jobs before?*
- *What is your typical workday like?*
- *What functions do you enjoy doing the most?*
- *What did you like about your boss? Dislike?*
- *Which job did you enjoy the most? Why? Which job did you enjoy the least? Why?*
- *Have you ever been fired? Why?*

YOUR CAREER GOALS

- *Why do you want to join our organization?*

- *Why do you think you are qualified for this position?*
- *Why are you looking for another job?*
- *Why do you want to make a career change?*
- *What ideally would you like to do?*
- *Why should we want to hire you?*
- *How would you improve our operations?*
- *What is the lowest pay you will take?*
- *How much do you think you are worth for this job?*
- *What do you want to be doing five years from now?*
- *How much do you want to be making five years from now?*
- *What are your short-range and long-range career goals?*
- *If you could choose your job and organization, where would you go?*
- *What other types of jobs are you considering? Other companies?*
- *When will you be ready to begin work?*
- *How do you feel about relocating, traveling, working overtime, and spending weekends in the office?*
- *What attracted you to our company?*

YOUR PERSONALITY AND OTHER CONSIDERATIONS

- *Tell me about yourself.*
- *Where are your major weaknesses? Your major strengths?*
- *What causes you to lose your temper?*
- *What do you do in your spare time? Any hobbies?*
- *What types of books do you read?*
- *What role does your family play in your career?*
- *How well do you work under pressure? In meeting deadlines?*
- *Tell me about your management philosophy.*
- *How much initiative do you take?*
- *What types of people do you prefer working with?*
- *How _____ (creative, analytical, tactful, etc.) are you?*
- *If you could change your life, what would you do differently?*
- *Who are your references?*

With each question you should develop positive answers which emphasize your *strengths*. Remember, the interviewer wants to know about your *weaknesses*. For example, if the interviewer asks you *"What are your weaknesses?"* turn this negative question into a positive by answering something like this:

"I sometimes get so involved with my work that I neglect

*my family as well as forget to do some of the more mun-
dane things in life, such as mow the lawn or repair the TV.
I guess I'm somewhat of a workaholic."*

What employer could hold this negative against you? You have
taken a negative and raised the expectations of the employer by
basically saying you are a hard and persistent worker; he will get
more for his money than expected.

Other questions may appear to be illegal, but some employers
ask them nonetheless:

- *Are you married, divorced, separated or single?*
- *How old are you?*
- *Do you go to church regularly?*
- *Do you have many debts?*
- *Do you own or rent your home?*
- *What social and political organizations do you belong to?*
- *What does your spouse think about your career?*
- *Are you living with anyone?*
- *Are you practicing birth control?*
- *Were you ever arrested?*
- *How much insurance do you have?*
- *How much do you weigh?*
- *How tall are you?*

Be prepared to respond to these questions. Don't say *"That's an
illegal question and I refuse to answer it!"* While you may be per-
fectly right in saying so, this response lacks tact, which may be
what the employer is looking for. For example, if you are divorced
and the interviewer asks about your divorce, you might respond with
*"Does a divorce have a direct bearing on the responsibilities of
_____?"* Some employers may ask such questions just to see
how you answer or react under stress. For example, if an interviewer
asks if you are on the pill, he may want to see if you will blow your
top, become embarrassed, or keep your cool. We recommend keeping
your cool by responding with tact and humor:

> *"Yes, I take three pills a day — vitamins A, B, and C, and
> they make me especially fit for this job!"*

The interviewer will get the message, and you will have indicated
that you can handle stressful communication.

ASKING INTELLIGENT QUESTIONS

Think about possible questions to ask the interviewer. While he wants to know about you, you need to get information as well as indicate your interest by asking questions. Try to remember several of these questions.

- *What duties and responsibilities does this job entail?*
- *Where does this position fit into the organization?*
- *Is this a new position?*
- *What kind of person are you looking for?*
- *When was the last person promoted?*
- *What is the best experience and background for this position?*
- *Whom would I report to? Tell me a little about these people.*
- *Are you happy with them? What are their strengths and and weaknesses?*
- *What are your expectations for me?*
- *May I talk with present and previous employees about this job?*
- *What problems might I expect to encounter on this job? (efficiency, quality control, declining profits, internal politics, evaluation)*
- *What has been done recently in regards to _____?*
- *What is the normal pay range for this job?*
- *How did you get your job?*
- *How long have you been with this company?*
- *Tell me about promotions and advancement with your company.*
- *What might I expect for myself?* (Lathrop, 1977: 186-187).

COMMUNICATING NONVERBALLY

You should also prepare yourself according to the checklist of "dos" and "don'ts" we outlined under the role perspective. Most of these items are common sense. Your wardrobe should consist of clothes appropriate to the interview situation. For most professional jobs, this will mean wearing relatively conservative clothes – the blue or gray suit. Women should avoid looking sexy. Excessive jewelry and heavy make-up and perfume are discouraged.

Other nonverbal behaviors to sensitize yourself to are how you sit, stand, and listen. Practice greeting the interviewer. When you enter the office area, remove your coat. On meeting the interviewer, extend your hand; women should do the same, particularly when interviewing with a male. Next, sit when and where the interviewer indicates; don't rush to a seat as if you are in a hurry to get started and finished.

Be particularly sensitive to *your listening behavior*. While the interviewer expects more than single "yes" and "no" answers to his questions, she also needs nonverbal feedback in order to take you seriously. Indicate your attention and interest by maintaining frequent eye contact, nodding, smiling, and interjecting verbal responses. Listening is an active process, and effective listeners make others feel good about their communication.

ENDING INTERVIEWS AND PERFECTING SKILLS

Also practice ending an interview. Many people don't know when or how to close interviews. They go on and on until someone breaks an uneasy moment of silence with an indication that it is time to go. Normally an interviewer will initiate the close of the interview by standing, shaking hands, and thanking you for coming to the interview. Don't end by saying *"Goodbye and thank you."* At this stage, you should summarize the interview in terms of your interests, strengths, and goals. Restate your qualifications and continuing interest in working with the employer. At this point it is proper to ask the interviewer about his selection plans: *"When do you anticipate making your final decision?"* Follow this question with your final one: *"May I call you next week to inquire about my status?"* By taking the initiative in this manner, the employer will need to clarify your status soon and you will have an opportunity to talk to her further.

Often toward the end of an interview you will be asked for a list of references. Be sure to prepare such a list prior to the interview. Include the names, addresses, and phone numbers of four individuals who will give you positive professional and personal recommendations.

Whoever assists you in preparing for the interview should evaluate your performance. Practice the whole interviewing scenario beginning with entering the door to leaving at the end. You should sharpen your nonverbal communication skills and be prepared to give positive answers to questions as well as ask intelligent questions. The more you practice, the better prepared you will be for the real job interview.

INTERVIEWING BY TELEPHONE

Few people are effective telephone communicators. Much nonverbal communication between parties, such as eye contact and facial expression and gestures, is absent in telephone conversations. People who may be dynamic in face-to-face situations may be dull and boring over the telephone. Since critical communication relating to the interview will take place over the telephone, pay particular attention to how you handle your telephone communication.

There are two potential telephone situations relating to the interview. First, you may request an interview by calling an employer. Second, the employer calls you and conducts a screening interview over the phone. While the rules for both types of telephone conversations vary, there is consensus on certain practices.

When initiating a request for an interview, always know the name of the person you wish to contact. It is relatively simple to get the name. Make two phone calls, one to the receptionist or secretary and another to the person you want to speak to. When calling the receptionist or secretary, just ask for the name of the person you wish to contact. For example, ask *"Who is the head of the _____ department?"* On your second call talk directly to the person you wish to speak with.

Most often your telephone call will go through a secretary. There is no need to give the secretary much information other than *"I would like to speak with Mr. Casey. This is John Davis calling."* If the secretary wants more information about the nature of your business, tell her you wish to make an appointment to see him about some business. If she persists in trying to identify what exactly you want, tell her it is personal business. If this line of questioning fails and she won't put you through, try to call at odd times, such as one half hour before the office opens and a half hour after it closes. Many managers come to work early and leave later than their secretaries. During that time, no one is around to answer the telephone except the person you wish to have an interview with.

If you send a letter introducing yourself prior to this telephone call, your telephone introduction will be easier to handle. For example, try this:

> *"Hello, this is John Davis. I'm calling in regards to the letter I sent you last week. I mentioned I would call you today to inquire about the possibility of scheduling a meeting. You may recall my background and interests are in training and development. I would like to meet with you briefly to discuss. . ."*

However, if this is one of those "cold turkey" request-for-interview calls, you will have to take pot luck as we noted in the previous chapter. You will have trouble getting past the receptionist or secretary. Don't expect many employers to invite you to a job interview based on such a call. Be straightforward, assertive, and hope for the best. Try to avoid the "give-me-a-job" mentality of these calls. Use some opening statements to ease the aggressiveness of this call:

"I heard about the innovative work you are doing in technical training. . ."

"I've always wanted to learn more about opportunities with your organization. Would it be possible for us to get together briefly to discuss your training needs?"

"I was told you might know someone who would be interested in my background: 10 years of increasingly responsible training and development experience. . ."

It is best to write these opening statements on a piece of paper and refer to them in your conversation. Avoid a lengthy phone conversation. You do not want to turn this into a job interview. You want to schedule an interview. If the individual asks you interview-type questions, do your best to stress your strengths and specify an interview time.

Remember, your telephone voice will be a slightly higher pitch than your normal voice. Therefore, lower your pitch and speak in a moderate volume and rate. If you vary your volume, rate, and pitch for emphasis, you will sound relatively enthusiastic and interesting over the telephone (Einhorn, Bradley, and Baird: 68).

The second type of telephone encounter is the unexpected call from the employer. Many employers conduct a preliminary telephone screening interview prior to inviting the finalists to the job interview. If you get one of these calls, be prepared; expect the employer to try to probe your weaknesses. After all, she needs to eliminate a certain number of finalists. The questions will be similar to those asked in the formal interview. Again try to sound enthusiastic, interested, and positive. Stress your strengths and try to arrange a formal interview. Keep your list of questions near the telephone so that you also can interview the employer.

Many employers will probe the salary question with you on the phone. They want to know if they can afford you or if you have a realistic salary expectation. While it is best to leave this question until the second or third interview, be prepared to answer it over the telephone. Since you should know the salary range for the position based upon your research, either quote the high end of the range as the bottom of your range or, better still, mention to the interviewer that you are open to the salary question at this point. You need more information about the position, and out of fairness to the employer, he needs to know more about your value. This will give you a lead into requesting an interview.

You can prepare for these telephone conversations by role playing with a friend. Tape-record the conversation, but do not look at each other during the conversation. Have someone else critique the tape and discuss how you might improve the telephone interview.

HANDLING EMPLOYERS' SUSPICIONS AND OBJECTIONS

Most employers are suspicious of candidates, and rightfully so. Employment realities teach them some hard facts of life, such as encountering dishonest applicants. Therefore, you must learn how to overcome their suspicions and objections to hiring you.

While employers may not directly ask you these questions, they think about them nonetheless:

- *Why should I hire you?*
- *What do you really want?*
- *What can you really do for me?*
- *What are your weaknesses?*
- *What problems will I have with you?*

Underlying these questions are specific employers' objections to hiring you:

- *You're not as good as you say you are; you probably hyped your resume or fudged about yourself.*
- *You just want a job and security.*
- *Career changers are bad risks in this business.*
- *You have weaknesses like the rest of us. Is it alcohol, sex, drugs, shiftlessness?*
- *You'll probably want my job in another 5 months.*

Employers raise such suspicions and objections because you are an unknown quantity. After all, they have probably made poor hiring decisions before.

It is difficult to trust strangers in the employment game. Indeed, there is an alarming rise in the number of individuals lying on resumes; the number is likely to increase in a tight job market. Approximately one-fifth of all credentials checked for verification at Stanford University, for example, are found to be falsifications. The Harvard Business School receives four or five fraudulent inquiries a week during their recruiting season. One-third of all investigations conducted by the National Credential Verification Service in Minneapolis turn out to be falsifications. Even John Molloy, the respected image consultant, recommends that you lie on your resume if you have an unexplained time gap (Molloy, 1982: 74). Given such behaviors, employers don't want to repeat their mistakes if they can help it.

How do you best handle employers' objections? You must first recognize their biases and stereotypes and then *raise* their expectations. You do this by stressing your strengths and avoiding your weaknesses. You must be impeccably honest in doing so. Take, for example, the question *"Why are you leaving your present job?"* If you have been fired and you are depressed, you might blurt out all your problems:

> *"I had a great job, but my crazy boss began cutting back on personnel because of the recent slump in company sales. I got the axe along with three others."*

You might be admired for your frankness, but this answer is too negative; it reveals the wrong motivations for seeking a job with the employer. Essentially you are saying you are unemployed and bitter because you were fired. A better answer would be:

> *"My position was abolished because of budget reductions. However, I see this as a new opportunity for me to use the skills I acquired during the past 10 years to improve profits. Having worked regularly with people in your field, I'm now anxious to use my experience to contribute to a growing company."*

Another question reflecting objections to hiring you is:

> *"Your background bothers me somewhat. You've been with that company for 10 years. You know, it's different working in this company. Why should I hire you?"*

A positive way to respond is:

"I understand your hesitation in hiring someone with my background. And I agree with you. Many people don't function well in a different occupational setting. But I don't believe I have that problem. I'm used to working with people. I work until the job gets done, which often means long hours and on weekends. I'm very concerned with achieving results. But most important, I've done a great deal of thinking about my goals. I've researched your company, products, and markets. From what I have learned, this is exactly what I want to do. I know I will do a good job as I have always done in the past."

Whatever you do, avoid confessing your weaknesses, negatives, or lack of experience. You must direct the interview toward your strengths and positives.

AFFECTING THE FINAL OUTCOME

The purpose of the initial job interview is to get a second job interview. The purpose of the second interview is to get a third and fourth interview or a job offer, depending on when the employer decides to stop interviewing. Once you have been interviewed, you should follow through to get nearer to the job offer.

One of the best follow-up methods is the thank-you letter. An example is included in Appendix C. After talking to the employer over the telephone or in a face-to-face interview, send a thank-you letter. This letter should be typed on good quality bond paper; typed letters look more professional than handwritten notes or letters. In this letter express your gratitude for the opportunity to interview. Re-state your interest in the position and highlight any particularly noteworthy points made in your conversation or anything you wish to further clarify. Close the letter by mentioning that you will call in a few days to inquire about the employer's decision. When you do this, the employer should remember you as a thoughtful person.

If you call and the employer has not yet made a decision, follow through with another phone call in a few days. Send any additional information to the employer which may enhance your application. You might also want to ask one of your references to call the employer to further recommend you for the position. However, don't engage in overkill by making a pest of yourself. You want to tactfully communicate two things to the employer at this point: (1) you are interested in the job, and (2) you will do a good job.

PROJECTING A POSITIVE IMAGE

Most employers quickly assess candidates' strengths and weaknesses based upon resumes and letters. If your resume and letter pass the 30 second test, you move on to the telephone interview. If you sufficiently impress the employer in the 10 minute telephone interview, you move on to the formal interview stage. At each step you must manage your image in order to make a positive impression. How you communicate your "qualifications" is as important as your job-related qualifications.

The interview is an image management activity. For example, interviewers normally make a positive or negative decision based upon the impression you make during the first 4 or 5 minutes of the interview. The major factors influencing this decision are your nonverbal cues communicated at the very beginning of the interview. Therefore, what you wear, how you look, the way you shake hands, how you smell, whether you are interested and enthusiastic, where and how you sit, and how you initiate the small talk are extremely important to the interviewer's decision; these factors may be more important than your answers to the interview questions. Your answers will tend to either reinforce or alter the initial impression.

While it may seem unfair for employers to make such snap decisions, it happens nonetheless. Accept it as an important reality of the job search, and learn to adjust your behavior to your best advantage. Remember those first five minutes may be the most critical moments in your job search and for your future job or career. Put your best foot forward with the most positive image you can generate.

Chapter Twelve
HANDLING THE MONEY QUESTION

Salary is one of the most important yet least understood considerations in the job search. Many individuals do well in handling all interview questions except the salary question. They are either too shy to talk about money, or they believe you must take what you are offered because salary is predetermined by employers. As a result, these applicants may be paid much less than they are worth. Over the years they will lose thousands of dollars by having failed to properly negotiate their salaries.

You are not likely to be offered a job before going through more than one interview. Once you receive a job offer, it is not final until your salary is determined.

In this chapter we demonstrate how you can establish and communicate your dollar value to the employers. This is important to know for reasons relating to finances and future advancement. If you negotiate from strength, you should do well in your negotiations. How you negotiate your salary also will affect your future relationship with the employer. As Haldane Associates note from years of salary negotiating experience,

Employees who have handled themselves well during their salary negotiations were treated with greater respect and were given more opportunities to advance within the organization. . . make sure that you are negotiating from

a position of competence and compatibility, not need or greed (Germann and Arnold: 158-159).

Above all, you must overcome the cultural constraint that *"nice people don't talk about salaries."* At the same time, don't go to the extremes of appearing greedy or having unrealistic expectations of your value.

CHANGING EXPECTATIONS

While most salary negotiation experts advise you how to get the highest salary possible by using various psychological techniques on employers, be prepared to face a new game in the 1980's. The rules for negotiating salaries appear to be changing, and the change may be in the employers' favor.

Employees today appear to have less flexibility in negotiating salaries than they did in the 1960's and 1970's. A new game is called "give backs." Employers, facing high personnel costs and declining productivity and profits, are asking employees to share some of the costs and losses; thus, employees may need to lessen annual salary demands or even take salary cuts. From the perspective of employees, give backs may save their jobs. This unprecedented salary movement has already begun in the auto, steel, and airline industries.

The no-growth and give back salary trends will influence individuals' bargaining positions with employers in the 1980's. Except in certain high-tech areas, employers know the job market is tight. They may think employees can be easily replaced by others who can do just as good a job but for less money. Since employers will be more likely to set a salary figure for a position and stick with it, salary negotiating techniques may have limited effect.

Therefore, be careful about playing hard-to-get with salary. You may instead need to lower your salary expectations. This is particularly true if you are leaving a $25,000 a year job. Don't expect to immediately move into a $30,000 or $35,000 job unless you are well connected. You may have to take another $25,000 job. And your salary may not increase much over the next few years because of the give back thinking of many employers as well as the increasing trend of tying salary increments to productivity measures. For instance, if you receive a $30,000 a year salary, will you generate $100,000 a year income for the organization in order to justify this salary? Since many people do not think in such cost-benefit terms about their salaries, they may not be prepared to talk realistically about their value to employers. Ask yourself this question: *"How much income will I generate for the employer?"* If you can answer this question with a specific figure, you have a good basis for justifying your salary expectations.

These salary trends stress that it is even *more* important to know how to negotiate salary in turbulent times. You don't want to be exploited by employers who feel they now have the upper hand because of high unemployment. Remember, they still have a problem — to find someone who will do a good job and cost them less in the long-run. Help solve the employer's problem by clearly communicating your value in dollars.

RAISING THE QUESTION

The salary question may arise at any time. For instance, if you respond to a classified ad, the employer may want you to state your *"expected salary."* An application form may request the same information. An unexpected telephone call from the employer, which turns into a formal telephone interview, may include the question of salary. And during the first interview the employer may want to know your salary expectations.

Employers like to raise the salary question early in order to screen candidates. Why, for example, should an employer waste his time inviting you to one, two, or three interviews without first knowing whether you are within his salary range? Hence, many employers will raise the salary question early in the game.

Your perspective will differ. You want to deal with the salary question toward the end — after you learn more about the job and the expectations of the employer. You don't want to prematurely eliminate yourself from consideration nor do you want to lock yourself into a low salary figure from which you can't negotiate. You want to negotiate as high a salary as possible. Finding yourself in this dilemma, what do you do?

ALTERNATIVE STRATEGIES

You face several choices. If you are asked to state a salary figure on an application form or in response to a classified ad, you take the chance of eliminating yourself from consideration by not stating a figure or by stating too high a figure. On the other hand, you limit your negotiating room by stating too low a figure. We recommend three different responses; you should choose the one that best responds to your situation. First, you will encounter some ads which appear to describe a $25,000 to $30,000 a year job, but you later find the employer is expecting to hire God for $12,000! If you don't state a salary figure, you may waste your time applying for such a position. If you state what you feel both you and the job are worth as a salary range of $25,000 to $30,000, you will eliminate yourself from consideration — which you probably want to do anyway.

Second, if the employer requests your *"expected salary,"* you can state *"open"* or *"negotiable."* Within certain limits, salary normally is negotiable. By doing this you are telling the employer that you have no specific salary expectations; you are willing to work with the employer on arriving at a mutually agreeable figure. If you do this, you won't prematurely eliminate yourself from consideration. However, you may waste time applying for that terrific $12,000 job.

Third, you can state a salary range. If the employer asks for your *"salary history,"* calculate a range by taking your present base salary and adding any additional income. For example, your *"salary history"* can be a salary range of $25,000 — your base — to $30,000 — your additional income. This gives the employer a true picture of your present income as well as provides flexibility for negotiating from various points within your range. On the other hand, if the employer asks for your *"expected salary,"* you can state any range you wish regardless of your present income. In this case, calculate what you figure both you and the job are worth. State your expectations as a range rather than a specific dollar figure. A salary range figure will give both you and the employer room for maximum negotiating flexibility, such as a $30,000 to $35,000 range.

These rules are equally valid for written applications, cover letters in response to ads, telephone interviews, and face-to-face interviews. If the employer wants you to state a figure during your first interview, state a range or stall for more information. If he persists, give him a range based upon your knowledge of salary and your feelings of worth. Assuming you are making a positive impression on the employer, the further into the interview the salary question is raised, the better your bargaining position in the end. Throughout the interviews you should be communicating to the employer that you are worth more than his initial salary expectation.

DETERMINING YOUR VALUE

You can determine salary figures by doing research on salary ranges for particular positions. Do this prior to the interview by talking to people who know about such salaries — other organizations, a salary and wage administrator, a similar employee — or by consulting publications which list salary ranges for comparable positions. You also must assess what you are worth, what you will be willing to take, and what you hope to be making in the next five years.

Don't forget that employers also do their homework on salary. Many will know your previous salary or have a close approximation based upon their knowledge of similar positions. Expect them to calculate their salary expectation for you by adding 10 to 15 percent to your last salary.

While you should not expect employers to exploit you, neither should you trust them to offer you what you are worth. *This is a business transaction — your talent for their money.* You want to persuade the employer to settle for the highest possible figure, because you are worth it, and because your new salary will influence future salary increments as well as salaries for future jobs.

NEGOTIATING A FINAL FIGURE

A standard salary negotiation scenario is for the employer to raise the question: *"What are your salary requirements?"* You can turn this question around by asking the employer: *"What is the normal range in your company for a position such as this as well as for someone with my qualifications?"* The employer will either get you to state a figure first by restating in another manner his original question or he will tell you his range. Expect a frank answer most of the time. If he indicates a range, the rest of the salary negotiation is relatively simple.

Having done your homework and thus knowing what you are worth and what the employer is willing to pay, you are now ready to do some friendly but earnest haggling over price. If, for example, the employer says his range for the position is $22,000 to $25,000, you might respond by saying *"$25,000 is within my range."* If his range is much more or less than you anticipated, avoid being emotional or overly positive or negative. Disregard his bottom figure and concentrate on working from the middle to the top of his range or by putting his top figure into the middle of your range. For example, if he says *"$22,000 to $25,000,"* you should move the top of his range into your negotiable $25,000 to $30,000 range. This gives common ground to negotiate from or to stall for later negotiations and other considerations. However, if the employer states a single figure, such as $23,000, multiply his figure by 25 percent and add this percentage to his original figure. His $23,000 figure now becomes your $29,000 expectation. Respond by saying *"I'm thinking more in terms of $29,000."* A $6,000 difference gives you room for negotiations. If you state $35,000 you may appear unreasonable, unless you can support this figure based upon your salary research on comparable positions.

Employers may praise their "benefits" package prior to talking about a cash figure. Be wary of such benefits. Most are standard and thus come with the job regardless of the salary figure you negotiate. Some benefits may be negotiable: travel time, office size and location, and equipment — the normal perks. Therefore, concentrate first on the salary figure and don't worry about the benefits — you'll get them anyway.

The salary negotiation techniques are not designed for you to outwit or take advantage of employers. Be prepared to justify in concrete terms why you think you are worth what you are asking. What exactly are you going to give the employer in exchange for your higher salary figure? The whole job search process should have prepared you for answering this question in detail.

RENEGOTIATING SALARY

Your initial salary figure will influence your future salaries. Indeed, many employers will figure your worth by finding out what you made in your last job and then adding 10 to 15 percent to that figure to arrive at your new salary. If you were a $12,000 a year teacher, you will be starting from a depressed salary level with such a calculation; you may have difficulty justifying a major salary increase in the eyes of most employers. In this case, you need to focus on your worth to the employer — not on what he can get you for. On the other hand, if you are coming from a $35,000 a year job to a $25,000 one, you must convince the employer that you will be happy with a salary decrease — if, indeed, you *can* live with it. Many employers will not expect you to remain long if you take such a salary cut; thus they may be reluctant to offer you a position.

To make sure your future salary will reflect your value, try to reach an agreement to renegotiate your salary at a later date, perhaps in another six to eight months. Use this technique especially when you feel the final salary offer is less than what you are worth, but you want to accept the job. Employers often will agree to this provision since they have nothing to lose and much to gain if indeed you are as productive as you tell them.

However, be prepared to renegotiate in both directions — up and down. If the employer does not want to give you the salary figure you want, you can create good will by proposing to negotiate the higher salary figure down after six months, if your performance does not meet the employer's expectations. On the other hand, you may accept his lower figure with the provision that the two of you will negotiate your salary up after six months, if you exceed the employer's expectations. It is preferable to start out high and negotiate down rather than start low and negotiate up.

Renegotiation provisions stress one very important point: you want to be paid on the basis of your performance. You demonstrate your professionalism; self-confidence, and competence by negotiating in this manner. More important, you insure that the question of your monetary value will not be closed in the future. Thus, as you negotiate the present, you also negotiate your future with this as well as other employers.

TIMING, LEVERAGING, AND CLOSING

Once you receive a job offer you should close the offer in a professional manner. Employers normally offer a job contingent upon reaching a salary agreement. An offer should never be accepted until you reach agreement on salary. At this point, timing is especially important in what you do.

Don't jump at an offer, because you may communicate a negative — you are needy. Take time to consider your options. Remember, you are committing your time and effort in exchange for money and status. Is this the job you really want? Take some time to think about the offer before giving the employer a definite answer. Giving you this time is common professional courtesy. But don't appear to be playing a game of hard-to-get and thus create ill will with your new employer.

While considering the offer, ask yourself several of the same questions you asked at the beginning of your job search:

- *What do I want to be doing five years from now?*
- *How will this job affect my personal life?*
- *Do I want to travel?*
- *Do I know enough about the employer and the future of the organization?*
- *Are there other jobs I'm considering which would better meet my goals?*

Accepting a job is serious business. You could be locked into it for a long time.

If you receive one job offer while considering another, you will be able to compare relative advantages and disadvantages. You also will have some external leverage for negotiating salary and benefits. While you should not play games, let the employer know you have alternative job offers. This communicates that you are in demand, others also know your value, and the employer's price is not the only one in town. Use this leverage to negotiate your salary, benefits, and job responsibilities.

If you get a job offer but you are considering other employers, let the others know you have a job offer. Telephone them to inquire about your status as well as inform them of the job offer. Sometimes this will prompt employers to make a hiring decision on you sooner than anticipated. In addition, you will be informing them that you are in demand; they should seriously consider you before you get away!

You could play a bluffing game by telling employers you have alternative job offers even though you don't. Some candidates do this and get away with it. We don't recommend this approach. Not only is it dishonest, it will work to your disadvantage if the employer learns that you were lying. But more important, you should be selling yourself on the basis of your strengths rather than your cleverness and greed. If you can't sell yourself by being honest, don't expect to get along well on the job. When you compromise your integrity, you compromise your value to others and yourself.

The whole point of our job search methods is to clearly communicate to employers that you are competent and worthy of being paid top dollar. If you follow our advice, you should do very well with employers in interviews and in negotiating your salary as well as working on the job.

PART III

Creating
New
Opportunities

Chapter Thirteen
KEEPING, REVITALIZING, AND ADVANCING CAREERS

Your present career decisions will affect your future career development. Throughout this book we have tried to prepare you for making critical career choices tomorrow, next month, next year, and 10 years from now. While we cannot predict your future, we do know you will gain greater control over it when you use our re-careering methods.

After negotiating the job offer, shaking hands, and feeling great for having succeeded in getting a job that is right for you, what's next? How do you get started on the right foot and continue to advance your career? In this chapter we suggest how to best handle your job and career future after congratulating yourself on a job search well done.

CONTINUING THE PROCESS

If you managed your interviews and salary negotiations in a professional manner, your new employer should view you in a positive light. At this point you should do two things. First, send your new employer a thank-you letter. Mention your appreciation for the professional manner in which you were hired and how pleased you are to be joining the organization. Reaffirm your goals and your commitment to producing results. This letter should be well received.

181

Employers seldom receive such thoughtful letters. and your re-affirmation helps ease the employer's fears of hiring an untested quantity.

The second thing you should do immediately is send thank-you letters to those individuals who assisted you with your job search, especially those with whom you conducted informational and re-ferral interviews. Tell them of your new position, thank them for their assistance, and offer your assistance in the future. Not only is this a nice and thoughtful thing to do, it also is a wise thing to do for your future.

Always remember your networks. You work with people who can help you in many ways. Take good care of your networks by sending a thank-you letter and keeping in contact. In another few years you may be looking for another position. In addition, people in your network may later want to hire you away from your present employer. Since they know what you can do and they like you, they may want to keep you informed of new opportunities. While you will be developing new contacts and expanding your network in your new job, your former contacts should be remembered for future reference. An occasional letter, New Years card, or telephone call are thoughtful things to do.

CONDUCTING ANNUAL CAREER CHECK-UPS

Much has been written on how to handle yourself on the job (Irish; Djeddah; Germann and Arnold; Korda; Kennedy; DuBrin). It is not necessary to repeat this advice except for a few important points which are often neglected. After three months on the job, you should know who's who, who has clout, whom to avoid, and how to get things done in spite of people and their positions. In other words, you will become inducted into the *informal structure* of the organization. You should become aware of this structure and utilize it to your advantage.

While it goes without saying that you should *perform* in your job, you need more than just performance. You should understand the informal organization, develop new networks, and use them to advance your career. This means conducting an *internal career advancement campaign* as well as *an annual career check-up.*

Don't expect to advance by sitting around and doing your job, however good you may be. Power is distributed in organizations, and politics often is ubiquitous. Learn the power structure as well as how to *play positive politics.* DeBrin and Kennedy outline in their books how you can play these games to your advantage.

After a while many organizations appear to be similar in terms of the quality and quantity of politics. Intensely interpersonal jobs are the most political. Indeed, people are normally fired because of politics — not incompetence. What do you do, for example, if you find yourself working for a tyrannical or incompetent boss or a jealous co-worker is out to get you?

We recommend an annual career check-up. Take out your resume and review it. Ask yourself several questions:

- Am I achieving my objective?
- Has my objective changed?
- Is this job meeting my expectations?
- Am I doing what I'm good at and enjoy doing?
- Is this job worth keeping?
- How can I best achieve career satisfaction either on this job or in another job or career?
- What other opportunities elsewhere might be better than this job?

Individuals should increasingly ask these questions in the turbulent job market of today and tomorrow.

Perhaps changing jobs is not the best alternative for you. If you encounter difficulties with your job, you should first assess the nature of the problem. Perhaps the problem can be resolved by working with your present employer. Many employers prefer this approach. They are learning that increased job satisfaction translates into less job stress and absenteeism as well as more profits for the company. Progressive employers want happy workers because they are productive employees. They view job-keeping and job-revitalization as excellent investments in their futures.

JOB-KEEPING AND POLITICS

Assuming you enjoy your work, how can you best ensure keeping your job as well as advancing your career in the future? What job-keeping skills should you possess for the career environments of today and tomorrow? How can you best avoid becoming a victim of cutbacks, politics, and terminations?

As we noted in Chapter Eleven, most employers want their employees to perform according to certain expectations. Hecklinger and Curtin (159) further expand these expectations into thirteen basic job-keeping skills:

1. *Ability to do the job well:* develop your know-how and competence.

2. *Initiative:* work on your own without constant direction.

3. *Dependability:* being there when you are needed.

4. *Reliability:* getting the job done.

5. *Efficiency:* being accurate and capable.

6. *Loyalty:* being faithful.

7. *Maturity:* handling problems well.

8. *Cheerfulness:* being pleasant to be with.

9. *Helpfulness:* willing to pitch in and help out.

10. *Unselfishness:* helping in a bind even though it is not your responsibility.

11. *Perseverance:* carrying on with a tedious project.

12. *Responsibility:* taking care of your duties.

13. *Creativity:* looking for new ways to solve your employer's problems.

While using these skills will not ensure job security, they will most likely enhance your security and potential for advancement.

A fourteenth job-keeping skill — managing your political environment — is one employers don't like to talk about. It may well be more important than all of the other job-keeping skills. Many people who get fired are victims of political assassinations rather than failures at meeting the bosses' job performance expectations or scoring well on the annual performance appraisal.

You must become politically sophisticated at the game of office politics in order to survive in many jobs. For example, what might happen if the boss you have a good working relationship with today is replaced tomorrow by someone you don't know or by someone you know but don't like? By no fault of your own — except having been associated with a particular mentor or patron — you may become a victim of the new bosses' house cleaning. Accordingly, you get a two-hour notice to clean out your desk and get out. Such political assassinations are common occurances in the publishing, advertising, and other businesses. In fact, one recent study found that 25 percent of fired executives had a new boss within the 18 month period preceding their firing (Bauerlein: 95)!

Eight survival tactics can be used to minimize the uncertainty and instability surrounding many jobs today. These survival tactics include:

1. *Learn to read danger signals:* Beware of cutbacks, layoffs, and firings before they occur. Adjust to the danger signals by securing your job or by looking for another job.

2. *Document your achievements:* Keep a record of what you accomplish — problems you solve, contributions you make to improving productivity and profits.

3. *Expand your horizons:* Become more aware of other areas in the company and acquire skills for performing other jobs. The more skills you have, the more valuable you will be to the company.

4. *Prepare for your next job:* Seek more training through:

   - apprenticeships
   - community colleges
   - weekend colleges
   - private, trade, or technical schools
   - home study through correspondence courses
   - industrial training programs
   - government training programs — U.S. Department of Agriculture
   - military training
   - cooperative education
   - four-year college or university

5. *Promote yourself:* Talk about your accomplishments with co-workers and supervisors — but don't boast. Keep them informed of what you are doing; let them know you are available for promotion.

6. *Attach yourself to a mentor or sponsor:* Find someone

in a position of influence and power whom you ad-
mire and who can help you acquire more responsibilities, skills, and advancement. Avoid currying favor.

7. *Continue informational interviewing:* Educate yourself
   as well as expand your interpersonal network of job
   contacts by regularly talking to people about their
   jobs and careers.

8. *Use your motivated skills:* Success tends to attract
   more success. Regularly use the skills you enjoy in
   different everyday settings (Hecklinger and Curtin:
   160-161).

The most important thing you can do now is to assess your
present situation as well as identify what you want to do in the
future with your career and life. You may conclude that your job
is not worth keeping!

We are not proposing disloyalty to employers or regular job-
hopping. Instead, we believe in the great American principle of
"self-interest rightly understood"; your first obligation is to yourself. No one owes you a job, and neither should you feel you owe
someone your career. As Irish notes, jobs and careers should not be
life sentences. Periodically assess your career health and feel free to
make changes when necessary:

> *Most professional people today have four or five
> "careers." They feel free to leave a job they do well to
> take another. And there is no great secret why they do
> it; these men and women know what they want. . . Young-
> er people stay at jobs they don't like because (a) they
> panic at the thought of finding another job; (b) they
> don't know what to do next; (c) they feel "loyal" to the
> person or organization they work for; (d) they don't feel
> free to do what they want* (Irish: 218).

Since many jobs change for the worse, it may not be worth
staying around for headaches and ulcers. If the organization does not
meet your career expectations, use the same job search methods that
got you into the organization. Be prepared to bail out for greener
pastures by doing your job research and conducting informational
and referral interviews. While the grass may not always be greener on
the other side, many times it is; you will know by conducting another job search.

REVITALIZING JOBS

Assuming you know how to survive on your job, what do you do if you feel burnout, experience high levels of job stress, or are just plain bored with your job? A job change, rather than resolving these problems, may lead to a repetition of the same patterns elsewhere. Techniques for changing the nature of your present job may prove to be your best option.

Most people will sometime experience what Kennedy (1980b: 13) calls the "Killer Bs": blockage, boredom, and burnout. What can individuals do to make their jobs less stressful, more interesting, and more rewarding? One answer is found in job-revitalization alternatives.

Job-revitalization involves changing work patterns. It requires you to take risks. Again, you need to evaluate your present situation, outline your career and life goals, and develop and implement a plan of action. A job-revitalization campaign may include meeting with your superior to develop an on-the-job career development plan. Set goals with your boss and discuss with him or her how you can best meet these goals on the job. If your boss is not familiar with career development and job-revitalization alternatives, suggest some of these options:

- Rotating jobs
- Redesigning your job
- Promotions
- Enlarging your job duties and responsibilities
- Sabbatical or leave of absence
- Part-time work
- Flextime scheduling
- Job sharing
- Retraining or educational programs
- Internship

Perhaps your supervisor can think of other options which would be acceptable to company policy as well as productive for both you and the organization.

More and more companies are recognizing the value of introducing career development programs and encouraging job-revitalization among their employees. They are learning it is more cost-effective to retain good employees by offering them new job options for career growth within the organization than to see them go. Such programs and policies are congruent with the productivity and profit goals of organizations. They are good management practices. As organizations in the 1980's and 1990's become more cost-conscious and employee-oriented, they will place greater emphasis on career development and job-revitalization.

BEING PREPARED

You should prepare yourself for the job realities associated with a society that is undergoing major structural changes. This means avoiding organizations, careers, and jobs that are declining as well as knowing what you do well and enjoy doing. It also means regularly acquiring the necessary training and retraining to function in a turbulent job market. And it means using your career planning skills to effectively re-career in the decades ahead. If you do this, you should be well prepared to turn turbulence into new opportunities and to acquire new jobs which will become exciting and satisfying challenges.

Chapter Fourteen
LOCATING THE RIGHT COMMUNITY

Where will you be working and living next year, five years, or 10 years from today? While you target specific employers, you also conduct your job search in particular communities. For some people, moving to another community is desirable for career and life style purposes. For others, unemployment would be preferred to leaving their community. Your job search must weigh the relative costs and benefits of relocating to a new community where job opportunities for someone with your skills may be plentiful.

In recent years economic development has shifted toward the Sunbelt and Rocky Mountain regions. Millions of job seekers will be migrating to these regions in the 1980's and 1990's in response to growing energy and high-tech industries. Perhaps you, too, will look toward these regions as you change jobs and careers in the future.

In this chapter we examine how to conduct both a long-distance and a community-based job search campaign. We include the case of Washington, D.C. to illustrate the importance of conducting community research as well as for identifying alternative job networks. Nowhere do we recommend that you pull up stakes and take to the road in search of new opportunities. Many people are doing so in the 1980's as they head for the reputed promised lands of Houston and Denver. Many of them remain unemployed, totally unprepared for the realities of today's job market. Don't ever take to the road until

189

you have done your homework by researching communities, organizations, and individuals as well as created the necessary bridges for contacting employers in a new community. More important, be sure you have the appropriate work-content skills for finding employment in specific communities.

TARGETING COMMUNITIES

Many people are attached to their communities. Friends, relatives, churches, schools, businesses, and neighborhoods provide an important sense of identity which is difficult to leave for a community of strangers. Military and diplomatic personnel — the truly transient groups in society — may be the only ones accustomed to moving to new communities every few years.

The increased mobility of society is partly due to the nature of the job market. Many people voluntarily move to where job opportunities are most plentiful. Thus, Dallas becomes a boom city with hundreds of additional cars entering the already congested freeways each week. The corporate structure of large businesses, with branches geographically spread throughout the national production and distribution system, requires the movement of key personnel from one location to another — much like military and diplomatic personnel.

When you begin your job search, you face two alternative community approaches. You can concentrate on a particular job, regardless of its geographic setting, or you can focus on one or two communities. The first approach, which we term *follow-the-job*, is widely used by migrant farm workers, cowboys, bank robbers, mercenaries, oil riggers, construction workers, newspaper reporters, college and university professors, and city managers. These people move to where the jobs are in their particular profession; some end up in boring communities.

If you follow-the-job, you will need to link into a geographically mobile communication system for identifying job opportunities. This often means subscribing to specialized trade publications, maintaining contacts with fellow professionals in other communities, or creatively advertising yourself to prospective employers through newspaper ads or letter blitzes.

On the other hand, you may want to *target a community*. This may mean remaining in your present community or locating a community you find especially attractive because of job opportunities, climate, recreation, and social and cultural environments. Regardless of rumored job opportunities, many people, for instance, would not move to the "Deep South" where the weather is hot and humid and the people display different linguistic, social, and cultural styles. The same is true for Southerners who are not particularly interested in moving to cold, dreary, and crime ridden northern cities. At the same time, Portland, Santa Fe, Colorado Springs, Salt Lake City, Dallas, Tulsa, St. Petersburg, Seattle, San Francisco, and San Diego are reputed to be the new promised land for many people. Oases of prosperity, these cities are on the community target list of many job seekers who find Buffalo, Detroit, Cleveland, Pittsburgh, Newark, Erie, Gary, and East St. Louis to be at the end of the earth!

We recommend using this second approach of targeting specific communities. The follow-the-job approach is okay if you are young, adventuresome, or desperate; you find yourself in a particularly geographically mobile profession; or your career takes precedence over all other aspects of your life. By targeting a community, your job search will be more manageable. Furthermore, moving to another community can be a liberating experience which will have a positive effect on both your professional and personal lives.

GROWING CITIES

Frictional unemployment — the geographic separation of underemployed and unemployed individuals from high labor demand regions and communities — should present new options for you. Numerous job opportunities may be available if you are willing to relocate.

Growing regions and communities are relatively predictable for the 1980's. During the 1970's, several metropolitan areas in Table 9 had the highest growth rates and many of the patterns continue into the 1980's. For example, large cities in the Northeast and North Central regions — especially in the states of Massachusetts, New York, Connecticut, Michigan, Ohio, Pennsylvania, and New Jersey — are in trouble because of declining industrial and population bases. Economic and demographic growth will continue in the South, Southwest, and the eight-state Rocky Mountain region. A few pockets of prosperity will be found in the Northeast, such as Boston's Route 128 which accounts for 20 percent of new factory employment in all of New England (Sivy: 76).

The growth communities for the 1980's are concentrated in the Sunbelt and Rocky Mountain regions. Seven of the 10 fastest growing states are in the Rocky Mountain region: Montana, Idaho, Wyoming, Colorado, New Mexico, Arizona, and Utah. The other

TABLE 9

GROWTH OF 40 LARGEST METROPOLITAN AREAS, 1970 - 1980

Rank	Metropolitan Area	Population, 1980	Percentage Increase (+) and Decrease (-)
1	New York	9,081,000	-9
2	Los Angeles-Long Beach	7,445,000	+6
3	Chicago	7,058,000	+1
4	Philadelphia	4,701,000	-3
5	Detroit	4,340,000	-2
6	San Francisco-Oakland	3,226,000	+4
7	Washington	3,042,000	+4½
8	Dallas-Fort Worth	2,964,000	+24
9	Houston	2,891,000	+45
10	Boston	2,760,000	-5
11	Nassau-Suffolk, N.Y.	2,604,000	+2
12	St. Louis	2,341,000	-3
13	Pittsburgh	2,260,000	-6
14	Baltimore	2,165,000	+4½
15	Minneapolis-St. Paul	2,109,000	+7
16	Atlanta	2,010,000	+26
17	Newark	1,964,000	-5
18	Anaheim-Santa Ana-Garden Grove, Calif.	1,926,000	+35½
19	Cleveland	1,895,000	-8
20	San Diego	1,857,000	+37
21	Denver-Boulder	1,614,000	+30
22	Seattle-Everett	1,601,000	+12
23	Miami	1,573,000	+24
24	Tampa-St. Petersburg	1,550,000	+42
25	Riverside-San Bernardino-Ontario, Calif.	1,538,000	+35
26	Phoenix	1,512,000	+56
27	Milwaukee	1,393,000	-1
28	Cincinnati	1,390,000	+0.2
29	Kansas City	1,322,000	+4
30	San Jose	1,290,000	+21
31	Buffalo	1,241,000	-8
32	Portland, Ore.	1,234,000	+22½
33	New Orleans	1,184,000	+13
34	Indianapolis	1,162,000	+4½
35	Columbus, Ohio	1,088,000	+7
36	San Antonio	1,070,000	+20½
37	Sacramento	1,011,000	+26
38	Fort Lauderdale-Hollywood	999,000	+61
39	Rochester	970,000	+1
40	Salt Lake City-Ogden	935,000	+33

SOURCE: *The Miami-Herald,* March 8, 1981: 32A, from *American Demographics.*

three are the Sunbelt states of Florida, Texas, and Oklahoma. Florida should be the fastest growing state in the 1980's. Several communities in the energy rich Rocky Mountain states will become boom towns. Communities with large concentrations of high-tech industries will continue to expand both demographically and economically.

Most of the 20 fastest growing cities are found in the Sunbelt. They are: Las Vegas, Austin, Tucson, Fort Lauderdale, Houston, Phoenix, Oxnard, Calif., Tacoma, San Diego, Anaheim, Tulsa, Salt Lake City, Portland, Ore., Seattle, Oklahoma City, Tampa, West Palm Beach, Baton Rouge, Riverside, Calif., and Orlando. The 10 most rapidly expanding metropolitan areas in terms of employment opportunities are Fort Lauderdale, Tucson, Houston, Phoenix, Austin, San Diego, Oxnard, Calif., Columbia, S.C., Tampa, and Albuquerque.

The new high-tech industries can be expected to locate in the Southern and Western regions where there are low taxes, few labor unions, and good educational institutions. While California's Silicon Valley south of San Francisco initially attracted high-tech industries and Boston remains a traditional center, new locational patterns are now emerging. The cities successfully recruiting new high-tech industries are Phoenix, Albuquerque, Austin, Colorado Springs, San Antonio, Dallas, and Raleigh-Durham, North Carolina.

Even though the overall growth predictions point to the Sunbelt and Rocky Mountain regions, these statistics should not deter you from considering older cities in the Northeast and North Central regions. After all, 2 million new jobs are created nationwide each year. New jobs will continue to develop in cities such as Chicago, Philadelphia, and New York; these are still the best places to pursue careers in the growing fields of banking, publishing, and advertising. Several communities in the Midwest will become major high-tech centers because of their well developed infrastructure of energy, transportation, and education supportive of new high-tech industries *(USA Today*, Nov. 23, 1982: 1B).

Community growth and decline trends should be considered as part of your job and career options. If you live in Detroit or Youngstown, Ohio, seriously consider relocating to a growth community. Depressed communities simply do not generate enough jobs for their populations. Many communities with populations of 100,000 to 500,000 offer a variety of employment and life style opportunities. For a systematic and critical examination of various characteristics of communities in the United States, see Thomas F. Bowman, George H. Giuliani, and M. Ronald Minge, *Finding Your Best Place to Live in America* and Richard Boyer and David Savageau, *Places Rated Almanac.* The latter book, for example, identifies

Atlanta as the overall best place to live and work.

SELECTING A LOCATION

You and your family must take into consideration several factors and questions when deciding on which communities to target
your job search:

- Where would you like to live for the next 5, 10, or 20 years?
- What is the relative cost of living?
- How attractive are the educational, social, and cultural
  activities?
- What are the economic and psychological costs of making
  a move?
- What job and career opportunities are there for us?
- How can we best conduct a job search in another com-
  munity?

Many people answer these questions by remaining in their
community or by targeting growth communities in the Rocky
Mountain and Sunbelt regions. The exodus from the declining
industrial cities in the Northeast and North Central regions to the
Sunbelt began in the 1960's, expanded in the 1970's, and continues
into the 1980's with the inclusion of the energy rich Rocky Mountain states. Many cities in these regions have abundant job opportunities for *skilled* workers. Targeting a job search in the metropolitan areas of Dallas-Fort Worth, Miami, San Diego, Los Angeles,
Phoenix, Fort Lauderdale-Hollywood, Denver-Boulder, Salt Lake
City-Ogden, and Atlanta may be a wise move. While these areas will
experience numerous problems over the next decade, their problems
are ones of growth — traffic congestion, pollution, city planning,
crime, and housing shortages — not ones of decline. We believe it
is better to experience the problems of growth than of decline. In a
situation of decline, your livelihood becomes threatened. In a situation of growth, your major problem may be fighting the traffic congestion in order to get to a job which offers a promising career.

If you find yourself in a declining community, seriously consider moving. Individuals in the financially troubled states and cities
of the Northeast and North Central regions — especially in Michigan
and Ohio — need to consider alternative communities. As population and industry decline in these areas, so too do job opportunities.
Many highly educated and talented individuals are staying around
too long in these communities driving taxi cabs, changing tires, and

flipping hamburgers in anticipation that prosperity is just around the corner.

New frontiers for renewed job and career prosperity exist in this country if you are willing to pack your bags and move. But remember, most of these frontiers require highly skilled individuals in the high-tech industries of today and tomorrow. If you don't possess the necessary skills, consider getting retraining before making a move. Unfortunately, many people making the moves today do not have the necessary skills.

Ironically, when people most need to make a move — during a period of hard times — they are least willing or able to make the move. Such a move appears riskier than during a period of prosperity. Furthermore, many people are locked into financial obligations, such as a mortgaged house which doesn't sell in a depressed housing market. If you find yourself locked in financially, you may want to consider taking an immediate financial loss in anticipation of renewed prosperity in a community which is actually experiencing prosperity. You may recoup your immediate losses within a year or two. However, you will have to pass through a transition period which can be difficult if you don't approach it in a positive, up-beat manner. Remember, there is life after Buffalo, Detroit, Cleveland, Newark, Pittsburgh, Boston, Philadelphia, New York, Chicago, and East St. Louis. Consider going to where there is a more promising future.

RESEARCHING FROM LONG DISTANCE

How do you target your job search on a particular community? If you decide to remain in your present community, your job search is relatively manageable on a day-to-day basis. If you target another community, you will need to conduct a long-distance job search which requires more extensive use of the mail and telephone as well as carefully planned visits to the community. In fact, you will probably use your job search time more efficiently with a long-distance campaign. In both situations, you need to conduct community research prior to initiating the major communication steps in your job search.

Most of your community research can be conducted in the library, as we noted in Chapter Nine. You need names, addresses, and phone numbers of potential employers. Use the major directories, as we identified in Chapter Nine, such as the *Dun & Bradstreet's Middle Market Directory* and *Who's Who in Commerce and Industry*. The Yellow Pages of telephone directories are especially useful sources for identifying the business and commercial structure of communities as well as for addresses and telephone numbers. The larger the community, the more specialized the businesses. For example, New York City has several businesses specializing in manufacturing manhole covers! At the same time, write to chambers of commerce for information on the community and to companies for annual reports and other organizational literature. Homequity will send you a package of information on housing and schools in any community by merely calling their toll free number: 800/243-1033. Homequity also publishes a useful booklet, *Personal Relocation Planning Guide*, to help you plan your move, including your career. To order a copy, send $15 to Homequity, 249 Danbury Rd., Wilton, CT 06897. United Van Lines (800/325-3870) will send you free information on 7,000 cities, and many banks will supply you with relocation information.

Part of your research may involve narrowing the number of communities you are considering. If you identify 10 alternative communities, outline a criteria from which to evaluate the 10 communities. Select three communities and initiate a writing campaign for more information. If at all possible, schedule a trip to the cities to get an on-site view or feel for the relative environments. Further try to narrow your choices by rank-ordering your preferences among the three communities. Concentrate most of your job search efforts on your top priority community.

Your next step is to develop a strategy for penetrating both the advertised and hidden job markets. If you are conducting a job search outside your present community, the advertised job market will be most accessible to you. However, you need to link into the hidden job market, where most of the good jobs are located. Doing this from a distance is somewhat difficult, but nonetheless it can be managed.

WORKING THE LOCAL JOB MARKET

The advertised job market is always the easiest to access. Buy a newspaper and read the classified ads. Contact an employment firm and they will eagerly assist you. Walk into a personnel office and they may permit you to fill out an application form.

If you target a community from a distance, begin by subscribing to a local newspaper; the Sunday edition will most likely meet your needs. This newspaper also will give you other important information on the community — housing market, economics, politics, society, culture, and recreation. Survey the help wanted ads to get a feel for the structure of the advertised job market. Remember, these are not necessarily indicative of the true employment picture in a community — only 20 to 30 percent of the job market. Write letters to various companies and ask about job opportunities. You also may want to contact one or more professional employment agencies or job search firms — preferably fee-paid ones — for job leads. But remember our warnings in Chapter Five about possible frauds and hucksters!

Efforts to penetrate the advertised job market should be geared toward uncovering the hidden job market. For example, in reading the Sunday newspaper, watch for names of important people in the society or "Living" section. You may want to contact some of these people by using an approach letter as we outlined in Chapters Nine and Ten. The employment agencies may give some indication of the general employment situation in the community — both advertised and hidden job markets. The chamber of commerce might be able to give you some job leads other than those advertised.

If you are conducting a long-distance job search, we recommend following the same procedures we outlined in Chapter Ten on networking. *Preparation* is the key to success. Do your research on potential employers, write letters, make phone calls, and schedule informational and referral interviews. The major difference in this situation is your timing. In addition, you need to give more information to your contacts. In your letter mention that you are planning to move to their community and would appreciate their advice on job opportunities for someone with your qualifications. Mention that you plan to visit the community on such and such a date and would appreciate an opportunity to discuss your job search plan at that time. In this case, enclose your resume with the letter and request a reply to your inquiry. Most people will reply and schedule an interview or refer you to someone else.

You should set aside one or two weeks — preferably more — for literally blitzing the community with informational and referral interviews. This requires doing a considerable amount of advance work. For example, use your present community to practice informational and referral interviewing. Contact employers in your area who are in similar positions. Many of them may give you referrals to friends and colleagues in your targeted community.

With limited contacts, you will probably need to use the "cold turkey" approach more frequently from a distance. You should make most of your key contacts at least four weeks before you plan to visit your targeted community. Within two weeks of your visit, you should have scheduled most of your interviews.

Try to schedule at least three interviews each day. You will probably do more because each interview will yield one or two referrals to others. Five interviews a day are manageable if you don't need to spend a lot of time traveling from one site to another. Plan to keep the sites near each other for each day. Within a two week period, you should be able to conduct 40 to 60 interviews. Use the weekends to research the community further. Contact a realtor who will be happy to show you around the community and inform you of different housing alternatives, neighborhoods, schools, taxes, public services, shopping centers, and a wealth of other community information. You should reserve the last two days for following up on referrals. Scheduling interviews with referrals will have to be made by telephone because of the time factor.

After concluding your one to two week visit, follow up your interviews with thank-you letters, telephone calls, and letters indicating continuing interest and requesting referrals.

If you receive an invitation to a formal job interview, be sure to clarify the financial question of who pays for the interview. Normally if the employer has requested the interview, the company pays the expense to and from the interview. However, if you have invited yourself to an interview by stating that you will be "in town," expect to pay your own expenses. If you are unclear about who initiated the interview, simply ask the employer *"How should we handle the travel expenses?"* You'll get a clarification, and there will be no misunderstanding.

IDENTIFYING OPPORTUNITY STRUCTURES

Each community has its own social, economic, political, and job market structure. Your job is to understand and utilize the particular job market structure in your targeted community. Therefore, we outline the case of Washington, D.C. for illustrative purposes. The principles for identifying and utilizing the institutional and personal networks will remain the same for most communities even though the individuals, groups, and institutions differ.

The degree of structure differs for every community. However, one thing is relatively predictable: most communities lack a coherent structure for processing job information efficiently and effectively. As Norton Long noted years ago, communities are structured like an *"ecology of games"* (Long: 252). The Yellow Pages of your telephone book best outline the different games. Banks, mortgage companies, advertising firms, car dealers, schools, churches, small businesses, industries, hospitals, law firms, governments, and civic and voluntary groups do their "own thing" and have their own internal power structure. No one dominates except in small communities which also are company towns — paper mills, mining companies, universities, or steel mills. At the same time, the groups overlap with each other because of economic, political, and social needs. The bank, for example, needs to loan money to the businesses and churches. The businesses, in turn, need the educational institutions. And the educational institutions need the businesses to absorb their graduates. Therefore, individuals tend to cooperate in seeing that people playing the other games also succeed. Members of school boards, medical boards, and the boardrooms of banks and corporations will overlap and give the appearance of a "power structure" even though power is structured in the loosest sense of the term. The game players compete and cooperate with each other as well as co-op one another. The structures they create are your *opportunity structures* for penetrating the hidden job market.

Take the example of Washington, D.C. The opportunity structures for your job search networks are relatively well defined in this city. While government is the major institution, other institutions are well defined in relation to the government. Within government, both the political and administrative institutions function as alternative opportunity structures in the Washington networks: congressional staffs, congressional committees, congressional subcommittees, congressional bureaucracy, executive staff, departments, independent executive agencies, and independent regulatory agencies. Outside, but clinging to, government are a variety of other groups and networks: interest groups, the media, professional associations, contractors, consultants, law firms, banks, and universities and colleges. As illustrated in Figure 6, these groups are linked to one another for survival and advancement. Charles Peters calls them "survival networks" which function in the "make believe world" of Washington, D.C. (Peters: 5,17). Ripley and Franklin (5-7) identify the key-political dynamics as "subgovernments," the interaction of interest groups, agencies, and congressional committees.

For years Washington insiders have learned how to use these "survival networks" and "subgovernments" to advance their careers. A frequent career pattern would be to work in an agency for three to four years. During that time, you would make important contacts on Capitol Hill with congressional staffs and committees as well as with private consultants, contractors, and interest groups. Your specialized knowledge on the inner workings of government is marketable to these other people. Therefore, you make a relatively easy job change from a federal agency to a congressional committee or to an interest group. After a few years here, you move to another group in the network. Perhaps you work on your law degree at the

FIGURE 6

WASHINGTON NETWORKS

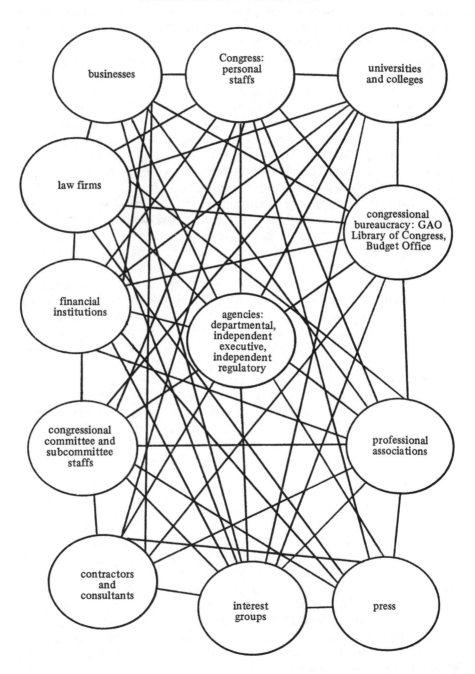

same time so that in another five years you can go into the truly growth industry in the city — law firms. The key to making these moves is the personal contact — whom you know. Particular attention is given to keeping a current SF-171 or resume, just in case an opportunity happens to come by for you. Congressional staff members usually last no more than two years; they set their sights on consulting and contracting firms, agencies, or interest groups for their next job move.

Whatever community you decide to focus your job search on, expect it to have its particular networks. Do as much research as possible to identify the structure of the networks as well as the key people who can provide access to various elements in the opportunity structures. Washington is not unique in this respect; it is just better known, and Washingtonians talk about it more because of their frequent job moves.

Chapter Fifteen
STARTING YOUR OWN BUSINESS

The 1980's and 1990's will be a period of entrepreneurship perhaps unprecedented in our history. Thousands of small businesses will develop in response to opportunities in the evolving high-tech society. As in the past, over 85 percent of all new jobs created in the private sector will be provided by these small business enterprises. Therefore, you should include small businesses as you target your job search. Doing this will require a great deal of research on your part since most small businesses do not have high visibility among job seekers.

One other alternative is to start your own business. Millions of people do. In the coming decades, millions more will opt for employing themselves as work becomes more decentralized, electronic cottages evolve, and advancement opportunities become increasingly limited in companies.

In fact, 500,000 to 600,000 new businesses are started each year. However, there also are grim business statistics for the would-be entrepreneur: 400,000 to 500,000 businesses fail each year; 50 percent fail after 38 months; and nearly 90 percent fail within 10 years. Unfortunately, the odds are against anyone becoming a successful entrepreneur.

Nonetheless, owning your business is a viable re-careering alternative to working for someone else if you approach business intelligently. Many people fail because they lack the necessary ingredients for success. In this chapter we outline the basics for getting started in owning your business and employing yourself.

TAKING RISKS

You will find few challenges riskier than starting your own business. At the same time, you may experience your greatest professional satisfaction in running your own business.

Starting a business means taking risks. First, you will probably go into debt and realize little income during the first two years you are building your business even though you had grandiose visions of becoming an overnight success. You may be under-capitalized or have overhead costs higher than anticipated. It takes time to develop a regular clientele. What profits you do realize are normally plowed back into the business in order to expand operations and guarantee larger future profits. Second, business is often a trial and error process in which it is difficult to predict or ensure outcomes. Due to unforeseen circumstances beyond your control, you may fail even though you work hard and make intelligent investment decisions. Third, you could go bankrupt and lose more than just your investments of time and money.

At the same time, owning your own business can be tremendously satisfying. It is the ultimate of independence. Being your own boss means you are in control, and no one can fire you. You are rewarded in direct proportion to your productivity. Your salary is not limited by a boss, nor are your accomplishments credited to others. Unless you decide otherwise, you are not wedded to an 8 to 5 work routine or a two week vacation. Depending on how successful your business becomes, you may be able to retire young and pursue other interests. You can turn what you truly enjoy doing, such as hobbies, into a profitable, rewarding, and fun career.

But such self-indulgence and gratification has costs. You will probably need at least $10,000 to $20,000 of start-up capital, or perhaps as much as $250,000, depending on the type of business you enter. No one will be sending you a paycheck every two weeks so you can regularly pay your bills. You may work 12 and 14 hour days, seven days a week, and have no vacation during the first few years. And you may become heavily indebted, experience frequent cash flow problems, and eventually have creditors descend on you.

Why, then, start your own business? If you talk to people who have worked for others and then started their own businesses, they will tell you similar stories. They got tired of drawing a salary while making someone else rich. They got bored with their work and hated the 8 to 5 routine. Some were victims of organizational politics. On a more positive note, many started businesses because they had a great idea they wanted to pursue or they wanted the challenge of independently accomplishing their own goals.

If you decide to go into business for yourself, be sure you know what you want to do and be willing to take risks. Don't expect to get rich overnight or sit back and watch your business grow on its own. Be prepared to work long and hard hours, experience disappointments, and challenge yourself to the limits.

There are few things that are more self-actualizing than running your own business. But you must have realistic expectations as well as a motivational pattern which is conducive to taking risks and being an entrepreneur. In Chapter Six you identified your motivational patterns and skills. If you like security, predictability, and stability, you probably are a candidate for a position where someone hands you a paycheck each week. If you read and believe in a get-rich-quick book which tries to minimize your risks and uncertainty, you probably have been ripped-off by an enterprising author who is getting rich writing books for naive people!

STRENGTHS OF SUCCESSFUL ENTREPRENEURS

How can you become self-employed and successful at the same time? No one has a magical success formula for the budding entrepreneur — only advice. We do know why many businesses fail, and we can identify some basic characteristics for success. Poor management and decision-making lie at the heart of business failures. Many people go into business without doing sufficient market research; they under-capitalize; they select a poor location; they incur extremely high and debilitating overhead costs; they lack commitment; they are unwilling to sacrifice; they can't read or count; and they lack interpersonal and salesmanship skills.

On the positive side, studies continue to identify something called "drive," or the need to achieve, as a key characteristic of successful entrepreneurs. Young achievers and successful entrepreneurs possess similar characteristics: *"A high energy level, restless, a willingness to work hard and take risks, a desire to escape from insecurity"* (Kellogg: 38). The findings of most studies of successful people, however, are inconclusive:

> *One study says originality, popularity, sociability, judgement, aggressiveness, the desire to excel, humor, cooperativeness, liveliness and athletic ability are factors essential*

> *to successful leadership. Another gives the following recipe for success: intelligence, verbalization skills, integrity, self-acceptance, leadership (defined as the ability to get things done), adaptability, such "accidental" factors as good health and good luck. Good grief — one study of successful men and women merely lists talent, luck and persistence. Another heralds hard work, period. . . Elsewhere, a more traditional study tells us that successful people set goals, make lists and believe in the American Dream. Another tells us that the ability to seize and recognize opportunity is important, that creativity, self-reliance, and willingness to accept responsibility are keys to success. The sea of speculation, however ill or well-defined, is vast* (Kellogg: 32-33).

Successful business people combine certain motivations, skills, and circumstances. Contrary to popular myths, you don't need to be rich or have an MBA or business experience to get started. If you are willing to gamble and are a self-starter, self-confident, an organizer, and you like people, you should consider this entrepreneurial alternative in your re-careering decisions. These characteristics along with drive, thinking ability, human relations, communication, technical knowledge, hard work, persistence, and good luck are essential ingredients for business success. If these are among your strengths, as identified in Chapter Six, you may be a good candidate for starting your own business with a high probability of success. If you feel you have recurring weaknesses in certain areas, you may want to consider finding a business partner who has particular complementary strengths for running a business.

KNOWING YOURSELF

There are many different ways to get started in business. You can buy into a franchise which can initially cost you $10,000 to $500,000. Advertisements in the *Wall Street Journal* are a good source for hundreds of franchise opportunities from flipping hamburgers to selling animals. You can join someone else's business on a full-time or part-time basis as a partner or employee in order to get some direct business experience. You can try your hand at a direct-sales business such as Amway, Shaklee, or Avon. Hundreds of new direct-sales businesses modeled after Amway's business methods are now marketing every conceivable product — soap, typewriters, canoes, motor oil, and milk. You can buy someone else's business or you can start your own business from scratch.

Your decision on how to get started in business should be based upon the data you generated on your skills and goals in Chapters Six and Seven. Do not go into business for negative reasons — fired, hate your job, can't find work. Unfortunately, many people go into business with totally unrealistic expectations as well as with little understanding of their own goals, skills, and motivations. For example, while it is nice to work around pretty clothes, owning a dress shop requires handling inventory and personnel as well as paying the rent and doing bookkeeping. Getting all those pretty dresses on the rack is hard work! Many people also don't understand how the business world works. It requires a great deal of interpersonal skill to develop and expand personal networks of creditors, clients, colleagues, and competitors.

Therefore, you should do two things before you decide to go into business. First, thoroughly explore your goals and motivations. The questions are familiar: What do you want to do? What do you do well? What do you enjoy doing? Second, research different types of businesses in order to better understand advantages, disadvantages, procedures, processes, and possible problems. Talk to business persons about their work. Try to learn as much as possible about the reality before you invest your time and money. Surprisingly, few people do this. Many people leap into a business that they think will be great and then later learn it was neither right for them nor did they have realistic expectations of what was involved. This is precisely why so many businesses fail each year.

You should approach business opportunities the same way you approach the job market: do research, develop networks, and conduct informational and referral interviews. Most business people, including your competition, will be happy to share their experiences with you and assist you with advice and referrals. Such research is absolutely invaluable. If you fail to do it initially, you will pay later on by making the same mistakes that millions of others have made in starting their own businesses in isolation of others. *Don't be high on motivation but low on knowledge and skills.*

EMERGING OPPORTUNITIES

Most business people will tell you similar stories of the reality of running your own business. Do your market research, spend long hours, plan, and be persistent. They also will give you advice on what businesses to avoid and what business routines you should be prepared to handle. For example, you probably should avoid these manufacturing and retailing businesses that had the highest failure rates during the beginning of the 1980's:

- *Manufacturing:* furniture, textiles, leather and shoes, apparel, electronic machinery

- *Retailing:* infant and children's wear, furniture and furnishings, sporting goods, women's ready-to-wear, photo equipment and supplies, menswear

Many service and high-tech businesses will be growing in the 1980's. Given the changing demographic structure — fewer young people, more elderly, the two career family — numerous opportunities are arising for small personal service businesses to meet the needs of the elderly and career-oriented families. Businesses relating to restaurants, home maintenance, health care, housing for the elderly, and mortuaries and cemeteries should expand considerably during the next two decades.

Opportunities are also available for inventive business persons who can make more productive use of busy peoples' time — fast foods, financial planning, and mail-order shopping. The information and high-tech revolutions are taking place at the same time two career families do not have time to waste standing in lines at banks, grocery stores, and department stores. Mail-order or computer assisted home and office-based shopping should increase dramatically during the next decade.

A service business is particularly attractive. It is easy to establish, it requires a small initial investment, and the bookkeeping is relatively simple. You can operate from your home and thus keep your overhead down (Kamoroff: 13-14).

Knowing these trends and opportunities is important, but they should not be the only determining factors in choosing a business. You should start with *yourself* by again trying to identify a business that is fit for you rather than one you think you might fit into.

PREPARING THE BASICS

You also need to consider several other factors before starting a business. Since a business requires financing, locating, planning, developing customer relationships, and meeting legal requirements, be prepared to address these questions:

1. *How can I best finance the business?* Take out a personal or business loan with a bank? Go into a partnership in order to share the risks and costs? Get a loan from the Small Business Administration?

2. *How much financing do I need?* Many businesses fail because they are under-capitalized. Others fail because of over spending on rent, furnishings, inventory, personnel, and advertising.

3. *Where is my market?* Just in this community, region, or nationwide? Mail-order businesses enable you to expand your market nationwide whereas retail and service businesses tend to be confined to particular neighborhoods or communities.

4. *Who are my suppliers?* How many must I work with? What about credit arrangements?

5. *Where is the best location for the business?* Do you need to open a store or operate out of your home? If you need a store or office, is it conveniently located for your clientele? "Location is everything" still best summaries the success of many businesses, especially McDonalds.

6. *How should the business be legally structured?* Sole proprietorship, partnership, or corporation? Each has advantages and disadvantages. A corporation has the best tax advantages.

7. *What licenses and permits do I need?* These consist of local business licenses and permits, federal employee identification numbers, state sales tax number, state occupational licenses, federal licenses and permits, and special state and local regulations which vary from state to state and from community to community. What type of insurance do I need? Fire, theft, liability, workers' compensation, and auto?

8. *How many employees do I need?* Can I do without personnel initially until the business expands? Should I use part-time and temporary help?

9. *What business name should I use?* If incorporated, is anyone else using the name? If a trade name, is it registered?

10. *What accounting system should I use?* Cash or accrual? Can I handle the books or do I need a part-time or full-time accountant?

11. *Do I need a lawyer?* What type of lawyer? What legal work can I do myself?

12. *How do I develop a business plan?* A business plan should include a definition of the business, a marketing strategy, operational policies, purchasing plans, financial statements, and capital raising plans.

GETTING USEFUL ADVICE

Choosing the right business for you is only one of many important decisions. For a good overview of these and other considerations in establishing a small business, see Bernard Kamoroff's *Small-Time Operator.* This book will provide you with all the basic information you need for starting your own business, including ledger sheets for setting up your books. Albert Lowry's *How to Become Financially Successful By Owning Your Own Business* also outlines the basics for both small-time and big-time operators. Several other books provide similar how-to advice for the neophyte entrepreneur:

David H. Bangs, Jr., and William R. Osgood, *Business Planning Guide* (Portsmouth, NH: Upstart Publishing Co., Inc. 1979).

Deaver Brown, *The Entrepreneur's Guide* (New York: Macmillan Publishing Co., 1980)

Norman Feingold and Leonard Perlman, *Making It On Your Own* (Washington, D.C.: Acropolis Books, Ltd., 1981)

Stuart Feldstein, *Home, Inc.* (New York: Grosset and Dunlap, 1981)

David E. Gumpert and Jeffry A. Timmons, *The Insider's Guide To Small Business Resources* (New York: Doubleday, 1981)

Alice Hower and Alfred Howard, *Turn Your Kitchen Into a Goldmine* (New York: Harper and Row, 1981)

The federal government will help you with several publications available through the Small Business Administration: 1441 L Street, NW, Washington, D.C. 20416, Tel. 202/753-6365. SBA field offices are located in 85 cities. The Consumer Information Center publishes a free booklet entitled *More Than a Dream: Running Your Own Business*: Dept. 616J, Pueblo, Colorado 81009. The Internal Revenue Service sponsors several one-day tax workshops for small businesses. Your local chamber of commerce also can give you useful information.

If you are interested in how to get started in a particular small business, write for information from the American Entrepreneurs Association, 2311 Pontius Avenue, Los Angeles, California 90064 or use their toll-free numbers: 800/421-2300 or 800/421-2345. This organization has a comprehensive set of services for starting small businesses. These include a business catalogue (free upon request), the magazine *Entrepreneur*, and "Start-A-Business Stores" located in Houston, Los Angeles, and Chicago. To help you get off in the right direction, this organization publishes 198 small business start-up and operation manuals which include businesses such as energy stores, video stores, seminars, pet cemeteries, health clubs, pizza parlors, travel agencies, dating services, rent-a-hot tub, furniture stripping, pipe shop, discos, and maid services. For a six-month free subscription to *Money Making Opportunities* magazine, which lists hundreds of mail-order ads, write to Money Making Opportunities, 11071 Ventura Blvd., Studio City, California 91604. These publications will give you a sampling of alternative businesses you can establish. However, beware of hucksters who may advertise in business magazines. Many want your money for "proven success" and "get-rich-quick" formulas that don't even work for the advertisers!

CONTINUING SUCCESS

The factors for operating a successful business are similar to the 20 principles we outlined in Chapter Five for conducting a successful job search. Once your initial start-up problems are solved, you must organize, plan, implement, and manage in relation to your goals. Many people lack these abilities. Some people are good at initially starting a business, but they are unable to follow through in managing day-to-day routines once the business is established. And others have the ability to start, manage, and expand businesses successfully.

Be careful about business success. Many business people become obsessed with their work, put in 12 and 14 hour days continuously, and spend seven day weeks to make the business successful. Unwilling to delegate, they try to do too much and thus become a prisoner to the business. The proverbial *"tail wagging the dog"* is a common phenomenon in small businesses. For some people, this life style feeds their ego and makes them happy. For others, the 8 to 5 routine of working for someone else on salary may look very attractive. Therefore, you must be prepared to change your life style when embarking on your own business. Your major limitation will be yourself. So think it over carefully, do your research, and plan, organize, implement, and manage for success. The thrill of independence and success is hard to beat!

Chapter Sixteen

FINDING PUBLIC EMPLOYMENT

Most of our discussion of re-careering has centered on finding employment in the private sector. While over 85 percent of all jobs are found there, another 15 million jobs are located in the public sector. With one of seven individuals working for federal, state, or local governments, public jobs constitute a major employment sector.

People seek public employment for two major reasons: security and good pay. Indeed, the average postal worker makes $25,000 a year and his or her job security is virtually guaranteed. Others avoid government employment altogether, because it is viewed as dull and low paying work. Whatever your view, keep in mind that someday you may work for a government agency. Public employment is a re-careering option.

If you are interested in finding public employment, this chapter will provide you with the basics for getting started with a job search aimed at government. We include this special chapter because the case of finding public employment differs somewhat from finding employment in the private sector. If you are particularly interested in working for the federal government in Washington, D.C., you should integrate this chapter with our earlier discussion of opportunity structures in Washington, D.C. (Chapter Fourteen).

MISPERCEPTIONS AND UNDERSTANDING

Government bureaucracies are often viewed in a pejorative sense — red tape, inefficiency, dull work, limited career opportunities, poor pay, and incompetence. Some government agencies and officials indeed fit these images, but many do not. Such stereotypes are equally valid for many private companies. Except during periods of recession, when businesses are forced to cutback and improve efficiency, the public and private sectors probably have comparable degrees of deadwood and inefficiency. One major difference is that it is often easier to get rid of employees in the private sector than in government.

Another side of government consists of numerous exciting, challenging, and well-paid career opportunities. Government is the largest single employer in the United States. It consists of 79,913 units of government, and approximately 500,000 politicians and 15 million employees. Altogether it encompasses 1 national, 50 state, 18,862 municipal, 3,042 county, 16,823 township, 15,174 school district, and 25,962 special district governmental units. While 15 million individuals are employed directly by government, millions of other individuals depend on government contracts and other forms of public largess for their livelihoods. In total, government may be responsible for employing more than 30 million individuals in both the public and private sectors.

The growth in government employment has been steady since World War II. Federal employment has remained relatively stable, increasing and decreasing by only a small percentage during the past three decades. Today, the federal bureaucracy consists of approximately 2.85 million civil servants.

The major growth in government has taken place at the state and local levels. Since 1950, state bureaucracies increased by 209 percent to 3.3 million employees; local bureaucracies grew by 174 percent to 8.8 million workers (Meier: 30-32).

Recent cutbacks in government programs instituted by the Reagan Administration have begun to be felt at all levels of government. Public employment in 1982 was down by 316,000 from 1981. Most of the personnel cuts were being made in financially troubled state and local government units. However, expansion of public employment continues in certain areas. We can expect, for example, the growth states of Florida, Texas, New Mexico, Utah, Arizona, Colorado, and Nevada to experience increases in state and local government employment into the 1990's. The federal government, despite terminating nearly 60,000 workers, continues to hire 1,200 new employees each day. Similar to the private sector, new job opportunities in government are most plentiful for individuals who have marketable skills. In government, computer, engineering, and health service skills remain in demand.

Although growth in public employment has subsided somewhat, employment opportunities still abound in government. After all, thousands of vacancies arise each week due to resignations, retirements, and deaths. Governments perform highly complex and technical functions which require a diversified and increasingly technical workforce. They hire in almost every occupational category found in the private sector. For example, the federal government employs undertakers, movie directors, and realtors along with typists, accountants, policy analysts, and managers. The federal government's workforce includes approximately 150,000 engineers and architects, 120,000 accountants and budget specialists, 120,000 doctors and health specialists, 87,000 scientists, 45,000 social scientists, and 2,700 veterinarians. The Department of Defense (960,116), Postal Service (660,014), and the Veterans Administration (228,285) together account for nearly two-thirds of the federal government workforce. The largest single category of employees at the state and local levels is educators. They constitute approximately 52 percent of this workforce, or nearly 5.5 million state and local employees; 2.6 million are teachers. Their numbers, however, are decreasing due to cutbacks in education (Krannich and Banis, 1981).

Outside of education, government salaries and benefits at the lower and middle levels — $10,000 to $30,000 — are comparable to, if not better than, those in the private sector. Take, for example, an assistant professor, with a Ph.D. and five years of teaching and administrative experience, who makes $20,000 a year teaching in a college or university. With the federal government, this individual would qualify for GS-13 or GS-14 positions which have a starting salary of $34,950 to $41,277. The federal government also provides several generous benefits which are not considered standard elsewhere. These include liberal vacation, sick leave, group life insurance, injury compensation, health benefits, and an excellent retirement program. At the local level, many city managers earn $50,000 to $70,000 a year. While few people get rich in the public service, few are ever poor.

Many people avoid government employment because they neither understand the opportunities available nor the formal and informal procedures for acquiring such employment. Some people believe you must have political "pull" to get a government job; others believe you must complete lengthy application forms, take examinations, and wait to be classified and chosen from someone's list of qualified candidates. Neither view is completely true. Political patronage is still well and alive in America, especially at the urban and county levels. Affirmative action and equal employment opportunity principles are acknowledged by most government units, but practices differ. Highly formalized merit personnel systems involving complicated examinations and selection procedures also operate, but to a greater degree at the federal level than at the state and local levels.

Acquiring government employment requires understanding both the formal and informal personnel systems. Thus, your job search campaign aimed at government bureaucracies should begin with this simple fact of life: learn *both* the formal and informal systems and how to integrate them into a successful campaign. While many of the job search skills you learned in previous chapters are directly applicable to government, you must also possess additional knowledge and skills in order to get a government job.

MANAGING FRAGMENTATION

Most of the personnel and budgetary growth in the public sector during the past 30 years has occurred at the state and local levels. As the functions of state and local governments have expanded, so too has the demand for greater professional expertise. In many cases, state and local government salaries exceed those of the federal government. And despite a nationwide trend toward restricting the growth of government — especially in the aftermath of California's Proposition 13 tax revolt and federal government cutbacks to states and localities — numerous employment opportunities with government remain. Demands for increased efficiency and effectiveness usually result in greater opportunities for highly trained experts and correspondingly fewer opportunities for unskilled workers. Furthermore, opportunities always are available in different fields given normal personnel turnovers due to job-hopping, resignations, retirements, and deaths.

Identifying employment opportunities and using job search strategies at the state and local levels are complicated by the numerous and diverse units of government. Each governmental unit has a formal personnel structure as well as informal recruitment practices. Separate personnel systems usually exist for blue-collar and white-collar employees. And, despite attempts to centralize and formalize hiring procedures, thousands of governmental units have characteristics similar to organizations in the private sector — they are decentralized, fragmented, and chaotic. Hiring practices follow these same characteristics. Therefore, *different governmental units cannot be approached with a universal job search strategy.* Instead, you must research the structure, functions, problems, and practices of each governmental unit that interests you and then adjust your strategies accordingly.

PLAYING THE JOB LISTING GAME

Information on job vacancies in government is fragmented. The federal government has particular information sources which we will review later. This discussion centers on job vacancy information for state and local governments.

Several job listing sources are available on thousands of units of government. Major professional associations, such as the American Society for Public Administration and the International City Management Association, include listings of job vacancies in their newsletters. Each professional group within government — planners, housing officials, financial officials, personnel administrators, public works officials, parks and recreation officials — has its own professional association which also publishes newsletters and journals with job listing sections. Periodicals such as *Advance Job Listings, Affirmative Action Register, American City and County, County News, The Job Finder, Law Enforcement News, Public Works, Tax Administrators News,* and *Western City* also feature classified ad sections of job vacancies for public employees. Two job banks — Mountain States' Job Bank and the New England Administrative-Professional-Technical Job Bank — provide job listing and resume services for employers and candidates seeking positions in local governments of selected states.

For a comprehensive listing of 260 job vacancy listing sources for public employees, see Daniel Lauber's *The Compleat Guide to Jobs in Planning and Public Administration.* This guide contains names, addresses, and telephone numbers of the major professional associations, periodicals, and job banks relevant to federal, state, and local governments. It can be obtained by sending $10 to Impact Publications, 10655 Big Oak Circle, Manassas, VA 22111, Tel. 703/ 361-7300.

However, use such job listings with caution. Your best strategy will be to identify where you want to work and then target particular government units or agencies by using both the formal (responding to job listings) and informal channels (conducting informational interviews). If you still want to go the traditional route of locating job vacancies and seeing if you can fit into the job specifications, then by all means play this job listing game.

ENTERING STATE AND LOCAL GOVERNMENTS

Even though each governmental unit differs, we can identify some general principles for orienting you to state and local government employment. First, political patronage still operates in many units of government. This is especially true in the case of rural county governments. Most state governments have reformed their personnel systems along the lines of the federal government's merit personnel system. Many city and urban county governments — especially large ones — also have developed highly formalized recruitment and promotion procedures; political patronage and political connections play a much diminished role today. While contacting an elected state representative, mayor, city councilman, ward leader, or county commissioner for employment assistance may be an acceptable procedure in some communities, it may be considered "tacky" to do so in other communities. Political "pull" can, in some settings, have adverse effects on your job search. It is best to research the *hiring cultures* of different units of government in order to learn what are both the proper and most effective methods for conducting a job search.

Regardless of the prevalence of political patronage or a highly formalized merit recruitment system, you still need to use the informal strategies we outlined in previous chapters. Begin with the knowledge that personnel departments have little clout in the actual hiring process, even though they have a great deal of public visibility. After all, personnel departments usually are one of the weakest units in government. Furthermore, officials sometimes move deadwood into the personnel department where they will be "safe" from damaging the rest of government operations. At the same time, political exiles or officials on the "outs" with others may get "promoted" to the personnel department.

Nonetheless, you should make contact with the personnel department. But do not expect it to be useful in your job search. Personnel departments usually hire people at the lowest levels, such as sanitation workers, janitors, and typists. This department does testing, processes the necessary papers involved in placing a new employee on the payroll, and engages in some training. Personnel departments also play an important gatekeeping function: they dissuade potential applicants from pursuing government employment with elaborate and complicated formal application and hiring procedures. Don't be discouraged with all the paper and personnel jargon thrown at you.

However, you may encounter exceptions to this general rule. Some governmental units have made special efforts to revitalize their personnel department by centralizing hiring decisions under an influential personnel director. Indeed, we know of a few city managers who have attempted to increase their overall control of the city bureaucracy by doing precisely this. Our best advice to you is: know thy organization!

The general pattern among state and local governments is to decentralize hiring decisions to the departmental or operating unit level. At this level personnel needs are first assessed, information on positions is most readily available, interviews are conducted, and hiring decisions are finalized. Knowing this pattern, your job search should consist of four major activities:

1. Research the governmental unit — beginning with an organizational chart — to identify who has the power to hire. The person with the power to hire will usually be the head of the unit.

2. Conduct an informational interview with the head of the department, operating unit, or whomever you have identified as having this power.

3. Leave a resume, ask to be referred, ask to be remembered, and send a nice thank-you letter.

4. Continue this same procedure throughout this and other governmental units.

By conducting these activities, you should be the first one to know if and when a vacancy occurs or a new position is created. If you are interviewed, receive a job offer, and accept, the final step will be to contact the personnel department. At that stage you will initiate the necessary paper work to be placed on the payroll.

If you encounter a governmental unit with a highly formalized "merit" personnel system, position vacancies will most likely be widely advertised in adherence with affirmative action and equal opportunity principles. In this case you will compete with other applicants who are mainly using the formal system. You will have an advantage over them, because you have made important informal contacts. Sometimes a position actually will be "wired" for you. This means the position description essentially is written around your specific qualifications so that you are, by definition, the best qualified applicant. "Wiring" positions is a notorious practice at all levels in government as well as in the private sector. Your informal prospecting, networking, and informational interviewing strategies may make it possible for you to be a subject of such "wiring." Again, you must know your particular organization, and this requires doing sufficient research on your targeted audience.

PURSUING FEDERAL EMPLOYMENT

Finding employment with the federal government is another matter. The federal government is a good example of unnecessary complexity. Its highly formalized personnel system and procedures are at best intimidating, and at worst misleading. Many people simply avoid the federal government because of the numerous barriers facing the prospective applicant. Moreover, politicians like to blame their inadequacies on the bureaucracy. New administrations usually intimidate agencies with talk about "freezes" and "cut backs." The bureaucracy grinds on nonetheless.

Lack of knowledge about how the feds operate — rather than objective analyses of opportunities — is perhaps the single most important disincentive for individuals seeking federal government employment. Waelde identifies four reasons for application failure:

- Lack of knowledge of the job openings.
- Failure to fully understand the application procedures.
- Submission of application forms that do not effectively represent the applicant.
- Lack of perseverance to follow through on the original objective — to get a better job — until success is achieved.

The federal government is shrouded in myths and mystery. Although federal employment has not expanded since World War II, an annual turnover of approximately 17 percent results in nearly 500,000 vacancies in the total civilian workforce of 2.85 million. Normally, the federal government hires approximately 1,500 employess each day. Large turnovers take place among highly skilled employees and managerial-level officials who leave government for more attractive opportunities in the private sector. Many senior level professionals in the GS-13 to GS-15 levels, as well as in the newly created super-grade Senior Executive Service (formerly GS-16 to GS-18 positions), face a serious problem of premature career closure. For example, Congress has placed a ceiling on federal government earnings at the $57,500 GS-15 level in Table 10. Consequently, if you become a GS-15 at age 40, your government career suddenly ends in terms of future monetary rewards. Because of this situation, many high-level government employees leave government service

TABLE 10
GENERAL SCHEDULE PAY SCALE FOR FEDERAL GOVERNMENT EMPLOYEES, 1983

RATES WITHIN GRADE AND WAITING PERIOD FOR NEXT INCREASE

GS	52 WEEKS			104 WEEKS			156 WEEKS			
	1	2	3	4	5	6	7	8	9	10
1	8676	8965	9254	9542	9831	10000	10286	10572	10585	10857
2	9756	9987	10310	10585	10703	11018	11333	11648	11963	12278
3	10645	11000	11355	11710	12065	12420	12775	13130	13485	13840
4	11949	12347	12745	13143	13541	13939	14337	14735	15133	15531
5	13369	13815	14261	14707	15153	15599	16045	16491	16937	17383
6	14901	15398	15895	16392	16889	17386	17883	18380	18877	19374
7	16559	17111	17663	18215	18767	19319	19871	20423	20975	21527
8	18339	18950	19561	20172	20783	21394	22005	22616	23227	23838
9	20256	20931	21606	22281	22956	23631	24306	24981	25656	26331
10	22307	23051	23795	24539	25283	26027	26771	27515	28259	29003
11	24508	25325	26142	26959	27776	28593	29410	30227	31044	31861
12	29374	30353	31332	32311	33290	34269	35248	36227	37206	38185
13	34930	36094	37258	38422	39586	40750	41914	43078	44242	45406
14	41277	42653	44029	45405	46781	48157	49533	50909	52285	53661
15	48553	50171	51789	53407	55025	56643	58261*	59879*	61497*	63114*
16	56945	58843*	60741*	62639*	64537*	66435*	68333*	70231*	72129*	
17	66708*	68932*	71156*	73380*	75604*					
18	78184*									

* Under section 5308 of title 5, United States Code, and Public Law 97-276, the rate actually paid as of the effective date of this schedule is $57,500.

each year for greener pastures with interest groups, consulting firms, contractors, and other businesses. Others may move into the Senior Executive Service in the hope of securing yearly bonuses as well as encountering renewed prosperity.

Another important aspect of federal employment is the fact that 85 percent of the federal government is located outside Washington, D.C. Working for the feds, therefore, does not necessarily mean working in Washington. The federal government is divided into 10 administrative regions with headquarters in Philadelphia, Boston, Chicago, Atlanta, St. Louis, Dallas, Denver, San Francisco, Seattle, and New York. Cities with 25,000 federal employees or more are listed in Table 11.

─────────── **TABLE 11** ───────────

CITIES WITH 25,000
FEDERAL EMPLOYEES OR MORE

Washington, DC/MD/VA	341,566
New York/NJ	93,376
Philadelphia/NJ	69,054
Chicago	68,726
Los Angeles - Long Beach	66,699
San Francisco	65,236
Baltimore	52,791
Boston	37,604
Norfolk - Virginia Beach	35,215
San Antonio	34,262
St. Louis, MO/IL	34,126
Atlanta	31,150
Detroit	29,560
Dallas - Ft. Worth	28,453
Oklahoma City	26,827

SOURCE: *Federal Personnel Guide*, 1981 edition, (Washington, DC.: Federal Personnel Publications, 1981), 116-118.

The higher level GS-13 through GS-15 positions are disproportionately found in the Washington home offices.

Washington, as we noted in our discussion of community networks in Chapter Fourteen, offers numerous opportunities for two career families and individuals wishing to fast-track their careers in both government and business. These opportunities are found within federal executive agencies as well as within the related congressional bureaucracy, congressional committee staffs, personal congressional staffs, interest groups, consulting firms, businesses, and universities. Indeed, more than 50 percent of the job opportunities in Washington now are found within the non-governmental "service" sector, which consists of *"law and public relations firms and the trade associations where the paid lobbyists work"* (Peters: 14). If you are considering employment in Washington, Chapter Fourteen provides the necessary basics for getting you started on a job search there.

If you pursue a federal government career and advance to the highest levels within the bureaucracy, you will encounter one major problem with federal salaries and benefits. They are generous at the lower and middle levels, but there are few increasing monetary rewards as you move near the top. Once reaching the GS-15 level, you may need to redefine your career goals and plan for another career change. If you move into the private sector, you may enter a $70,000 to $100,000 a year executive position or develop your own contracting and consulting business based upon your previous experience and contacts in government.

CONDUCTING A JOB SEARCH

You should begin your job search with the understanding that there is *both* a formal and informal system for getting a job with the federal government. Your success will depend on how well you relate the two systems. At the same time, you must understand that there is an incredible amount of decentralization, fragmentation, overlap, redundancy, and chaos within the federal government. For example, if your goal is a position in research and intelligence, the CIA is only one of many agencies performing these functions. The Defense Intelligence Agency in the Department of Defense, Intelligence and Research Bureau in the State Department, and the National Security Council in the Executive Office of the President essentially do the same type of work. Congress also gets in the act with its Federal Research Division within the Library of Congress. These agencies duplicate each other and contribute to the overall redundancy of the federal government.

Other occupations also are represented in numerous agencies which overlap and duplicate one another. If you are interested in investigative work, almost every department has its own police or investigative force — not just the FBI. If you are looking for personnel training opportunities, most agencies conduct training — not just the Office of Personnel Management. You will uncover this redundancy once you begin conducting informational interviews. Indeed, personnel at the CIA will tell you to talk to their friends at the Defense Intelligence Agency or the Intelligence and Research Bureau in the State Department – agencies they may have worked for prior to moving to the CIA.

Most people consider redundancy to be a waste of taxpayers' money. However, some observers view redundancy as a necessary and positive force: it contributes to the overall effectiveness of government by providing important internal checks and balances on policy (Landau). Whatever your interpretation, we recommend that you utilize overlap, duplication, and redundancy to your advantage by contacting several agencies for information and referrals on job opportunities.

Decentralization also should be used to your advantage. Your contacts should be developed with key personnel in the operating units. As previously noted, this is where most hiring decisions are made. Since units tend to be isolated from one another because of decentralization, you should conduct several informational interviews within and between agencies. In fact, it is not unusual to discover that one office does not know what another office is doing, even though it is in the same agency, housed in the same building, or located next door.

The formal structure of hiring in the federal government overlays as incredible amount of decentralization, fragmentation, and chaos. It presents a deceptive picture of a centralized, organized, coordinated, and efficient government personnel system. This image initially encourages people to apply but then intimidates would-be applicants sufficiently enough to dissuade many from following through. Do not be intimidated or dissuaded from achieving your objective; understand the system, and use it to your benefit.

The Office of Personnel Management (OPM), formerly known as the Civil Service Commission, is an independent executive agency. It stands at the apex of the federal government's merit personnel system. Many people – including some working within OPM – believe you must apply for federal jobs through this agency. This is true in many, but not most, cases. Despite OPM, most government agencies are able to hire their own personnel. Like most personnel departments or offices, OPM lacks political clout; it will most likely continue to do so in the foreseeable future.

However, you cannot by-pass the Office of Personnel Management altogether, because it does have some power and performs certain useful roles. OPM does engage in the normal personnel functions of testing, selecting, classifying, and training employees. But it

performs only some of these functions for agencies. Since the federal
personnel reforms of January 1980, OPM increasingly has been de-
centralizing these functions to each agency. But decentralization has
not been uniform. For example, some agencies are capable of hiring
whereas others are more dependent upon OPM for assistance. In
other cases, OPM's role increasingly is marginal to the hiring process.
Overall, OPM is likely to perform general support functions for
agencies, such as providing information and assisting in the selection
and training processes. Yet, even here, reality defies simple explana-
tion. As most insiders already know, the Department of Agriculture
conducts training programs for many agencies in competition with
OPM's training units. Indeed, if you are interested in training positions, there are probably more opportunities in the Department of
Agriculture than in the Office of Personnel Management. This is
another example of the ubiquitous decentralization, overlap, duplication, redundancy, and bureaucratic politics which permeate the
federal government.

OPM does perform one essential function for your job search
campaign: dispenses information on procedures and opportunities.
In addition to its 10 regional headquarters, OPM's Federal Job Information Centers (FJIC's) are located in 72 other cities which are
considered subregional centers or key geographical locations for
dispensing federal employment information. However, you should
approach these FJIC's with some degree of caution and healthy
skepticism. The major functions of FJIC's are to provide information on job opportunities in particular agencies, hand out application forms (FS-171's), and conduct testing for lower-level entry
positions (GS-1 through GS-5). OPM representatives at the FJIC's
will tell you to follow the formal procedures; most will deny the
existence of an informal system, or at best they will not endorse it.
This is understandable, because their job is to propagate the formal
system rather than help you learn the most effective methods for
penetrating the bureaucracy.

OPM will outline the formal system by telling you that the
best way to get a federal job is to do the following:

1. Go to the FJIC for listings of job openings and inform-
    ation on procedures for getting a federal job. This
    results in a pile of literature and a FS-171 form.
2. Complete your SF-171 — the federal government's
    version of an obituary resume or application form —
    and send it to OPM.
3. Take whatever examinations are required for your
    level of qualifications (Mid-Level or Senior-Level

positions do not require examinations — only a completed SF-171 for getting a rating).

4. Submit your application (usually the SF-171 and a
reference or performance evaluation) in response to
a position announcement.

5. Wait to be called for an interview and given a job
offer.

If you follow OPM's advice, your chances of getting a job are
about as good as applying to a newspaper want ad or standing in
line at an employment firm — about perhaps, five percent. However,
OPM does not tell you about one other mystery to this process.
Remember, the federal government hires about 1,500 people each
day. But the FJIC's only list a few of these positions and usually
only those positions available in their particular region or city as
well as all positions classified as Senior-Level (certain GS-13 through
GS-15 positions) and a few Senior Executive Service positions. In
other words, the FJIC's provide you with almost worthless information on the availability of jobs in particular agencies at your level of
qualifications. There is a good reason for this. OPM does not know
what positions are available beyond the limited number reported to
OPM. In fact, no one in the federal government knows all the positions vacant on a particular day, week, or month. The federal government simply does not keep such information on itself.

Given OPM's lack of information on specific job openings,
you must contact the personnel offices of each agency for a complete listing of vacancies. Alternatively, a private group — the Federal
Research Service, Inc. — every two weeks compiles and publishes a
listing of 2,500 to 3,000 vacant agency positions. While this publication is relatively comprehensive, it misses many positions which are
listed only on the bulletin boards of agency personnel offices, circulated to a limited number of government offices, or posted outside
agency cafeterias and snack bars.

Your alternatives to spending $4 for each issue of the "Federal
Career Opportunities Report" are most unattractive. The federal
job information structure definitely favors individuals who physically are located in Washington, D.C. and have the time and patience
to walk from one agency personnel office or cafeteria bulletin board
to another. If you live outside Washington, D.C., you encounter
serious problems. You can visit your FJIC every week or telephone
every agency every week for information on vacant positions. After
spending $200 a week on long-distance telephone calls, the $4 an
issue for the "Report" will seem cheap and convenient. Moreover,
you can avoid having to travel to an FJIC and stand in line for

rather questionable information. The FJIC is mainly designed to help people apply for the GS-1 and GS-5 entry-level positions or for blue-collar positions. Visit the FJIC's, but beyond acquiring a copy of the FS-171, don't expect them to be useful in your job search. Again, the federal government is highly decentralized and fragmented within and between agencies. Your job will be to centralize and coordinate those aspects of the federal government job market that interest you. No one — including private employment and executive search firms — can do this for you.

USING THE INFORMAL SYSTEM

The informal federal hiring system is similar to the informal system we have discussed throughout this book. Since agencies continually face personnel problems because of normal turnover, they must recruit periodically. A personnel need is first identified in the operating unit and then communicated through the chain of command and eventually to a personnel office where it is formally announced in accordance with merit, affirmative action, and equal opportunity considerations. During the lengthy formal process of announcing the position, gathering SF-171's, and selecting candidates, agency personnel often try to hedge against uncertainty by looking for qualified personnel in the informal system. This means giving information on the vacancy to friends and acquaintances in their networks in the hope of attracting qualified candidates. Fearing the unknown, officials often welcome an opportunity to meet informally with a candidate, especially in the format of an informational interview.

If your timing is right, you may uncover a pending vacancy in an operating unit. Again, the personnel office will be the last to learn about the vacancy in the agency. Furthermore, the position description may be written around your resume and SF-171 or the agency may assist you in customizing your SF-171 in line with the position description. If agency personnel send you to their personnel office to rework your SF-171, this is a good signal that you are under serious consideration for a position. Although we have no accurate figures on the phenomenon of "wiring" positions, it probably occurs in many GS-13 and above positions. Irish estimates that 95 percent of these positions are filled through agency "promotion" (Irish: 205). Such practices arise from certain personnel fears of agencies. Many agency heads wish to avoid leaving critical personnel problems to chance decisions of low-level officials in personnel offices. If many applicants knew about this informal system, they would be outraged. But, then, if taxpayers knew how much government officials earn, many of them, too, would be outraged!

The informal system consists of following the same general job search steps we outlined earlier as well as adapting them to the federal government setting:

1. Research federal agencies.
2. Focus on a few agencies for intensive research.
3. Conduct informational interviews with agency personnel -- use your resume *and* SF-171.
4. Apply for agency vacancies with a customized SF-171.
5. Arrange interview with the hiring supervisor.

Revising Hawkins 1978 model of the federal employment process in Figure 7 (Hawkins: 114), we outline the formal and informal systems of federal employment as well as the relationship between the two for positions at the GS-9 to GS-15 levels.

We believe it is best not to mobilize partisan political "pull" with agencies. Bureaucrats in general do not like to respond to blatant political pressures from elected officials. Such strategies may work wonders at the state and local levels where the "good old boys" are still powerful — but be careful with the feds. There are exceptions, however. Perhaps you know a congressman who is on a powerful budget or appropriations committee affecting a particular agency. The congressman and his or her legislative assistants may know key people in the agency, and they will write you a standard letter of introduction. But do not expect miracles to happen with such a letter or by dropping names of big shots. In fact, the President of the United States only directly controls 2,000 of 2.85 million civilian government positions. Even the President may not be able to help you with the relatively autonomous and resistant bureaucracy!

Federal bureaucrats understand and thrive on the informal system, but political patronage and political pull are considered tacky, if not illegal, these days. In this respect, government bureaucrats are no different from their counterparts in other organizations: the informal system continues to yield more reliable and trustworthy information than the formal system. Thus, the hiring goals of most government agencies are similar to those of the private sector: hire the most qualified person who is *competent, intelligent, honest,* and *likable.* Indeed, the 1980 personnel reforms, which are based upon the model of the private sector, already have decentralized many hiring decisions to the agency level. In this sense, conducting a job search with the federal government is remarkably similar to conducting a job search in the private sector.

FIGURE 7

RELATIONSHIP OF FORMAL AND INFORMAL FEDERAL EMPLOYMENT PROCESSES

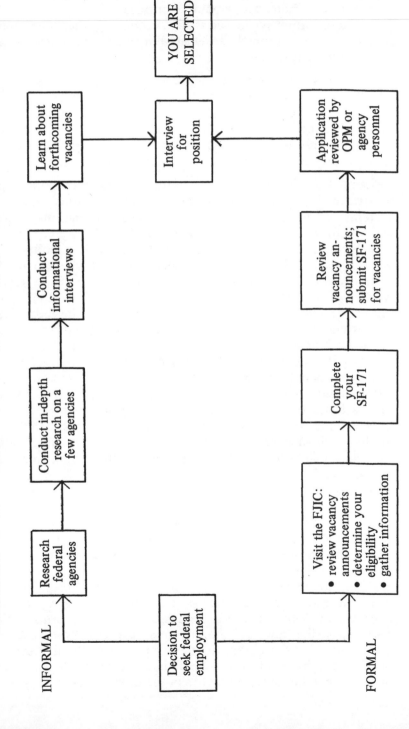

RESEARCHING AGENCIES

Three books should be useful for planning your overall job search campaign targeted at the federal government. David Waelde's *How to Get a Federal Job or Survive a RIF* (Washington, D.C.: FEDHELP Publications, 1982, $15) is the best "how to" book on federal government employment. He outlines both the formal and informal structure of federal employment, the role of OPM, how to complete the SF-171, and how to apply for a specific federal job.

James E. Hawkin's *The Uncle Sam Connection: The Insider's Guide to Federal Employment* (Chicago, Ill.: Follett Publishing Co., 1978, $4.95) is also a comprehensive treatment of both the formal and informal federal government employment processes. Compared to Waelde's book, this book says essentially the same thing, is a bit dated, and has less "how to" material on developing an effective SF-171.

Patricia B. Wood's *The 171 Workbook* (Washington, D.C.: Workbooks, Inc., 1979, $12.95), is by far the most comprehensive in-depth treatment of how to complete the SF-171. If followed carefully, this step-by-step guide should result in producing an outstanding SF-171 which would normally cost $100 or more if completed through a professional service or workshop.

Our final recommended resource is the "Federal Career Opportunities Report" which is published bi-weekly by the Federal Research Service, Inc. It lists approximately 2,500 to 3,000 job vacancies in agencies throughout the federal government. This is the only such listing available. You can subscribe to it on the following plans: $4 per issue, $21 for 6 bi-weekly issues, $40 for 12 bi-weekly issues, and $78 for 26 bi-weekly issues. Write to the following address for subscription information:

Federal Research Service, Inc.
P. O. Box 1059
Vienna, Virginia 22180
Attn: Subscription Manager

The federal bureaucracy is an extremely large and complex organization consisting of departments, independent executive agencies, and independent regulatory commissions. As we noted earlier, agency functions overlap and redundancy is well institutionalized throughout the bureaucracy. Understanding who does how much of what and where requires a major research effort on your part.

Your research should initially focus on the structure, functions, and problems of individual agencies. While conducting this research, you need to identify the names, addresses, and telephone numbers of key individuals within the agencies. For a good introduction to the federal government, start with the *U.S. Government Manual* (Washington, D.C.: U.S. Government Printing Office). A new edition of this book is published each year and can be purchased for around $13. It presents organizational charts of each agency as well as brief summaries of federal agency duties and responsibilities. However, your best research tool will be the *Federal Yellow Book* (Washington, D.C.: Washington Monitor). This is a loose leaf notebook published in revised form every six months. It breaks down all types of government agencies by listing the names, addresses, and telephone numbers of key agency personnel. Other useful research sources to consult are the *Federal Phone Book* and copies of individual agency directories. If you write or call an agency for information on its structure, functions, and activities, you may receive a wealth of information including an annual report outlining specific accomplishments of the agency. Many agencies also have in-house journals or newsletters which you may be able to examine in a library or personnel office of an agency.

Another good source of information on an agency will be conversations with former or present employees of the agency or a congressional staff member or interest group representatives who have contacts with the agency. Ask these people about the functions and problems of the particular agency, and who might be the best person within the agency to target for conducting an informational interview. Acquiring key names, addresses, and telephone numbers should be your primary research goal.

WRITING AN EFFECTIVE SF-171

The SF-171 is to government what the resume, curriculum vitae, and application form are to the rest of the world. It is the most important marketing tool in your job search with the federal government. Criticized for being too long, and not particularly informative, and rumored to be replaced with a less intimidating form, the SF-171 lives on nonetheless. It probably will continue to draw similar criticism and live on into the foreseeable future.

The SF-171 can be intimidating, long, and less than revealing of your qualifications — but only if you let it become so. Despite the criticisms, you need to grin and bear the SF-171 and, in the process, restructure it to communicate much more than it was originally intended to communicate. If you complete the SF-171 according to our advice, you will overcome one of the major obstacles to acquiring federal employment. Remember, the purpose of a resume and application form is to advertise yourself. You must communicate as clearly as possible your qualifications to your prospective employer.

The SF-171 is a four-page application form. It appears deceptively simple to complete, but it is an extremely complex document for those who know its value. Many people pay $100 or more to have professionals assist them in completing the SF-171. Others are able to complete the form in less than an hour by filling in the blanks in long hand. Those who know the importance of the SF-171 should spend hours — indeed a few days — in putting together an effective SF-171.

There are two keys to developing an effective SF-171. First, you should customize the SF-171 beyond its standard four-page length. Second, you should utilize a functional-skills vocabulary in describing your experience. If you describe your experience on the SF-171 in the same manner you describe it in a functional resume (Chapter Eight), your SF-171 will conform to the best advice available on how to write an effective SF-171. At the same time, you may wish to consult the SF-171 sections of Waelde's and Wood's books for excellent step-by-step guidance in developing an effective SF-171. The remainder of this section refers to specific sections on the SF-171.

Your SF-171 also should be customized. We recommend two customizing methods. First, expand the length of each section (experience, honors, special qualifications) in order to include more information. You can do this by clipping and pasting the section headings to separate sheets of paper. Copies of these new sheets become customized sections of your SF-171. Complete these expanded sections in as much detail as possible. The "experience" section is the most critical, and it requires your best creative writing effort. In this section you should stress your direct and transferable abilities, skills, and talents as you did when writing a functional resume.

Overall, try to keep the length of your customized SF-171 to ten pages or less. After completing this new form, you will have a generalized SF-171 which you can use for other Federal applications. Be sure to keep a master copy — preferably the original — from which you can make additional copies to be sent to agencies. Leave items 1, 2, 13, "Signature," and "Date" blank on your master SF-171. When you submit a copy of your SF-171 in response to an agency vacancy, complete these vacant items at that time. It is best to use an electric typewriter with a carbon ribbon so that your original and reproductions will look as professional as possible.

Another way to customize the SF-171 is to rewrite the "experience" sections to respond specifically to the qualifications outlined
in a particular job vacancy announcement. Read each announcement
carefully and then use similar skills terminology in your SF-171. If
you customize your SF-171 in this manner, you must retype the
"experience" sections for each vacancy announcement. While this is
a time consuming process, it is the most effective approach for ad-
dressing the exact qualifications for a particular position.

If you need further assistance in completing the SF-171, examine Waelde's and Wood's books on the subject. However, our
advice on writing functional resumes will substitute for most of
their advice.

PROSPECTING AND NETWORKING

Conducting informational interviews within the federal government should follow the same principles we outlined in Chapter
Ten on prospecting and networking. Begin with a list of desired
agencies and positions as well as the names of individuals who know
people or who actually work within your targeted agencies. Contacting these people for information and referrals is the best way of
gaining access to agencies and uncovering employment opportunities.

If you don't know people who know key agency personnel,
the cold turkey approach also will work relatively well. Consult the
Federal Yellow Book or an agency directory for names, addresses,
and telephone numbers. Telephone or write key individuals for
informational interviews in your desired agencies. Request a brief
meeting to discuss your professional interests. The approach letter
should follow the guidelines we discussed earlier.

When making an appointment for an informational interview,
be sure you do not ask someone for a job. Stress that you are gathering information on opportunities in your area of interest and expertise. You will probably flatter whomever you contact by the mere
fact you are asking for their advice; you are recognizing the person
as an "expert" who can assist you.

In most cases, you will be successful in arranging an appointment for an informational interview. Moreover, most people will be
gracious and willing to assist you with advice and referrals. this is
perhaps one reason why federal officials often are criticized for
being "too accommodating" to the public as well as for developing
their own interest group clientele.

Informational interviews within government agencies should be conducted in the same manner as any other informational interview: *ask for advice, ask to be referred, and ask to be remembered.* Within a few days after the interview, send a thank-you letter in which you communicate genuine gratitude for the assistance. Continue building your network of new contacts by conducting several informational interviews. In so doing, you will learn a great deal about the federal employment process — both formal and informal. Accordingly, you should be one of the first persons to learn of vacancies related to your qualifications in the agencies you target.

ADVANCING WITHIN AND BEYOND GOVERNMENT

After you acquire a position within a federal agency, do an excellent job, and attach yourself to people who are moving ahead. At the same time, plan to move on to other positions within this or other agencies. Job-hopping within the federal government is a common practice — moreso in Washington, D.C. than elsewhere.

Always remember your friends and the importance of developing your networks both on and off the job. These networks will be the key to advancing your career within the government. At the same time, be sure to maintain and develop good relationships with agency clientele, particularly organizations doing contract work, interest groups, and congressional committee and staff members. Many of these individuals and groups may play critical future roles in advancing your career. You may later want to further advance your career by moving out of government into more lucrative and professionally rewarding private organizations. Be prepared to once again change jobs and perhaps explore a new and related career. When this time comes, read *Moving Out of Government* (Krannich, 1982).

Chapter Seventeen

TAKING ACTION FOR RESULTS

Chapter Five linked planning and organizing to the implementation process. In this final chapter we again return to the question of implementation. For it is this question which will largely determine whether you will get results from this book.

YOU MUST IMPLEMENT

Reading a book without putting it into practice is a waste of your time and money. To do this would be unfortunate, particularly when the subject deals with something so important as your career and your future. This should not happen to you.

The methods we outlined in previous chapters have worked for thousands of individuals who have paid $1,500 to $10,000 to get similar information from the high-paid professionals. While you may want to see a professional for assistance at certain steps in your job search, if you are self-motivated you can do everything on your own with a minimum expenditure of money. The major cost will be your time and effort.

But you must make the effort and take the *risk of implementing* this book. Re-careering takes work and is a risky business. You try something new and place your ego on the line. You subject yourself to the possibility of being rejected several times. And this is precisely the major barrier you will encounter to effective implementation. For many people are unwilling to take more than a few rejections.

WELCOME REJECTIONS

Planning is the easy part of any task. You can set goals and outline a course of action divorced from the reality of actually doing it. But if you don't take action, you will not get your expected results. You must implement if you want desired results.

Once you take action, be prepared for rejections. Employers will tell you *"Thank you — we'll call you,"* but they never do. Other employers will tell you *"We have no positions available at this time for someone with your qualifications"* or *"You don't have the qualifications necessary for this position."*

Rejections are a normal part of the process of finding employment. More important, you must be rejected before you will be accepted. Expect 10 rejections or "noes" for every acceptance or "yes" you receive. If you quit after five or eight rejections, you prematurely end your job search. If you persist in collecting two to five more "noes," you will likely receive a "yes." Most people quit prematurely because their ego is not prepared for more rejections. Therefore, you should welcome rejections as you seek more and more acceptances.

ACTION PLANNING

Your planning must be closely linked to implementation. As we noted in Chapter Five, action planning is necessary from the very beginning of your job search. Put together a large three-month calendar in which you *identify specific tasks and expected outcomes* for each day and week. Refer to Figure 3 in Chapter Five for identifying your tasks and dates. A task such as *"contact 10 employers for informational interviews during the week of June 10"* should be followed by an expected outcome — *"conduct two job interviews during the week of June 29 and receive a job offer during the week of July 5."* By doing this, you link your goals to activities and outcomes; you will thus have a basis for evaluating your progress as well as for making necessary adjustments for improving your job search.

Once you have implemented this book, evaluate your careering skills by once again completing the exercise in Table 7 (Chapter Five) on your level of careering competencies. You should score under 40 points on this exercise.

RE-CAREERING IN YOUR FUTURE

The continuing transformation of American society will require millions of individuals to re-career in the years ahead. The nature of jobs and careers are changing as the workplace becomes transformed due to the impact of new technology. Many career fields in demand today may well be glutted tomorrow.

Throughout this book we have emphasized the importance of *being prepared* for turbulent times. The age of the generalist armed with job search skills alone is passing. The emerging society requires a new type of *generalist-specialist* who is trained for today's technology, *flexible* enough to be retrained in tomorrow's technology, and *adaptive* to new jobs and careers that will arise today and tomorrow. In other words, the society needs more and more generalist-specialists who welcome change by being willing and able to re-career. Knowing and practicing the job search skills outlined in this book, these people also are continuously learning new work-content skills in order to better position themselves in tomorrow's job market. *They transform their careering skills into re-careering competencies*.

You should be prepared to develop and practice re-careering competencies for the decades ahead. We recommend one final re-careering action on your part. Make an effort to *learn one new skill each year*; the skill can be related to work, family, community, or a hobby such a building bookcases, operating different computer software packages, repairing appliances, or remodeling your home. If you do this, you will be better prepared for making the career transitions necessary for functioning effectively in turbulent times!

REFERENCES

Aslanian, Carol B. and Henry M. Brickell
    1979   *Americans in Transition: Life Changes as Triggers to Adult Learning*. New York: The College Board.

Azrin, Nathan H. and Victoria A. Besalel
    1980   *Job Club Counselor's Manual*. Baltimore, MD: University Park Press.

Bauerlein, Chuck
    1980   "If the Ax Falls." *The Graduate*, 95-97.

Bluestone, Barry and Bennett Harrison
    1982   *The Deindustrialization of America*. New York: Basic Books.

Bolles, Richard Nelson
    1981   "The 'Warp' in the Way We Perceive Our Life in the World of Work." *Training and Development Journal*. 11:20-27.
    1980   *What Color is Your Parachute?* Berkeley, CA: Ten Speed Press.
    1978   *Three Boxes of Life*. Berkeley, CA: Ten Speed Press.

Boyer, Richard and David Savageau
  1981 *Places Rated Almanac: Your Guide to Finding the Best Place to Live in America.* Chicago: Rand McNally.

Bowman, Thomas F., George H. Giuliani, and M. Randal Minge
  1981 *Finding Your Best Place to Live in America.* West Babylon, NY: Red Lion Books.

Breitmayer, William F.
  1982 "All About Ads." *National Business Employment Weekly* (January) 24: 14-16.

Brown, Deaver
  1980 *The Entrepreneur's Guide.* New York: Macmillan Publishing Co.

Choate, Pat and Noel Epstein
  1982 "Workers of the Future, Retool! Nothing to Lose But Your Jobs." *Washington Post* (May 9) :D1 and D5.

Crystal, John C. and Richard N. Bolles
  1974 *Where Do I Go From Here With My Life?* Berkeley, CA: Ten Speed Press.

Djeddah, Eli
  1978 *Moving Up.* Berkeley, CA: Ten Speed Press.

Drucker, Peter
  1980 *Managing in Turbulent Times.* New York: Harper and Row.

DuBrin, Andrew J.
  1978 *Winning at Office Politics.* New York: Van Nostrand Reinhold Co.

Einhorn, Lois J., Patricia Hayes Bradley, John E. Baird, Jr.
  1982 *Effective Employment Interviewing.* Glenview, IL: Scott, Foresman, and Co.

Eisen, Jeffrey
  1978 *Get the Right Job Now!* Philadelphia and New York: J. B. Lippincott Co.

Feingold, Norman and Leonard Perlman
1981 *Making It on Your Own*. Washington, DC: Acropolis Books, Ltd.

Feldstein, Stuart
1981 *Home, Inc*. New York: Grosset and Dunlap.

Ferguson, Marilyn
1980 *The Acquarian Conspiracy: Personal and Social Transformation in the 1980s*. Los Angeles: J.P. Tarcher.

Germann, Richard and Peter Arnold
1980 *Bernard Haldane Associates' Job & Career Building*. New York: Harper and Row.

Gray, Ernest A.
1981 *Successful Business Resumes*. Boston, MA: CBI Publishing Co.

Gumpert, David E. and Jeffry A. Timmons
1981 *The Insider's Guide to Small Business Resources*. New York: Doubleday.

Haldane, Bernard
1960 *How to Make a Habit of Success*. Washington, DC: Acropolis Books Ltd.

Hawkins, James E.
1978 *The Uncle Sam Connection: An Insider's Guide to Federal Employment*. Chicago: Follett Publishing Co.

Hecklinger, Fred J. and Bernadette M. Curtin
1982 *Training for Life: A Practical Guide to Career and Life Planning*. Dubuque, IA: Kendall/Hunt Publishing Co.

Hedberg, Augustin
1982 "How to Change Your Life." *Money*, (May), 44-53.

Holland, John L.
1973 *Making Vocational Choices: A Theory of Careers*. Englewood Cliffs, NJ: Prentice-Hall, Inc.

Hower, Alice and Alfred Howard
1981 *Turn Your Kitchen Into a Goldmine*. New York: Harper and Row.

Irish, Richard K.
   1978   *Go Hire Yourself an Employer.* Garden City, NJ: Anchor
          Press.

Jackson, Carole
   1981   *Color Me Beautiful.* New York: Ballantine Books.

Kamoroff, Bernard
   1981   *Small-Time Operator.* Laytonville, CA: Bell Springs
          Publishing.

Kellogg, Mary Alice
   1978   *Fast Track: The Superachievers and How They Make It
          to Early Success, Status and Power.* New York: McGraw-
          Hill.

Kennedy, Marilyn
   1980a *Office Politics.* Chicago: Follett Publishing Co.
   1980b *Career Knockouts.* Chicago: Follett Publishing Co.

Komar, John J.
   1979   *The Interview Game: Winning Strategies of Job Seekers.*
          Chicago: Follett Publishing Co.

Korda, Michael
   1977   *Success!* New York: Ballantine Books.

Krannich, Caryl Rae
   1982   *Interview for Success.* Manassas, VA: Impact Publications.

Krannich, Ronald L.
   1983   "Are Job Clubs For You?" *National Business Employment
          Weekly* (January 9): 11-12.
   1982   *Moving Out of Government: A Guide to Surviving and
          Prospering in the 1980's.* Manassas, VA: Impact Publica-
          tions.

Krannich, Ronald L. and William J. Banis
   1982   *High Impact Resumes and Letters.* Manassas, VA: Impact
          Publications.
   1981   *Moving Out of Education: The Educator's Guide to Career
          Management and Change.* Chesapeake, VA: Progressive
          Concepts Inc.

Lakein, Alan
1973   *How to Get Control of Your Time and Life.*   New York:
Signet Books.

Landau, Martin
1969   "Redundancy, Relationality, and the Problem of Duplication and Overlap." *Public Administration Review* 29:
346-358.

Lathrop, Richard
1977   *Who's Hiring Who.* Berkeley, CA: Ten Speed Press.

LeBoeuf, Michael
1979   *Working Smart.* New York: Warner Books.

Lewis, Judy and Joanne Nicholson
1981   "Color — The Missing Link," pp. 70-84 in Jacqueline
Thompson (ed.), *Image Impact.* New York: A&W Publishers, Inc.

Lin, Nan, Paul Dayton, and Peter Greenwald
1978   "Analyzing the Instrumental Use of Relations in the
Context of Social Structure." *Sociological Methods and
Research* 7:149-166.

Long, Norton
1958   "The Local Community as an Ecology of Games." *American Journal of Sociology* 64:251-261.

Lowry, Albert J.
1981   *How to Become Financially Successful By Owning Your
Own Business.* New York: Simon and Schuster.

MacKenzie, R. Alex
1972   *The Time Trap.* New York: AMACOM.

Meier, Kenneth J.
1979   *Politics and the Bureaucracy.* North Scituate, MA: Dux-
bury Press.

Merritt, Giles
1982   "The Job Gap." *World Press Review* (December).

Molloy, John T.
    1981   *Live for Success.* New York: William Morrow and Co.
    1977   *The Woman's Dress for Success Book.* New York: Warner
            Books.
    1975   *Dress for Success.* New York: Warner Books.

Naisbitt, John
    1982   *Megatrends: Ten New Directions Transforming Our Lives.*
            New York: Warner Books.

Peters, Charles
    1980   *How Washington Really Works.* Reading, MA: Addison-
            Wesley.

Riley, Robert T.
    1978   *How to Manage Your Time Successfully.* Dallas, TX:
            The Drawing Board, Inc.

Ripley, Randall B. and Grace A. Franklin
    1976   *Congress, The Bureaucracy, and Public Policy.* Homewood,
            IL: The Dorsey Press.

Rogers, Edward J.
    1982   *Getting Hired.* Englewood Cliffs, NJ: Prentice-Hall.

Scheele, Adele
    1979   *Skills for Success: A Guide to the Top for Men and Wo-
            men.* New York: Ballantine Books.

Sivy, Michael
    1981   "Putting Money Into the Boom Regions." *Money* 2:74-82.

Solmon, Lewis, Nancy L. Ochsner, and Margo-Lea Hurwicz
    1979   *Alternative Careers for Humanities Ph.Ds: Perspectives of
            Students and Graduates.* New York: Praeger Publishers.

Souerwine, Andrew H.
    1978   *Career Strategies: Planning for Personal Achievement.*
            New York: AMACOM.

Stanat, Kirby W.
    1977   *Job Hunting Secrets & Tactics.* Chicago: Follett Pub-
            lishing Co.

Stump, Robert W.
   1980   "Transferable Skills and Job Changes," pp. 87-111 in
          Judith W. Spring (ed.), *Issues in Career and Human Re-
          source Development.* Madison, WI: American Society for
          Training and Development.

Toffler, Alvin
   1980   *The Third Wave.* New York: Bantam Books.

U.S. Department of Labor
   1982   *Occupational Outlook Handbook.* Washington, DC:
          Bureau of Labor Statistics.
   1982   *Economic Projections to 1990.* Washington, DC: Bureau
          of Labor Statistics.
   1980   *Occupational Projections and Training Data*, 1980 Edi-
          tion. Washington, DC: Bureau of Labor Statistics.

Waelde, David
   1982   *How to Get a Federal Job or Survive a RIF.* Washington,
          DC: FEDHELP Publications.

Wiant, A.A.
   1980   *Occupational Change and Transferable Skills: The Em-
          ployers' Viewpoint.* Columbus, OH: The National Center
          for Research in Vocational Education.

Wood, Patricia B.
   1979   *The 171 Workbook.* Washington, DC: Workbooks, Inc.

Appendix A
EMPLOYMENT PROJECTIONS TO 1990

Based on an analysis of 235 occupations, the following figures present employment data for 1978 as well as project average annual job changes to the year 1990. The data are based on the research for the 1980-81 *Occupational Outlook Handbook*. The occupational clusters correspond to the 13 used in the *Handbook*: industrial production and related occupations; office occupations; service occupations; education and related occupations; sales occupations; construction occupations; occupations in transportation activities; scientific and technical occupations; mechanics and repairers; health occupations; social scientists; social service occupations; and performing arts, design, and communications occupations.

EMPLOYMENT, 1978 AND 1990 (projected), AND AVERAGE ANNUAL OPENINGS, BY OCCUPATION, 1978-1990

Occupation	Estimated employment, 1978	Projected employment 1990	Percent change, 1978 - 1990	Annual average openings
Industrial production and related occupations:				
Foundry occupations:				
Patternmakers	3,700	3,900	5.2	120
Molders.	21,000	22,100	5.2	400
Coremakers	12,000	12,600	5.2	300

244

Employment, 1978 and 1990 (projected), and average annual openings, by occupation, 1978-1990 — Continued

Occupation	Estimated employment, 1978	Projected employment 1990	Percent change, 1978 - 1990	Annual average openings
Machining occupations:				
All-round machinists	484,000	584,000	20.7	14,500
Instrument makers				
(mechanical).	6,000	6,900	17.1	200
Machine tool operators.	542,000	609,000	12.4	14,000
Setup workers				
Setup workers (machine tools)	65,000	81,000	24.6	1,600
Tool-and-die makers	170,000	210,000	23.5	5,300
Printing occupations:				
Bookbinders and bindery				
workers.	69,000	70,000	1.3	2,500
Compositors.	181,000	158,000	-12.8	5,800
Electrotypers and				
stereotypers	2,000	N/A	N/A	N/A
Lithographers	28,000	45,000	61.1	900
Photoengravers	8,000	7,500	-6.3	200
Printing press operators				
and assistants	167,000	182,000	8.9	3,800
Other industrial production				
and related occupations:				
Assemblers.	1,164,000	1,662,000	43.0	35,000
Automobile painters	42,000	54,000	27.2	1,000
Blacksmiths	11,000	7,000	-36.4	600
Blue-collar worker				
supervisors.	1,671,000	1,925,000	16.0	48,000
Boilermaking occupations . .	37,000	56,000	46.2	1,500
Boiler tenders	71,000	71,000	0	2,800
Electroplaters	40,000	40,000	0	800
Forge shop occupations . . .	77,000	80,100	3.6	1,800
Inspectors				
(manufacturing).	771,000	909,000	18.0	23,500
Millwrights.	95,000	118,000	25.0	2,800
Motion picture				
projectionists	11,000	10,500	-4.5	800
Ophthalmic laboratory				
technicians.	26,400	32,200	22.0	900
Photographic laboratory				
occupations	57,000	68,000	20.0	1,800
Power truck operators	363,000	458,000	24.0	6,000
Production painters.	133,000	158,000	19.0	3,100
Stationary engineers	179,000	186,000	4.0	7,100
Wastewater treatment plant				
operators (sewage plant				
operators)	112,000	N/A	N/A	N/A
Welders.	679,000	907,000	33.6	16,000
Office occupations:				
Clerical occupations:				
Bookkeeping workers.	1,830,000	2,045,000	11.8	78,000
Cashiers	1,400,000	2,100,000	49.7	60,500

Employment, 1978 and 1990 (projected), and average annual openings, by occupation, 1978-1990 — Continued

Occupation	Estimated employment, 1978	Projected employment 1990	Percent change, 1978 - 1990	Annual average openings
Collection workers	78,000	95,000	21.8	3,200
File clerks	273,000	335,000	22.6	11,400
Hotel front office clerks.	79,000	98,000	24.9	3,700
Office machine operators.	160,000	201,000	26.2	6,200
Postal clerks	260,000	210,000	-19.0	6,000
Receptionists	588,000	752,000	27.9	27,000
Secretaries and stenographers	3,684,000	5,357,000	45.4	167,000
Shipping and receiving clerks.	461,000	567,000	23.0	13,200
Statistical clerks.	377,000	475,000	26.0	15,300
Stock clerks	507,000	600,000	18.3	15,200
Typists	1,044,000	1,246,000	19.4	42,000
Computer and related occupations:				
Computer operating personnel.	666,000	665,000	-.2	12,600
Programmers.	247,000	320,000	29.6	3,100
Systems analysts	182,000	250,000	37.4	2,200
Banking occupations:				
Bank clerks	505,000	760,000	50.5	24,000
Bank officers and managers.	330,000	510,000	54.5	13,000
Bank tellers	410,000	455,000	11.0	13,000
Insurance occupations:				
Actuaries.	9,000	12,000	32.4	250
Claim representatives. . . .	169,000	237,000	40.5	4,650
Insurance agents, brokers, and underwriters	568,000	682,000	20.0	20,500
Administrative and related occupations:				
Accountants.	985,000	1,275,000	29.4	37,000
Buyers	115,000	142,000	23.5	5,200
City managers	3,300	5,000	52.0	200
College student personnel workers	55,000	N/A	N/A	N/A
Credit managers	49,000	56,000	14.3	1,600
Hotel managers and assistants	168,000	193,000	14.9	6,800
Lawyers	487,000	609,000	25.0	27,000
Marketing research workers.	24,000	N/A	N/A	N/A
Personnel and labor relations workers	405,000	473,000	16.8	11,000
Public relations workers . .	185,000	269,000	24.4	4,900
Purchasing agents	185,000	267,000	44.3	6,600
Urban regional planners	17,000	22,000	30.0	350

Employment, 1978 and 1990 (projected), and average annual openings, by occupation, 1978-1990 — Continued

Occupation	Estimated employment, 1978	Projected employment 1990	Percent change, 1978 - 1990	Annual average openings
Service occupations:				
Cleaning and related occupations:				
Building custodians	2,251,000	2,704,000	20.1	138,000
Hotel housekeepers and assistants	20,000	29,000	49.9	1,200
Pest controllers	31,500	44,500	42.0	1,400
Food service occupations:				
Bartenders	282,000	369,000	30.9	14,300
Cooks and chefs.	1,186,000	1,564,000	31.9	55,000
Dining room attendants and dishwashers	455,000	741,000	62.8	13,000
Food counter workers . . .	463,000	648,000	39.9	19,000
Meatcutters	204,000	187,000	-8.3	6,600
Waiters and waitresses . . .	1,383,000	1,635,000	18.2	49,000
Personal service occupations:				
Barbers.	121,000	140,000	15.7	8,100
Bellhops and bell captains	20,000	19,000	-5.0	700
Cosmetologists	542,000	624,000	15.1	22,000
Funeral directors and embalmers	45,000	45,000	0.0	2,200
Private household service occupations:				
Private household workers.	1,162,000	893,000	-23.2	68,000
Protective and related service occupations:				
Correction officers	110,000	153,000	38.9	9,500
FBI special agents.	8,000	N/A	N/A	N/A
Firefighters	220,000	270,000	21.0	3,600
Guards	550,000	820,000	50.0	50,000
Police officers	450,000	550,000	22.7	8,000
State police officers.	47,000	59,000	26.0	800
Construction inspectors (government)	20,000	30,000	50.0	1,400
Health and regulatory inspectors (government)	100,000	122,000	24.6	3,800
Occupational safety and health workers.	80,000	N/A	N/A	N/A
Other service occupations:				
Mail carriers	245,000	260,000	6.0	6,000
Telephone operators	311,000	290,000	-6.8	11,700
Education and related occupations:				
Teaching occupations:				
Kindergarten and elementary school teachers	1,322,000	1,652,000	24.9	58,500

Employment, 1978 and 1990 (projected), and average annual openings, by occupation, 1978-1990 — Continued

Occupation	Estimated employ- ment, 1978	Projected employ- ment 1990	Percent change, 1978 - 1990	Annual average openings
Secondary school teachers	1,087,000	861,000	-20.8	26,000
College and university faculty	673,000	611,000	-9.2	16,000
Teacher aides	342,000	519,000	51.8	11,000
Library occupations:				
Librarians	142,000	160,000	12.7	6,500
Library technicians and assistants	172,000	195,000	13.4	6,700
Sales occupations:				
Automobile parts counter workers.	97,000	119,000	22.1	2,400
Automobile sales workers.	158,000	200,000	26.5	6,900
Automobile service advisors.	25,000	30,400	22.1	600
Gasoline service station attendants	340,000	322,000	-5.6	6,800
Manufacturers' sales workers.	402,000	499,000	24.0	13,700
Models	60,000	N/A	N/A	N/A
Real estate agents and brokers.	555,000	670,000	20.7	40,000
Retail trade sales workers	2,851,000	3,785,000	32.8	148,000
Route drivers	195,000	190,000	-2.9	4,100
Securities sales workers. . .	109,000	120,000	10.0	4,600
Travel agents.	18,500	30,000	62.2	950
Wholesale trade sales workers.	840,000	958,000	14.0	30,000
Construction occupations:				
Bricklayers, stonemasons, and marblesetters	205,000	220,000	7.3	4,900
Carpenters	1,253,000	1,390,000	10.9	47,000
Cement masons and terrazzo workers	82,000	110,000	32.5	2,100
Construction laborers. . . .	860,000	970,000	12.8	39,000
Drywall installers and finishers	82,000	N/A	N/A	N/A
Electricians (construction).	290,000	350,000	20.7	7,900
Elevator constructors. . . .	17,000	N/A	N/A	N/A
Floor covering installers . .	88,000	110,000	25.0	1,400
Glaziers (construction). . .	19,000	25,000	31.6	500
Insulation workers	51,000	65,000	27.5	1,000
Ironworkers	78,000	104,000	33.3	1,900
Lathers	23,000	N/A	N/A	N/A
Operating engineers (construction machinery operators). . .	581,000	820,000	41.4	16,000

Employment, 1978 and 1990 (projected), and average annual
openings, by occupation, 1978-1990 — Continued

Occupation	Estimated employment, 1978	Projected employment 1990	Percent change, 1978 - 1990	Annual average openings
Painters and paperhangers .	504,000	572,000	13.5	21,000
Painters.	484,000	550,000	13.6	20,000
Paperhangers.	20,000	22,000	10.0	1,300
Plasterers.	28,000	30,000	7.1	900
Plumbers and pipefitters . .	428,000	513,000	19.9	13,000
Roofers.	114,000	140,000	22.8	2,300
Sheet-metal workers	70,000	90,000	28.6	1,800
Tilesetters	33,000	45,000	36.4	800
Occupations in transportation activities:				
Air transportation occupations:				
Air traffic controller	21,000	26,000	23.9	300
Airplane mechanics.	132,000	145,000	10.1	2,400
Airplane pilots.	76,000	110,000	43.9	1,000
Flight attendants	48,000	76,000	56.2	2,500
Reservation and passenger agents.	56,000	64,000	15.0	1,500
Merchant marine occupations:				
Merchant marine officers.	13,500	13,000	-3.7	750
Merchant marine sailors.	24,800	16,000	-36.9	450
Railroad occupations:				
Brake operators	66,000	67,000	1.3	1,500
Conductors	37,000	39,000	6.2	1,500
Locomotive engineers . . .	34,000	37,000	9.6	1,700
Shop trades	76,000	71,000	-6.7	2,500
Signal department workers.	12,800	14,100	10.0	350
Station agents	5,900	2,400	-59.6	100
Telegraphers, tele- phoners, and tower operators.	9,700	6,800	-30.2	300
Track workers.	59,000	59,000	0.0	1,400
Driving occupations:				
Intercity busdrivers.	23,500	23,700	.08	475
Local transit busdrivers. . .	77,000	91,000	18.9	1,900
Local truckdrivers.	1,720,000	2,040,000	18.4	38,000
Long-distance truckdrivers	584,000	689,000	18.0	12,800
Parking attendants	44,000	50,000	13.6	2,700
Taxicab drivers	94,000	94,000	0	4,300
Scientific & technical occupations:				
Conservation occupations:				
Foresters.	31,200	38,000	20.6	900
Forestry technicians	13,700	17,300	26.0	400
Range managers	3,700	4,700	27.0	100
Soil conservationists	9,300	11,400	21.7	250

Employment, 1978 and 1990 (projected), and average annual openings, by occupation, 1978-1990 — Continued

Occupation	Estimated employment, 1978	Projected employment 1990	Percent change, 1978 - 1990	Annual average openings
Engineers.	1,136,000	1,441,000	26.8	21,000
Aerospace	60,000	70,000	20.7	900
Agricultural	14,000	17,800	26.8	300
Biomedical.	4,000	5,100	26.8	75
Ceramic	14,000	17,800	26.8	250
Chemical.	53,000	63,000	20.0	900
Civil.	155,000	190,000	22.8	4,900
Electrical	300,000	364,000	21.5	5,100
Industrial.	185,000	233,000	26.0	4,000
Mechanical.	195,000	232,000	19.1	4,400
Metallurgical.	16,500	21,300	29.0	350
Mining	6,000	9,500	58.3	300
Petroleum	17,000	23,400	37.6	350
Environmental scientists:				
Geologists	31,000	42,000	35.5	800
Geophysicists	11,000	14,600	35.5	300
Meteorologists	7,300	8,800	20.0	200
Oceanographers	3,600	4,400	21.6	75
Life science occupations:				
Biochemists	20,000	25,000	25.5	450
Life scientists	215,000	280,000	28.4	6,100
Soil scientists	3,500	4,200	20.7	120
Mathematics occupations:				
Mathematicians	33,500	37,000	9.9	700
Statisticians	23,000	31,100	35.2	800
Physical scientists:				
Astronomers.	2,000	2,100	5.0	30
Chemists.	143,000	178,000	24.0	3,200
Physicists	44,000	48,000	8.9	700
Other scientific and technical occupations:				
Broadcast technicians. . . .	40,000	N/A	N/A	N/A
Drafters	296,000	367,000	24.0	5,100
Engineering and science technicians.	600,000	760,000	25.1	10,500
Food technologists	15,000	17,000	12.0	350
Surveyors and surveying technicians.	62,000	74,000	20.0	1,300
Mechanics and repairers:				
Telephone craft occupations:				
Central office craft occupations	135,000	130,000	-3.7	1,400
Central office equipment installers	21,400	18,000	-15.9	200
Line installers and cable splicers	59,000	60,000	2.1	500
Telephone and PBX installers and repairers	115,000	135,000	17.5	1,300

Employment, 1978 and 1990 (projected), and average annual
openings, by occupation, 1978-1990 — Continued

Occupation	Estimated employment, 1978	Projected employment 1990	Percent change, 1978 - 1990	Annual average openings
Other mechanics & repairers:				
Air-conditioning, refrigeration and heating mechanics.	210,000	245,000	16.7	5,300
Appliance repairers	145,000	180,000	24.1	4,000
Automobile body repairers	185,000	235,000	28.0	3,500
Automobile mechanics . .	860,000	1,060,000	22.7	21,000
Boat engine mechanics . . .	20,000	24,000	23.9	600
Bowling-pin machine mechanics	6,200	N/A	N/A	N/A
Business machine repairers	63,000	98,000	56.0	1,250
Computer service technicians.	63,000	121,000	92.5	600
Electric sign repairers. . . .	15,000	18,000	20.0	400
Farm equipment mechanics	62,000	77,000	24.2	2,200
Furniture upholsterers . . .	29,000	29,000	0	1,100
Industrial machinery repairers	655,000	1,085,000	66.0	22,000
Jewelers	32,000	N/A	N/A	N/A
Locksmiths	15,000	N/A	N/A	N/A
Maintenance electricians.	300,000	385,000	28.3	8,500
Motorcycle mechanics . . .	13,000	N/A	N/A	N/A
Piano and organ tuners and repairers.	8,000	8,800	10.0	600
Shoe repairers	22,000	21,000	-4.5	1,700
Television and radio service technicians	131,000	166,000	26.7	3,200
Truck and bus mechanics	165,000	210,000	27.0	3,500
Vending machine mechanics	23,000	N/A	N/A	N/A
Watch repairers	19,000	N/A	N/A	N/A
Health occupations:				
Dental occupations:				
Dentists	120,000	155,000	29.2	2,500
Dental assistants.	150,000	225,000	50.0	4,700
Dental hygienists	35,000	65,000	85.7	3,500
Dental laboratory technicians.	47,000	70,000	48.9	900
Medical practitioners:				
Chiropractors	18,000	21,000	17.2	1,250
Optometrists.	21,000	26,000	25.2	1,100
Physicians and osteo- pathic physicians	405,000	560,000	38.1	6,000
Podiatrists	8,100	12,500	53.7	250
Veterinarians	33,500	45,000	35.6	700

Employment, 1978 and 1990 (projected), and average annual openings, by occupation, 1978-1990 — Continued

Occupation	Estimated employment, 1978	Projected employment 1990	Percent change, 1978 - 1990	Annual average openings
Medical technologist, technician, and assistant occupations:				
Electrocardiograph technicians.	20,000	N/A	N/A	N/A
Electroencephalographic technologists and technicians.	7,000	10,500	49.9	200
Emergency medical technicians.	115,000	N/A	N/A	N/A
Medical laboratory workers.	210,000	265,000	26.2	10,200
Medical record technicians and clerks	50,000	65,000	30.0	3,600
Operating room technicians.	35,000	53,000	49.9	1,200
Optometric assistants. . . .	15,000	21,500	42.4	700
Radiologic (X-ray) technologists.	100,000	140,000	40.0	5,700
Respiratory therapy workers.	50,000	77,500	55.0	2,700
Nursing occupations:				
Registered nurses	1,060,000	1,570,000	49.6	42,000
Licensed practical nurses.	518,000	840,000	62.2	34,000
Nursing aides, orderlies, and attendants.	1,037,000	1,575,000	52.0	49,000
Therapy and rehabilitation occupations:				
Occupational therapists.	15,000	30,000	100.0	1,200
Occupational therapy assistants.	10,000	15,000	50.0	700
Physical therapists	30,000	45,000	50.0	1,400
Physical therapist assistants and aides	12,500	15,000	20.0	200
Speech pathologists and audiologists	32,000	60,000	87.5	1,600
Other health occupations:				
Dietitians.	35,000	50,000	42.9	2,000
Dispensing opticians	17,600	24,300	38.1	600
Health services administrators	180,000	282,000	57.1	9,900
Medical record administrators	12,500	15,000	20.0	700
Pharmacists	135,000	185,000	37.0	3,600
Social scientists:				
Anthropologists	7,000	8,600	23.1	200
Economists	130,000	183,000	39.2	3,500
Geographers	10,000	12,300	22.6	300
Historians	23,000	23,000	0.0	700

Employment, 1978 and 1990 (projected), and average annual
openings, by occupation, 1978-1990 — Continued

Occupation	Estimated employment, 1978	Projected employment 1990	Percent change, 1978 - 1990	Annual average openings
Political scientists	14,000	16,100	13.8	350
Psychologists	130,000	171,000	32.1	3,200
Sociologists	19,000	20,700	8.1	500
Social service occupations:				
Counseling occupations:				
School counselors	45,000	50,000	11.1	1,300
Employment counselors	6,100	N/A	N/A	N/A
Rehabilitation counselors	19,000	N/A	N/A	N/A
College career planning and placement counselors	5,000	N/A	N/A	N/A
Other social service occupations:				
Cooperative extension service workers	16,000	18,000	12.5	475
Homemaker-home health aides	110,000	185,000	70.0	29,000
Social service aides	134,000	160,000	18.3	5,500
Social workers.	385,000	475,000	24.2	14,000
Performing arts, design, and communications occupations:				
Performing artists:				
Actors and actresses	13,400	18,000	34.3	450
Dancers.	8,000	11,000	37.5	300
Musicians.	127,000	177,000	39.4	4,700
Singers	22,000	31,000	40.9	800
Design occupations:				
Architects	54,000	77,000	42.6	2,100
Display workers.	44,000	59,000	35.3	2,000
Floral designers	56,000	76,000	35.2	2,500
Industrial designers	13,000	15,300	17.5	350
Interior designers	79,000	95,000	20.9	2,200
Landscape architects	14,000	20,500	45.8	550
Photographers.	93,000	107,000	15.0	2,700
Communications occupations:				
Newspaper reporters	45,000	53,000	19.6	1,700
Public relations workers.	131,000	163,000	24.4	4,900
Radio and television announcers.	27,000	33,500	22.2	350
Technical writers	24,000	N/A	N/A	N/A

SOURCE: *Occupational Projections and Training Data,* (Washington DC: U.S. Department of Labor, Bureau of Labor Statistics, 1980), 83-91.

Appendix B
RESUMES

The following resume examples represent the five most common types of resumes: traditional chronological, improved chronological, combination, functional, and resume letter. The same fictitious individual is used in order to demonstrate how one person's qualifications can be presented in these different formats.

The *traditional chronological resume* includes a hodge-podge of information on the individual's history. Chronology is the guiding organizational principle for this resume. It tends to display the individual's weaknesses rather than strengths. For example, it lacks a job objective, includes such negatives as "divorced," "terminated," and "bartender." The usual statistics on height, weight, birth, and health do not enhance this resume. Hobbies are irrelevant, and references may be in for a surprise when the employer calls them unexpectedly.

Subsequent resume examples follow key organizational principles discussed in Chapter Eight: focus on an objective; state most important information first; include only information strengthening the objective; and layout is attractive and eye pleasing.

The *improved chronological resume* stresses skills and accomplishments but organizes them chronologically. A functional skills vocabulary is used for summarizing each position. Inclusive dates are placed at the end of each position summary, because they are the least important consideration but employers expect dates nonetheless.

The *combination resume* stresses skills and accomplishments ("Areas of Effectiveness") in relation to an objective as well as includes a chronological work history section. A personal statement appears in order to give the resume a distinctive personal quality. A second page, "Supplemental Information," is attached to further strengthen the major thrust of the resume as well as provide more specific content for the functional skills and work history categories.

Functional resumes stress the job objective, education, skills, and accomplishments. Work history is purposefully absent because in most cases the person using this type of resume has little job-related experience. Education is normally placed immediately after the objective for similar reasons — educational experience is more relevant to the objective than work-related experience.

The *resume letter* targets a particular position by stressing one's skills and accomplishments in direct relation to an employer's position. This is a good device to use if your general resume does not specifically address an employer's needs. It is a good way to create flexibility in your job search campaign. However, if an employer requests a resume, you should send one accompanied by a cover letter.

For examples of other resumes, both typeset and typewriter produced in different formats, see *High Impact Resumes and Letters* (Krannich and Banis, 1982: 113-118).

Traditional Chronological Resume

```
                              RESUME

James C. Astor                          Weight:  190 lbs.
4921 Tyler Drive                        Height:  6'0"
Washington, D.C. 20201                    Born:  June 2, 1947
                                        Health:  Good
                               Marital Status:  Divorced

EDUCATION

   1976-1977:  M.A., Vocational Counseling, Virginia Commonwealth University,
               Richmond, Virginia.
   1965-1969:  B.A., Psychology, Roanoke College, Salem, Virginia.
   1961-1965:  High School Diploma, Richmond Community High School, Richmond,
               Virginia.

WORK EXPERIENCE

   6/13/77 to 2/22/82:  Supervisory Trainer, GS-12, U.S. Department of Labor,
        Washington, D.C.  Responsible for all aspects of training.  Terminated
        because of budget cuts.
   9/10/75 to 11/21/76:  Bartender, Johnnie's Disco, Richmond, Virginia.
        Part-time while attending college.
   4/3/73 to 6/2/75:  Counselor, Virginia Employment Commission, Richmond,
        Virginia.  Responsible for interviewing unemployed for jobs.  Resigned
        to work full-time on Master's degree.
   8/15/70 to 6/15/72:  Guidance counselor and teacher, Petersburg Junior High
        School, Petersburg, Virginia.
   2/11/68 to 10/6/68:  Cook and Waiter, Big Mama's Pizza Parlor, Roanoke,
        Virginia.  Part-time while attending college.

PROFESSIONAL AFFILIATIONS

   American Personnel and Guidance Association
   American Society for Training and Development
   Personnel Management Association
   Phi Delta Pi

HOBBIES

   I like to play tennis, bicycle, and hike.

REFERENCES

   David Ryan, Chief, Training Division, U.S. Department of Labor, Washington,
        D.C. 20012, (212)735-0121.
   Dr. Sara Thomas, Professor, Department of Psychology, George Washington
        University, Washington, D.C. 20030, (201)621-4545.
   Thomas V. Grant, Area Manager, Virginia Employment Commission, Richmond,
        Virginia 26412, (804)261-4089.
```

Improved Chronological Resume

JAMES C. ASTOR

4921 Tyler Drive
Washington, D.C. 20011   212/422-8764

OBJECTIVE: A training and counseling position with a computer firm,
where strong administrative, communication, and planning
abilities will be used for improving the work performance
and job satisfaction of employees.

EXPERIENCE: U.S. Department of Labor, Washington, D.C.
Planned and organized counseling programs for 5,000 employees.
Developed training manuals and conducted workshops on interpersonal skills, stress management, and career planning; resulted
in a 50 percent decrease in absenteeism. Supervised team of
five instructors and counselors. Conducted individual counseling and referrals to community organizations. Advised government agencies and private firms on establishing in-house
employee counseling and career development programs. Consis-
tently evaluated as outstanding by supervisors and workshop
participants. 1977 to present.

Virginia Employment Commission, Richmond, Virginia.
Conducted all aspects of employment counseling. Interviewed,
screened, and counseled 2,500 jobseekers. Referred clients
to employers and other agencies. Coordinated job vacancy and
training information for businesses, industries, and schools.
Reorganized interviewing and screening processes which
improved the efficiency of operations by 50 percent. Cited
in annual evaluation for "outstanding contributions to improving relations with employers and clients." 1973-1975.

Petersburg Junior High School, Petersburg, Virginia.
Guidance counselor for 800 students. Developed program of
individualized and group counseling. Taught special social
science classes for socially maladjusted and slow learners.
1970-1972.

EDUCATION: M.A., Vocational Counseling, Virginia Commonwealth University,
Richmond, Virginia, 1977.

B.A., Psychology, Roanoke College, Salem, Virginia, 1969.

REFERENCES: Available upon request.

Combination Resume

———————————— JAMES C. ASTOR ————————————

4921 Tyler Drive
Washington, D.C. 20011   212/422-8764

OBJECTIVE: A training and counseling position with a computer firm,
                    where strong administrative, communication, and planning
                    abilities will be used for improving the work performance
                    and job satisfaction of employees.

AREAS OF EFFECTIVENESS

ADMINISTRATION: Supervised instructors and counselors. Coordinated job
                    vacancy and training information for businesses, indus-
                    tries, and schools.

COMMUNICATION: Conducted over 100 workshops on interpersonal skills,
                    stress management, and career planning. Frequent guest
                    speaker to various agencies and private firms. Experi-
                    enced writer of training manuals and public relations
                    materials.

PLANNING: Planned and developed counseling programs for 5,000
                    employees. Reorganized interviewing and screening
                    processes for public employment agency. Developed
                    program of individualized and group counseling for
                    community school.

WORK HISTORY: Supervisory Trainer, U.S. Department of Labor, Washington,
                    D.C., 1977 to present.

                    Counselor, Virginia Employment Commission, Richmond,
                    Virginia, 1973-1975.

                    Guidance counselor and teacher, Petersburg Junior High
                    School, Petersburg, Virginia 1970-1972.

EDUCATION: M.A., Vocational Counseling, Virginia Commonwealth
                    University, Richmond, Virginia, 1977.

                    B.A., Psychology, Roanoke College, Salem, Virginia, 1969.

PERSONAL: Enjoy challenges and working with people . . . interested
                    in productivity . . . willing to relocate and travel.

Combination Resume – continued

```
SUPPLEMENTAL INFORMATION                              JAMES C. ASTOR
```

Continuing Education and Training

* Completed 12 semester hours of computer science courses.
* Attended several workshops during past three years on employee counseling and administrative methods:

> "Career Development for Technical Personnel," Professional
> Management Association, 3 days, 1980.
>
> "Effective Supervisory Methods for Training Directors,"
> National Training Associates, 3 days, 1982.
>
> "Training the Trainer," American Society for Training and
> Development, 3 days, 1981.
>
> "Time Management," U.S. Department of Labor, 3 days, 1980.
>
> "Career Development for Technical Personnel," Professional
> Management Associates, 3 days, 1980.
>
> "Counseling the Absentee Employee," American Management
> Associations, 3 days, 1979.

Training Manuals Developed

* "Managing Employee Stress," U.S. Department of Labor, 1981.
* "Effective Interpersonal Communication in the Workplace," U.S.
  Department of Labor, 1979.
* "Planning Careers Within the Organization," U.S. Department of Labor,
  1980.

Research Projects Completed

* "Employee Counseling Programs for Technical Personnel," U.S. Department
  of Labor, 1981. Incorporated into agency report on "New Directions in
  Employee Counseling."
* "Developing Training Programs for Problem Employees," M.A. thesis,
  Virginia Commonwealth University, 1977.

Professional Affiliations

* American Personnel and Guidance Association
* American Society for Training and Development
* Personnel Management Association

Educational Highlights

* Completing Ph.D. in Industrial Psychology, George Washington University,
  Washington, D.C., 1984.
* Earned 4.0/4.0 grade point average as graduate student.

Functional Resume

JAMES C. ASTOR

4921 Tyler Drive	Washington, D.C. 20011	212/422-8764

OBJECTIVE: A training and counseling position with a computer firm, where strong administrative, communication, and planning abilities will be used for improving the work performance and job satisfaction of employees.

EDUCATION: Ph.D. in process, Industrial Psychology, George Washington University, Washington, D.C.

M.A., Vocational Counseling, Virginia Commonwealth University, Richmond, Virginia, 1977.

B.A., Psychology, Roanoke College, Salem, Virginia, 1969.

AREAS OF EFFECTIVENESS:

Administration

Supervised instructors and counselors. Coordinated job vacancy and training information for businesses, industries, and schools.

Communication

Conducted over 100 workshops on interpersonal skills, stress management, and career planning. Frequent guest speaker to various agencies and private firms. Experienced writer of training manuals and public relations materials.

Planning

Planned and developed counseling programs for 5,000 employees. Reorganized interviewing and screening processes for public employment agency. Developed program of individualized and group counseling for community school.

PERSONAL: Enjoy challenges and working with people . . . interested in productivity . . . willing to relocate and travel.

REFERENCES: Available upon request.

Resume Letter

4921 Tyler Drive
Washington, D.C. 20011
March 15, 1982

Doris Stevens
STR Corporation
179 South Trail
Rockville, Maryland 21101

Dear Ms. Stevens:

STR Corporation is one of the most dynamic computer companies in the nation. In addition to being a leader in the field of small business computers, STR has a progressive employee training and development program which could very well become a model for other organizations. This is the type of organization I am interested in joining.

I am seeking a training position with a computer firm which would utilize my administrative, communication, and planning abilities to develop effective training and counseling programs. My experience includes:

<u>Administration</u>: Supervised instructors and counselors. Coordinated job vacancy and training information for businesses, industries, and schools.

<u>Communication</u>: Conducted over 100 workshops on interpersonal skills, stress management, and career planning. Frequent guest speaker to various agencies and private firms. Experienced writer of training manuals and public relations materials.

<u>Planning</u>: Planned and developed counseling programs for 5,000 employees. Reorganized interviewing and screening processes for public employment agency. Developed program of individualized and group counseling for community school.

In addition, I am completing my Ph.D. in industrial psychology with emphasis on developing training and counseling programs for technical personnel.

Could we meet to discuss your program as well as how my experience might relate to your needs? I will call your office on Tuesday morning, March 23, to arrange a convenient time to meet with you.

I especially want to show you a model employee counseling and career development program I recently developed. Perhaps you may find it useful for your work with STR.

Sincerely yours,

James C. Astor

Appendix C
LETTERS

The following examples cover the major types of letters you will write during your job search campaign. An example of a resume letter is not included because it is a subject of Appendix B.

The *cover letter* is in response to a classified ad. Following the principle of providing "cover" for advertising the resume, this letter mainly highlights interest. The writer takes the initiative to contact the employer by requesting an interview.

The *approach letters* represent two different situations. In the first letter the writer uses a referral to introduce herself. In the second example the writer introduces herself without prior contacts — the "cold turkey" approach. The writers in both examples are careful not to suggest that they are looking for a job through this individual. Instead, they want information and advice.

The *thank-you letters* are written for several occasions. The four examples include post-job interview, post-informational interview, job rejection, and job offer acceptance situations. In each case, the thank-you letter should communicate enthusiasm and thoughtfulness. When you write such letters, avoid the standard thank-you language. Make your letter express *you* rather than a model of a good letter.

You will find other occasions for writing letters which are not included with our examples. These might include sending a thank-you letter in response to information received over the telephone or through the mail or when declining a job offer or terminating employment for another job (Krannich and Banis, 1982: 130-131). The principles of good letter writing also pertain to these situations.

Cover Letter

2842 South Plaza
Chicago, Illinois 60228
March 12, 1982

David C. Johnson
Director of Personnel
Bank of Chicago
490 Michigan Avenue
Chicago, Illinois 60222

Dear Mr. Johnson:

The accompanying resume is in response to your listing in the Chicago Tribune for a loan officer.

I am especially interested in this position because my experience with the Small Business Administration has prepared me for understanding the financial needs and problems of the business community from the perspectives of both lenders and borrowers. I wish to use this experience with a growing and community-conscious bank such as yours.

I would appreciate an opportunity to meet with you to discuss how my experience will best meet your needs. My ideas on how to improve small business financing may be of particular interest to you. Therefore, I will call your office on the morning of March 17 to inquire if a meeting can be scheduled at a convenient time.

I look forward to meeting you.

Sincerely yours,

Joyce Pitman

Approach Letter: Referral

821 Stevens Points
Boston, MA 01990
April 14, 1982

Terri Fulton
Director of Personnel
TRS Corporation
6311 W. Dover
Boston, MA 01991

Dear Ms. Fulton:

   Alice O'Brien suggested that I contact you about my
interest in personnel management. She said you are one of
the best people to talk to in regard to careers in personnel.

   I am leaving government after seven years of increasingly
responsible experience in personnel. I am especially interested in working with a large private firm. However, before
I venture further into the job market, I want to benefit from
the experience and knowledge of others in the field who might
advise me on opportunities for someone with my qualifications.

   Perhaps we could meet briefly sometime during the next
two weeks to discuss my career plans. I have several questions
which I believe you could help clarify. I will call your office
on Tuesday, April 22, to schedule a meeting time.

   I look forward to discussing my plans with you.

                              Sincerely yours,

                              Katherine Kelly

Approach Letter: Cold Turkey

2189 West Church Street
New York, NY 10011
May 3, 1982

Patricia Dotson, Director
Northeast Association for
   the Elderly
9930 Jefferson Street
New York, NY 10013

Dear Ms. Dotson:

I have been impressed with your work with the elderly. Your organization takes a community perspective in trying to integrate the concerns of the elderly with those of other community groups. Perhaps other organizations will soon follow your lead.

I am anxious to meet you and learn more about your work. My background with the city Volunteer Services Program involved frequent contact with elderly volunteers. From this experience I decided I preferred working primarily with the elderly.

However, before I pursue my interest further, I need to talk to people with experience in gerontology. In particular, I would like to know more about careers with the elderly as well as how my background might best be used in the field of gerontology.

I am hoping you can assist me in this matter. I would like to meet with you briefly to discuss several of my concerns. I will call next week to see if your schedule permits such a meeting.

I look forward to meeting you.

Sincerely,

Carol Timms

Thank-You Letter: Post-Informational Interview

9910 Thompson Drive
Cleveland, Ohio 43382
June 21, 1982

Jane Evans, Director
Evans Finance Corporation
2122 Forman Street
Cleveland, Ohio 43380

Dear Ms. Evans:

Your advice was most helpful in clarifying my
questions on careers in finance. I am now reworking
my resume and have included many of your thoughtful
suggestions. I will send you a copy next week.

Thanks so much for taking time from your busy
schedule to see me. I will keep in contact and
follow through on your suggestion to see Sarah Cook
about opportunities with the Cleveland-Akron Finance
Company.

Sincerely,

Daryl Haines

Thank-You Letter: Post-Job Interview

```
                              2962 Forrest Drive
                              Denver, Colorado 82171
                              May 28, 1982


Thomas F. Harris
Director, Personnel Department
Coastal Products Incorporated
7229 Lakewood Drive
Denver, Colorado 82170

Dear Mr. Harris:

     Thank you again for the opportunity to interview for the
marketing position.  I appreciated your hospitality and enjoyed
meeting you and members of your staff.

     The interview convinced me of how compatible my background,
interests, and skills are with the goals of Coastal Products
Incorporated.  My prior marketing experience with the Department
of Commerce has prepared me to take a major role in developing
both domestic and international marketing strategies.  I am
confident my work for you will result in increased profits
within the first two years.

     For more information on the new product promotion program
I mentioned, call David Garrett at the Department of Commerce;
his number is 202/726-0132.  I talked to Dave this morning and
mentioned your interest in this program.

     I look forward to meeting you again.

                              Sincerely,


                              Tim Potter
```

Thank-You Letter: Job Rejection

```
                                    564 Court Street
                                    St. Louis, MO 53167
                                    April 29, 1982



Ralph Ullman, President
S. T. Ayer Corporation
6921 Southern Blvd.
St. Louis, MO 53163

Dear Mr. Ullman:

    I appreciated your consideration for the Research Associate
position. While I am disappointed in not being selected, I
learned a great deal about your corporation, and I enjoyed
meeting with you and your staff.  I felt particularly good about
the professional manner in which you conducted the interview.

    Please keep me in mind for future consideration.  I have a
strong interest in your company.  I believe we would work well
together.  I will be closely following the progress of your
company over the coming months.  Perhaps we will be in touch
with each other at some later date.

    Best wishes.

                            Sincerely,


                            Martin Tollins
```

Thank-You Letter: Job Offer Acceptance

7694 James Court
San Francisco, CA 94826
June 7, 1982

Judith Greene
Vice President
West Coast Airlines
2400 Van Ness
San Francisco, CA 94829

Dear Ms. Greene:

I am pleased to accept your offer, and I am looking forward to joining you and your staff next month.

The customer relations position is ideally suited to my background and interests. I assure you I will give you by best effort in making this an effective position within your company.

I understand I will begin work on July 1. If, in the meantime, I need to complete any paper work or take care of any other matters, please contact me.

I enjoyed meeting with you and your staff and appreciated the professional manner in which the hiring was conducted.

Sincerely,

Joan Kitner

Appendix D
RE-CAREERING RESOURCES

During the past 10 years hundreds of books have been written to help individuals find employment. While many of these books are excellent, others are of questionable quality. This section lists some of the better quality books.

The following books represent a variety of resources available on how to find employment, change careers, and function effectively in the world of work. The topics correspond to most of the re-careering subjects addressed in this book. Many of the books are found in libraries or bookstores. Others may be difficult to find. For your convenience, you can order many of the titles directly from Impact Publications:10655 Big Oak Circle, Manassas, Virginia 22111, Tel. 703/361-7300. Order information is included at the end of this book.

1. **FUTURE JOBS AND CAREERS**

Applegath, John, *Working Free: Practical Alternatives to the 9 to 5 Job* (New York: AMACOM, 1982).
Drucker, Peter, *Managing in Turbulent Times* (New York: Harper and Row, 1980).
Feingold, Norman and Norma Reno Miller, *Emerging Careers: New Occupations for the Year 2000 and Beyond* (Garrett Park, MD: Garrett Park Press, 1983).

Ferguson, Marilyn, *The Acquarian Conspiracy: Personal and Social Transformation in the 1980s* (Los Angeles: J.P. Tarcher, 1980).

Kennedy, Marilyn, *Career Knockouts: How to Battle Back* (Chicago: Follett Publishing Co., 1980).

Krannich, Ronald L., *Re-Careering in Turbulent Times* (Manassas, VA: Impact Publications, 1983).

Naisbitt, John, *Megatrends: Ten New Directions Transforming Our Lives* (New York: Warner Books, 1982).

Toffler, Alvin, *The Third Wave* (New York: Bantam Books, 1980).

2. JOB TRAINING AND EMPLOYMENT FIELDS

Feingold, S. Norman and Glenda Hansard-Winkler, *900,000 Plus Jobs Annually: Published Sources of Employment Listings* (Garrett Park MD: Garrett Park Press, 1982).

Gates, Anita, *90 Most Promising Careers for the 80's* (New York: Monarch Press, 1981).

Hegyi, Albert P., *Should You Get an MBA?* (Englewood Cliffs, NJ: Prentice-Hall, 1982).

Heller, Dorothy Kunkin and June Bower, *The Woman's Computer Book* (Washington, DC: Acropolis Books, 1983).

Mainstream Access Inc., *The Banking Job Finder* (Englewood Cliffs, NJ: Prentice-Hall, 1981).

Mainstream Access Inc., *The Data Processing/Information Technology Job Finder* (Englewood Cliffs, NJ: Prentice-Hall, 1981).

Mainstream Access Inc., *The Energy Job Finder* (Englewood Cliffs, NJ: Prentice-Hall, 1981).

Mainstream Access Inc., *The Insurance Job Finder* (Englewood Cliffs, NJ: Prentice-Hall, 1982).

Mainstream Access Inc., *The Public Relations Job Finder* (Englewood Cliffs, NJ: Prentice-Hall, 1981).

Mainstream Access Inc. *The Publishing Job Finder* (Englewood Cliffs, NJ: Prentice-Hall, 1981).

Mainstream Access, *The Real Estate Job Finder* (Englewood Cliffs, NJ: Prentice-Hall, 1981).

Maresca, Carmela C., *Careers in Marketing: A Woman's Guide* (Englewood Cliffs, NJ: Prentice-Hall, 1982).

Mullins, Carolyn J. and Thomas W. West, *The Office Automation Primer: Harnessing Information Technologies for Greater Productivity* (Englewood Cliffs, NJ: Prentice-Hall, 1982).

Pickens, Judy E., *The Freelancer's Handbook* (Englewood Cliffs, NJ: Prentice-Hall, 1981).

Sessions, Laura Steibel, *How to Break into Data Processing* (Englewood Cliffs, NJ: Prentice-Hall, 1982).

Ulrich, Heinz and J. Robert Connor, *The National Job-Finding Guide* (Garden City, NY: Doubleday & Co., 1981).

Yeomans, William N., *Jobs '82-'83* (New York: Perigee/Putnam's, 1982).

3. JOB STRESS AND BURNOUT

Cooper, Cary L., *The Stress Check: Coping With the Stresses of Life and Work* (Englewood Cliffs, NJ: Prentice-Hall, 1980).

Greenberg, Herbert M., *Coping With Job Stress: A Guide for All Employers and Employees* (Englewood Cliffs, NJ: Prentice-Hall, 1980).

McGuigan, F.J., *Calm Down: A Guide to Stress and Tension Control* (Englewood Cliffs, NJ: Prentice-Hall, 1981).

Leatz, Christine Ann, *Unwinding: How to Turn Stress into Positive Energy* (Englewood Cliffs, NJ: Prentice-Hall, 1981).

Maslach, Christina, *Burnout — The Cost of Caring* (Englewood Cliffs, NJ: Prentice-Hall, 1982).

Palmer, Stuart, *Role Stress: How to Beat Everyday Tension* (Englewood Cliffs, NJ: Prentice-Hall, 1981).

Welch, I. David, Donald C. Mederos and George A. Tate, *Beyond Burnout: How to Prevent and Reverse the Effects of Stress on the Job* (Englewood Cliffs, NJ: Prentice-Hall, 1982).

4. TERMINATION

Coulson, Robert, *The Termination Handbook* (New York: The Free Press, 1981).

Cowle, Jerry, *How to Survive Getting Fired — And Win!* (Chicago: Follett Publishing Co., 1979).

May, John, *The RIF Survival Handbook* (Washington, DC: Tilden Press, 1982).

Morin, William J. and Lyle Yorks, *Outplacement Techniques: A Positive Approach to Terminating Employees* (New York: AMACOM, 1982).

Peskin, Dean B., *A Job Loss Survival Manual* (New York: AMACOM, 1981).

Preston, Paul, *Employer's Guide to Hiring and Firing: Strategies, Tactics & Legal Considerations* (Englewood Cliffs, NJ: Prentice-Hall, 1982).

5. GENERAL CAREER AND LIFE PLANNING

Billingsley, Edmond, *Career Planning and Job Hunting for Today's Student: The Nonjob Interview Approach* (Santa Monica, CA: Goodyear Publishing Co., Inc. 1978).

Bolles, Richard Nelson, *The Three Boxes of Life: And How to Get Out of Them* (Berkeley, CA: Ten Speed Press, 1982).

Bolles, Richard Nelson, *What Color is Your Parachute?* (Berkeley, CA: Ten Speed Press, 1982).

Bolton, Robert H., *People Skills: How to Assert Yourself, Listen to Others, and Resolve Conflicts* (Englewood Cliffs, NJ: Prentice-Hall, 1979).

Boros, James M. and Robert Parkinson, *How to Get a Fast Start in Today's Job Market* (Englewood Cliffs, NJ: Prentice-Hall, 1982).

Crystal, John C. and Richard N. Bolles, *Where Do I Go From Here With My Life?* (Berkeley, CA: Ten Speed Press, 1974).

Djeddah, Eli, *Moving Up* (Berkeley, CA: Ten Speed Press, 1978).

Eisen, Jeffrey, *Get the Right Job Now!* (Philadelphia and New York: J. B. Lippincott Co., 1978).

Figgins, Ross, *The Job Game: Playing to Win* (Englewood Cliffs, NJ: Prentice-Hall, 1980).

Figler, Howard, *The Complete Job-Search Handbook* (New York: Holt, Rinehart, and Winston, 1979).

Fox, Marcia R., *Put Your Degree to Work* (New York: W.W. Norton Co., 1979).

Germann, Richard and Peter Arnold, *Bernard Haldane Associates' Job & Career Building* (New York: Harper and Row, 1980).

Haldane, Bernard, *How to Make a Habit of Success* (Washington, DC: Acropolis Books Ltd., 1960).

Haldane, Bernard, and Jean, and Lowell Martin, *The Young People's Job Finding Guide* (Washington, DC: Acropolis Books Ltd., 1981).

Hecklinger, Fred J. and Bernadette M. Curtin, *Training for Life: A Practical Guide to Career and Life Planning* (Dubuque, IA: Kendall/Hunt Publishing Co., 1982).

Irish, Richard K., *Go Hire Yourself an Employer* (Garden City, NY: Anchor Press, 1978).

Jackson, Tom, *Guerrilla Tactics in the Job Market* (New York: Bantam Books, 1980).

Jackson, Tom and Davidyne Mayleas, *The Hidden Job Market of the 80's* (New York: Quadrangle/The New York Times Book Co., 1980).

Jameson, Robert, *The Professional Job Changing System* (Parsippany, NJ: Performance Dynamics, 1978).

Kline, Linda and Lloyd L. Feinstein, *Career Changing: The Worry-Free Guide* (Boston: Little, Brown, and Co., 1982).

Lathrop, Richard, *The Job Market* (Washington, DC: The National Center for Job-Market Studies, 1978).

Lathrop, Richard, *Who's Hiring Who* (Berkeley, CA: Ten Speed Press, 1977).

Management Development Institute, *Career Dimensions I and II* (Croton-on-Hudson, NY: General Electric Company, 1982).

Mitchell, Joyce Slayton Mitchell, *Stopout: Working Ways to Learn* (Garrett Park, MD: Garrett Park Press, 1978).

Noer, David, *How to Beat the Employment Game* (Berkeley, CA: Ten Speed Press, 1975).

Petit, Ron, *The Career Connection* (Harrisonburg, VA: Professional Development Services, 1982).

Rogers, Edward J., *Getting Hired* (Englewood Cliffs, NJ: Prentice-Hall, 1982).

Souerwine, Andrew H., *Career Strategies: Planning for Personal Achievement* (New York: AMACOM, 1978).

Stanat, Kirby W., *Job Hunting Secrets & Tactics* (Chicago: Follett Publishing Co., 1977).

Thain, Richard J., *The Mid-Career Manual* (Englewood Cliffs, NJ: Prentice-Hall, 1982).

6.   SKILLS AND ASSESSMENT TECHNIQUES

Bolles, Richard Nelson, *The Quick Job-Hunting Map* (Berkeley, CA: Ten Speed Press, 1979).

Holland, John L., *Making Vocational Choices: A Theory of Careers* (Englewood Cliffs, NJ: Prentice-Hall, Inc., 1973).

Miller, Arthur F. and Ralph T. Mattson, *The Truth About You: Discover What You Should Be Doing With Your Life* (Tappan, NJ: Fleming H. Revell Co., 1977).

Pearson, Henry G., *Your Hidden Skills: Clues to Careers and*

Future Pursuits (Wayland, MA: Mowry Press, 1981).

Scheele, Adele, *Skills for Success: A Guide to the Top For Men and Women* (New York: Ballantine Books, 1979).

Sjogren, D.D., *Occupationally Transferable Skills and Characteristics: Review of Literature and Research* (Columbus, OH: The National Center for Research in Vocational Education, 1977).

Wiant, A.A., *Occupational Change and Transferable Skills: The Employer's Viewpoint* (Columbus, OH: The National Center for Research in Vocational Education, 1980).

7. ORGANIZING TIME

Lakein, Alan, *How to Get Control of Your Time and Life* (New York: Signet Books, 1973).

LeBoeuf, Michael, *Working Smart* (New York: Warner Books, 1979).

Lebov, Myrna, *Practical Tools and Techniques for Managing Time* (Englewood Cliffs, NJ: Prentice-Hall, 1982).

MacKenzie, R. Alex, *The Time Trap* (New York: AMACOM, 1972).

Reynolds, Helen and Mary E. Tramel, *Executive Time Management: Getting 12 Hours Work Out of an 8-Hour Day* (Englewood Cliffs, NJ: Prentice-Hall, 1982).

Riley, Robert T., *How to Manage Your Time Successfully* (Dallas, TX: The Drawing Board, Inc. 1978).

8. RESUMES AND LETTERS

Beigeleisen, J. I., *Job Resumes: How to Write Them, How to Present Them, Preparing for Interviews* (New York: Grosset and Dunlap, 1976).

Dickhut, Harold, *The Professional Resume and Job Search Guide* (Chicago: Management Counselors, Inc. 1978).

Jackson, Tom, *The Perfect Resume* (Garden City, NJ: Anchor Books, 1981).

Krannich, Ronald L. and William J. Banis, *High Impact Resumes and Letters* (Manassas, VA: Impact Publications, 1982).

McLaughlin, John and Stephen Merman, *Writing a Job-Winning Resume* (Englewood Cliffs, NJ: Prentice-Hall, 1980).

Ulrich, Heinz, *How to Prepare Your Own High Intensity Re-*

sume (Englewood Cliffs, NJ: Prentice-Hall, 1982).

9. NETWORKING

Kleiman, Carol, *Women's Networks* (New York: Lippincott and Crowell Publishers, 1980).

Stern, Barbara B., *Is Networking For You: A Working Woman's Alternative to the Old Boy System* (Englewood Cliffs, NJ: Prentice-Hall, 1980).

Welsh, Mary Scott, *Networking: The Great New Way for Women to Get Ahead* (New York: Harcourt Brace Jovanovich, 1980).

10. JOB CLUBS

Azrin, Nathan H. and Victoria A. Besalel, *Job Club Counselor's Manual* (Baltimore, MD: University Park Press, 1980).

11. DRESS AND APPEARANCE

Molloy, John T., *Live For Success* (New York: William Morrow and Co., 1981).

Molloy, John T., *The Woman's Dress for Success Book* (New York: Warner Books, 1977).

Molloy, John T., *Dress for Success* (for men) (New York: Warner Books, 1975).

Thompson, Jacqueline (ed.), *Image Impact* (New York: A & W Publishers, Inc., 1981).

Wallach, Janet, *Working Wardrobe: Affordable Clothes That Work for You* (Washington, DC: Acropolis Books, 1981).

12. INTERVIEWING

The Catalyst Staff, *Marketing Yourself: The Catalyst Guide to Successful Resumes and Interviews* (New York: Bantam Books, 1981).

Einhorn, Lois J., Patricia Hayes Bradley, and John E. Baird, Jr., *Effective Employment Interviewing* (Glenview, IL: Scott, Foresman, and Co., 1982).

Genua, Robert L., *The Employer's Guide to Interviewing:*

Strategy and Tactics for Picking a Winner (Englewood Cliffs, NJ: Prentice-Hall, Inc., 1971).

Komar, John J., *The Interview Game: Winning Strategies of Job Seekers* (Chicago: Follett Publishing Co., 1979).

Krannich, Caryl Rae, *Interview for Success* (Manassas, VA: Impact Publications, 1982).

Merman, Stephen and John McLaughlin, *Out-Interviewing the Interviewer: The Job-Winning Script for Success* (Englewood Cliffs, NJ: Prentice-Hall, 1982).

Midley, H. Anthony, *Sweaty Palms: The Neglected Art of Being Interviewed* (Belmont, CA: Lifetime Learning Publications, 1978).

Robertson, Jason, *How to Win in a Job Interview* (Englewood Cliffs, NJ: Prentice-Hall, 1978).

13. SALARY NEGOTIATIONS

Chastain, Sherry, *Winning the Salary Game* (New York: John Wiley and Sons, Inc., 1980).

Harrop, David, *Paychecks: Who Makes What* (New York: Harper and Row, 1981).

Kennedy, Marilyn Moat, *Salary Strategies: Everything You Need to Know to Get the Salary You Want* (New York: Rawson Wade, 1982).

Wright, John W., *The American Almanac of Jobs and Salaries* (New York: Avon, 1982).

14. POLITICS

DuBrin, Andres J., *Winning at Office Politics* (New York: Van Nostrand Reinhold Co., 1978).

Kennedy, Marilyn Moat, *Office Politics* (Chicago: Follett Publishing Co., 1980).

15. COMMUNITIES

Bowman, Thomas F., George H. Giuliani, and M. Rondal Minge, *Finding Your Best Place to Live in America* (West Babylon, NY: Red Lion Books, 1981).

Boyer, Richard and David Savageau, *Places Rated Almanac: Your Guide to Finding the Best Places to Live in America*

(Chicago: Rand McNally, 1981).

Bernstein, Bruce and James Udell, *Places and Spaces: '82-'83 Housing Almanac* (New York: Grosset and Dunlap, 1982).

16. STARTING A BUSINESS

Bangs, David H. Jr., and William R. Osgood, *Business Planning Guide* (Portsmouth, NH: Upstart Publishing Co., Inc., 1979).

Brown, Deaver, *The Entrepreneur's Guide* (New York: Macmillan Publishing Co., 1980).

Feingold, Norman and Leonard Perlman, *Making It On Your Own* (Washington, DC: Acropolis Books, Ltd., 1981).

Feldstein, Stuart, *Home, Inc.* (New York: Grosset and Dunlap, 1981).

Gumpert, David E. and Jeffry A. Timmons, *The Insider's Guide to Small Business Resources* (New York: Doubleday, 1981).

Hower, Alice and Alfred Howard, *Turn Your Kitchen Into a Goldmine* (New York: Harper and Row, 1981).

Jackson, Stanley G., *How to Proceed in Business — Legally: The Entrepreneur's Preventive Law Guide,* Federal Edition (Englewood Cliffs, NJ: Prentice-Hall, 1982).

Mancuso, Joseph R., *How to Prepare and Present a Business Plan* (Englewood Cliffs, NJ: Prentice-Hall, 1982).

Morine, John, *Riding the Recession: How Your Business Can Prosper Despite Shrinking Markets, High Inflation, and the Up's and Down's of Today's Economy* (Englewood Cliffs, NJ: Prentice-Hall, 1982).

Pritchard, Robert and Bruce Bradway, *Strategic Planning and Control Techniques for Profit: A Handbook for Small Business Owners* (Englewood Cliffs, NJ: Prentice-Hall, 1982).

Simmons, James G., *Creative Business Financing: How to Make Your Best Deal When Negotiating Equipment Leases and Business Loans* (Englewood Cliffs, NJ: Prentice-Hall, 1982).

17. WOMEN

Catalyst, *What to Do With the Rest of Your Life: The Catalyst Career Guide for Women in the '80s* (New York:

Simon and Schuster, 1980).

Doss, Martha Merrill (ed.), *The Directory of Special Opportunities for Women* (Garrett Park, MD: Garrett Park Press, 1981).

Douglas, Leslie Stone, *Women in Business* (Englewood Cliffs, NJ: Prentice-Hall, 1982).

Landau, Suzanne and Geoffrey Bailey, *How Working Women Win Top Jobs: and Landau Strategy* (New York: Playboy Paperbacks, 1980).

Lee, Nancy, *Targeting the Top: Everything a Woman Needs to Know to Develop a Successful Career, in Business, Year After Year* (New York: Doubleday and Co., 1980).

McCaslin, Barbara S. and Patricia P. NcNamara, *Be Your Own Boss: A Woman's Guide to Planning and Running Her Business* (Englewood Cliffs, NJ: Prentice-Hall, 1980).

Mitchell, Charlene and Thomas Burdick, *The Competitive Edge: Success Strategies for Women Based on Studies by the Harvard Business School* (Washington, DC: Acropolis Books, 1983).

Mouat, Lucia, *Back to Business: A Woman's Guide to Reentering the Job Market* (New York: Signet/New American Library, Inc., 1980).

Petit, Ron, *Women and the Career Game* (Harrisonburg, VA: Professional Development Services, 1983).

Shields, Laurie, *Displaced Homemakers: Organizing for a New Life* (New York: McGraw-Hill Book Co., 1981).

18. MINORITIES

Cole, Katherine W. (ed.), *Minority Organizations: A National Directory* (Garrett Park, MD: Garrett Park Press, 1979).

Directory of Career Resources for Minorities (Santa Monica, CA: Ready Reference Press, 1980).

Johnson, Willis L. (ed.), *Directory of Special Programs for Minority Group Members: Career Information Services, Employment Skills Banks, Financial Aid Services —* Third Edition (Garrett Park, MD: Garrett Park Press, 1980).

Swann, Ruth V. (ed.), *Financial Aid for Minority Students* (Garrett Park, MD: Garrett Park Press, 1981).

19. EDUCATION

Furniss, W. Todd, *Reshaping Faculty Careers* (Washington, DC: American Council on Education, 1981).

Krannich, Ronald L. and William J. Banis *Moving Out of Education: The Educator's Guide to Career Management and Change* (Chesapeake, VA: Progressive Concepts Inc., 1981).

Miller, Anne, *Finding Career Alternatives for Teachers: A Step-by-Step Guide to Your New Career* (New York: Apple Publishing Co., 1979).

Miller, Jean M. and Georgianna M. Dickinson, *When Apples Ain't Enough* (Sacramento, CA: Jalmar Press, Inc., 1980).

Pollack, Sandy, *Alternative Careers for Teachers* (Harvard, MA: Harvard Common Press, 1979).

20. GOVERNMENT

Dumbaugh, Kerry and Gary Secota, *Capitol Jobs: An Insider's Guide to Finding a Job in Congress* (Washington, DC: Tilden Press, 1982).

Hawkins, James E., *The Uncle Sam Connection: An Insider's Guide to Federal Employment* (Chicago: Follett Publishing Co., 1978).

Krannich, Ronald L., *Moving Out of Government: A Guide to Surviving and Prospering in the 1980's* (Manassas, VA: Impact Publications, 1982).

Lauber, Daniel, *The Compleat Guide to Jobs in Planning and Public Administration* (Evanston, IL: Planning/Communications, 1982).

Petit, Ron, *From the Military to a Civilian Career* (Harrisonburg, VA: Professional Development Services, 1983).

Waelde, David, *How to Get a Federal Job or Survive a RIF* (Washington, DC: FEDHELP Publications, 1982).

Wood, Patricia B., *The 171 Workbook* (Washington, DC: Workbooks, Inc., 1979).

Zehring, John William, *Careers in State and Local Government* (Garrett Park, MD: Garrett Park Press, 1980).

21. INTERNATIONAL

Beckmann, David M. and Elizabeth Anne Donnelly, *The Over-*

seas List, Opportunities for Living and Working in Developing Countries (Minneapolis: Augsburg Publishing House, 1979).

Kocher, Eric, *International Jobs: Where They Are, How to Get Them* (Reading, MA: Addison-Wesley, 1979).

Phelps, Cathy S., *The Guide to Moving Overseas* (Lemont, PA: Guide, 1978).

Sheehan, Gerard F. (ed.), *Careers in International Affairs* (Washington, DC: Georgetown University, 1982).

SUBJECT INDEX

AUTHOR INDEX

289

THE AUTHOR

Ronald L. Krannich is President of Development Concepts Incorporated, a career development, management, and publishing firm. He has a Ph.D. in political science and public administration. A former university professor, he is a noted lecturer, consultant, and writer. He has conducted workshops and seminars on career development, cutback management, and outplacement and has completed several research projects in the United States and abroad. Widely published in major journals, his most recent books include *Moving Out of Education: The Educator's Guide to Career Management and Change, High Impact Resumes and Letters,* and *Moving Out of Government: A Guide to Surviving and Prospering in the 1980's.* He can be contacted through the publisher or through Educational Services Group, 5201 Leesburg Pike, Suite 900, Falls Church, VA 22041, Tel. 703/379-2900.

ORDER FORM

NAME _____

ADDRESS _____

_____

CITY _____ STATE _____ ZIP _____

	QUANTITY	PRICE	TOTAL
FUTURE JOBS AND CAREERS			
Applegath - *Working Free*	_____	$15.95	_____
Drucker - *Managing in Turbulent Times*	_____	$14.95	_____
Feingold/Miller - *Emerging Careers*	_____	$11.95	_____
Krannich - *Re-Careering in Turbulent Times*	_____	$ 8.95	_____
JOB TRAINING AND EMPLOYMENT FIELDS			
Feingold/Hansard-Winkler - *900,000 Plus Jobs Annual*	_____	$11.95	_____
Hegyi - *Should You Get an MBA?*	_____	$ 8.95	_____
Heller/Bower - *Woman's Computer Book*	_____	$18.95	_____
Mainstream - *The Banking Job Finder*	_____	$ 9.95	_____
Mainstream - *The Data Processing/ Information Technology*	_____	$ 8.95	_____
Mainstream - *The Energy Job Finder*	_____	$10.95	_____
Mainstream - *The Insurance Job Finder*	_____	$ 9.95	_____
Mainstream - *The Public Relations Job Finder*	_____	$ 8.95	_____
Mainstream - *The Publishing Job Finder*	_____	$ 9.95	_____
Mainstream - *The Real Estate Job Finder*	_____	$ 9.95	_____
Maresca - *Careers in Marketing* (Women)	_____	$10.95	_____
Mullins/West - *The Office Automation Primer*	_____	$11.95	_____
Pickens - *The Freelancer's Handbook*	_____	$ 8.95	_____
Sessions - *How to Break into Data Processing*	_____	$ 8.95	_____
JOB STRESS AND BURNOUT			
Cooper - *The Stress Check*	_____	$ 8.95	_____
Greenberg - *Coping With Job Stress*	_____	$ 8.95	_____
McGuigan - *Calm Down*	_____	$ 8.95	_____
Leatz - *Unwinding*	_____	$ 8.95	_____
Maslach - *Burnout — The Cost of Caring*	_____	$ 8.95	_____
Palmer - *Role Stress*	_____	$ 8.95	_____
Welch/Mederos/Tate - *Beyond Burnout*	_____	$ 9.95	_____

TERMINATION	QUANTITY	PRICE	TOTAL
May - *The RIF Survival Handbook*	_____	$ 8.95	_____
Morin/Yorks - *Outplacement Techniques*	_____	$18.95	_____
Peskin - *A Job Loss Survival Manual*	_____	$14.95	_____
Preston - *Employer's Guide to Hiring and Firing*	_____	$ 9.95	_____

GENERAL CAREER AND LIFE PLANNING

Bolton - *People Skills*	_____	$ 8.95	_____
Boros - *How to Get a Fast Start in Today's Job Market*	_____	$ 8.95	_____
Figgens - *The Job Game*	_____	$ 8.95	_____
Haldane/Martin - *Young People's Job-Finding Guide*	_____	$10.95	_____
Hecklinger/Curtin - *Training for Life*	_____	$19.95	_____
Mitchell - *Stopout*	_____	$ 9.95	_____
Petit - *The Career Connection*	_____	$ 8.95	_____
Rogers - *Getting Hired*	_____	$ 8.95	_____
Thain - *The Mid-Career Manual*	_____	$ 8.95	_____

ORGANIZING TIME

Lebov - *Practical Tools and Techniques for Managing Time*	_____	$ 8.95	_____
Reynold/Tramel - *Executive Time Management*	_____	$ 8.95	_____

RESUMES AND LETTERS

Dickhut - *The Professional Resume and Job Search Guide*	_____	$ 9.95	_____
Krannich/Banis - *High Impact Resumes and Letters*	_____	$ 8.95	_____
McLaughlin/Merman - *Writing a Job-Winning Resume*	_____	$ 8.95	_____
Ulrich - *How to Prepare Your Own High Intensity Resume*	_____	$ 9.95	_____

NETWORKING

Stern - *Is Networking For You?*	_____	$ 8.95	_____

INTERVIEWING

Genua - *The Employer's Guide to Interviewing*	_____	$ 8.95	_____
Krannich - *Interview for Success*	_____	$ 8.95	_____
Merman/McLaughlin - *Out-Interviewing the Interviewer*	_____	$ 8.95	_____
Robertson - *How to Win a Job Interview*	_____	$ 8.95	_____

STARTING A BUSINESS	QUANTITY	PRICE	TOTAL
Feingold/Perlman - *Making It On Your Own*	_____	$14.95	_____
Jackson - *How to Proceed in Business –*			
Legally	_____	$11.95	_____
Mancuso - *How to Prepare and Present a*			
Business Plan	_____	$11.95	_____
Morine - *Riding the Recession*	_____	$ 8.95	_____
Pritchard/Bradway - *Strategic Planning*			
and Control Techniques for Profit	_____	$12.95	_____
Simmons - *Creative Business Financing*	_____	$14.95	_____

WOMEN

Doss - *The Directory of Special*			
Opportunities for Women	_____	$19.95	_____
Douglas - *Women in Business*	_____	$ 8.95	_____
Mitchell/Burdick - *The Competitive Edge*	_____	$16.95	_____
McCaslin - *Be Your Own Boss*	_____	$10.95	_____
Petit - *Women and the Career Game*	_____	$ 8.95	_____

DRESS AND APPEARANCE

Wallach - *Working Wardrobe*	_____	$16.95	_____

MINORITIES

Cole - *Minority Organizations*	_____	$29.95	_____
Johnson - *Directory of Special Programs*			
for Minority Group Members	_____	$20.95	_____
Swann - *Financial Aid for Minority*			
Students	_____	$20.95	_____

EDUCATION

Krannich/Banis - *Moving Out of Education*	_____	$14.95	_____
Miller - *Finding Career Alternatives*			
for Teachers (book)	_____	$12.95	_____
Miller - *Finding Career Alternatives*			
for Teachers (audio-cassette program)	_____	$49.95	_____
Pollack - *Alternative Careers for Teachers*	_____	$ 8.95	_____

GOVERNMENT

Dambaugh/Secota - *Capitol Jobs*	_____	$ 8.95	_____
Krannich - *Moving Out of Government*	_____	$14.95	_____
Lauber - *The Compleat Guide to Jobs in*			
Planning and Public Administration	_____	$10.95	_____
Petit - *From the Military to a*			
Civilian Career	_____	$ 8.95	_____
Waclde - *How to Get a Federal Job*	_____	$15.95	_____
Zehring, *Careers in State and Local*			
Government	_____	$11.95	_____

INTERNATIONAL QUANTITY PRICE TOTAL

Sheehan - *Careers in International
Affairs* _____ $10.95 _____

- Virginia residents add 4% state sales tax. _____

TOTAL ═══

NOTE: Institutions may order by purchase order, official letterhead, or telephone. Orders from individuals must be prepaid by check, money
order, or credit card. Telephone orders accepted with credit card
number.

☐ I enclose my check or money order for $ _____ made
payable to IMPACT PUBLICATIONS.

☐ Please charge $ _____ to my credit card:

☐ Visa   ☐ MasterCard

Card # _____ Expiration Date _____

Signature _____ Date _____

SEND YOUR ORDER TO: IMPACT PUBLICATIONS
10655 Big Oak Circle
Manassas, VA 22111
Tel: 703/361-7300

SPECIAL $2.00 BONUS OFFER

You may deduct $2.00 from the purchase price of any single title
of your choice if you enclose this coupon with your order.

NAME _____ Date _____